Leading Agile Teams

by Doug Rose

Library of Congress Cataloging-in-Publication Data

Rose, Doug (Agile coach), author.
Leading agile teams / by Doug Rose.
pages cm
ISBN 978-1-62825-092-3 (pbk. : alk. paper) -- ISBN 1-62825-092-5 (pbk. : alk. paper)
1. Teams in the workplace--Management. 2. Project management. 3. Organizational change--Management. I. Title.
HD66.R6496 2015
658.4'022--dc23
2015029560

ISBN: 978-1-62825-092-3

Published by: Project Management Institute, Inc.
14 Campus Boulevard
Newtown Square, Pennsylvania 19073-3299 USA
Phone: +610-356-4600
Fax: +610-356-4647
Email: customercare@pmi.org
Internet: www.PMI.org

PMI Publications welcomes corrections and comments on its books. Please feel free to send comments on typographical, formatting, or other errors. Simply make a copy of the relevant page of the book, mark the error, and send it to: Book Editor, PMI Publications, 14 Campus Boulevard, Newtown Square, PA 19073-3299 USA.

To inquire about discounts for resale or educational purposes, please contact the PMI Book Service Center.

PMI Book Service Center
P.O. Box 932683, Atlanta, GA 31193-2683 USA
Phone: 1-866-276-4764 (within the U.S. or Canada) or
+1-770-280-4129 (globally)
Fax: +1-770-280-4113
Email: info@bookorders.pmi.org

The paper used in this book complies with the Permanent Paper Standard issued by the National Information Standards Organization (Z39.48—1984).

10 9 8 7 6 5 4 3 2

For Velena & Leo

Table of Contents

Acknowledgments

First, I'd like to thank my wife, Jelena. She tirelessly read and reread dozens of drafts for this book. Without her support I would have never been able to finish. Her quiet optimism and invaluable criticism were key ingredients to completing this work. She made finishing this book a wonderful experience.

I'd also like to thank my son Leo. While finishing this book I was able to join his elementary school parent drop-off. Each morning was a joy. He patiently let me go right up to the classroom wearing my okay-for-home jeans.

I'd like to thank my friends at the University of Chicago. Many of the ideas for this book were gleaned from the give-and-take that I get from being an adjunct instructor. I'd like to especially thank Director of Business and Professional Programs Katherine Locke.

I have also enjoyed my relationship with Emory University. They have a great project management program and I learned a lot from their student professionals. I want to give a special thank you to Syracuse University for hiring me as part of their adjunct faculty. Their School of Information Studies is top-ranked for a reason. Thank you to Director of Learning Systems Peggy Takach and Interim Dean Jeff Stanton.

Most of this book was the product of years of gainful employment at several wonderful companies. Thank you for allowing me to come to your organizations and add real value. I'm always amazed at the enthusiasm these employees bring to the transition. There is a wealth of human energy out there in campuses and office parks. Thank you for giving me the opportunity to try and tap it.

I want to thank lynda.com and LinkedIn for the terrific opportunity to create their video training courses. Special thanks go to Director of Business & Education Content Jolie Miller, Manager of Content Production Jeff Layton, and Content Manager Kathe Sweeney.

Writing a book is hard work. Fortunately, there are many great people who can help. Thanks to David Gregory for proofreading and editing. Adriana Danaila created many of the illustrations in this book. Jennie Routley created the original layout and design. Of course, thank you to the Project Management Institute and Publications Production Supervisor Barbara Walsh for helping me publish this book. I also want to thank Kim Shinners and Monica Zaleski for helping bring this book to print.

Thank you to my parents and siblings for letting me turn their Boca Raton retirement home into my writer's sanctuary. I was able to write some of this book while sitting on the balcony at the Vistas home for active seniors. It's amazing how much easier it is to relax while writing next to a pool filled with laughing octogenarians. It puts impending deadlines into perspective. I enjoyed the company of many of the residents in the community. Special thanks to Joe for connecting the dots for me with his illuminating views on "runaway communism," progressive taxation, and "government-funded gluten."

Finally, I'd like to thank the agile community. Their contributions to this book are too numerous to count. Their ideas are cited on many of these pages. It's wonderful to be part of a community that embraces new ideas. There is not much dogma in the agile community. The framework gets remixed all the time. It's that vibrant flexibility that makes agile coaching such interesting work.

Why You Should Buy This Book

When I was in grade school, I was deeply suspicious of animal fables. I found it very unsettling to read about their barnyard bargaining—the shadowy back-and-forth between cats, dogs, swans, rats, and foxes. Why were they always negotiating?

"Will you sing me a song for a slice of cheese?" Or "could you give me a ride so I can cross the river?"

I remember wondering why our four-legged "friends" were always colluding in our absence.

But after many years, one of the old stories stuck with me. I'm reminded of it when I work with agile teams.

In the fable, there was a small village with a marauding cat harassing the local mice. The mice convened a meeting to solve the problem. They floated some good ideas in the meeting. Finally, the mice settled on attaching a bell to the cat's collar. That way they could run anytime they heard the cat's distant jingling.

It was a brilliant idea. It was the perfect plan. The mice congratulated themselves on a job well done. But just as they were closing the meeting, a mouse stood up and raised its paw. "That's a terrific idea," the mouse said, "but whose job is it to put the bell on the cat?"

This book is for the team whose job it is to put the bell on the cat.

Big changes are decided in executive meetings. But they're started, driven, and implemented by teams. The teams are where your transformational changes will sink or swim. There will be a lot of legwork, a lot of grassroots effort to push the ball forward.

Many of the meetings you'll endure will be with coworkers and mid-level managers. Most agile teams do not have the authority to overrule key decision makers. That means you won't be able to force any changes. There will be a lot of explaining and a lot of compromise.

Certain key tenets of agile are a sharp departure from how most organizations operate. Is your company ready for self-organized teams? Will you be able to throw away your Gantt charts and scheduled milestones? Are the project managers ready to cede some control? That will be your bell to hang.

This book will show you how to align agile methods to your organization. At the same time, you'll see how to stay true to the agile values. It is a practical guide for your bottom-up organizational change.

This book takes the team's perspective of starting agile. It is written specifically for the developers, project managers, product owners, and ScrumMasters who struggle with shoehorning agile into a traditional organization. These are the people who will do most of the legwork in getting agile up and running. Even teams with executive support still have to drive grassroots efforts to make agile fit.

The way your team works today may not be the same way it works in a few years. Some decisions will have long-term consequences and others are a good compromise in order to find a more agile way of working. This book will help you identify these forks and make suggestions on the best course to follow.

There are many books on agile methods. Some of these go into the details about specific practices. Others are a good introduction to the agile approach. What many of these books have in common is that they're about the *how.* They have an engineer's perspective on *how* to apply agile practices. They're about the steps you need to follow to be more agile. Their assumption is that if you build a great process, the benefits will follow.

A practical approach is important, but there isn't enough on the reasoning and pitfalls in making a large-scale organizational change. Most agile teams also need an understanding of the *why*. They need to see the benefits of making this large-scale transformation. This will help the team stay motivated. It will also give them the tools they need to explain agile to the rest of the organization.

You'll see a similar pattern throughout the chapters. Each agile practice will follow three steps. You'll see how you do it, then *why* you do it. Finally there's a tie into how this practice fits into a larger organization change.

Included in this book are many of the files you'll need for the meetings.[1] There's an introduction to the agile slide deck. You'll have spreadsheets for your first product backlog. There is a sample chart for reporting. There's even an example agile project charter. These will be your tools to convince your coworkers. These slides and reports will help show why agile is an improvement over the status quo.

One theme you'll see throughout this book is that transforming to agile is hard but doable. It's a bit like trying to get into better physical shape. The rules are simple. You should eat less and spend time at the gym. What's tricky is the strategy and tricks for changing your mindset. Agile really is a new way of thinking about your work.

You'll be much happier with agile if you take the time to plan the change. It isn't like spreading magic dust—a little sprinkle, everyone smiles, and then you're agile. It's a long, hard push.

Most organizations change with the grace of a turning cruise ship. Each day you hope to move the ship a little bit forward. I hope this book will help you set the direction and give you the support you need to get there.

[1] Find supporting files on http://www.dougenterprises.com/

Chapter 1

The Road Ahead

One misconception about agile is that it is just a collection of new practices that were dreamed up in some multibillion-dollar high-tech company. Many organizations see it as the next big thing. The thought process is as simple as, "We're a high-tech company and high-tech companies use agile, so we need to be agile."

These organizations tend to see agile as a few new things to do. They don't view it as a widespread organizational change.

You can see this from the feedback about agile transformations. Many organizations are trying agile practices but most are finding it challenging to change their overall culture.

Over the last few years, the agile software vendor VersionOne has put out a survey on the current state of agile. Their eighth version of the survey had about 3,500 respondents.

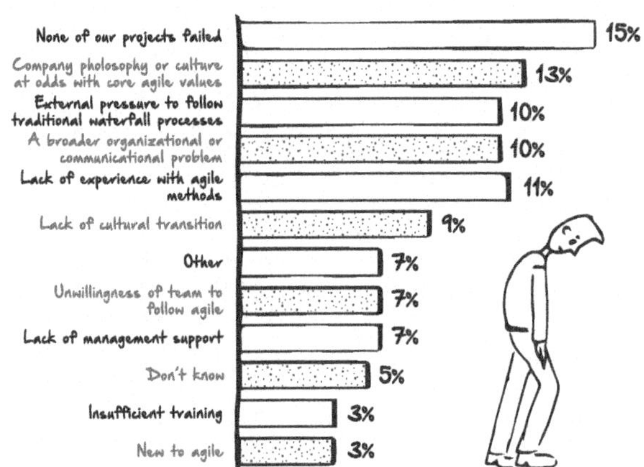

The respondents skewed heavily toward larger organizations. Seventy-five percent of the respondents came from companies that had between 100 and 1,000 employees. Of that group, about 85% reported that one or more of their agile initiatives had failed.

These findings strongly suggest that it wasn't the projects that failed. Instead, it was the cultural mismatch that caused many of the problems. Eighty-five percent of the organizations simply didn't accept that agile was a legitimate way to deliver software.

If you look at the results, you'll see at least half of the 85% failed because of well-established cultural norms. What this suggests is twofold. First, it seems like a lot of organizations started their initiative before they had a solid understanding of agile. Second, it suggests that after they started the initiative, it didn't sit well with the rest of the organization.

That's a pretty big problem. For one, it means that only a small percentage of agile initiatives are changing organizations. It also means that initiatives that do fail may be creating groups that are less inclined to retry.

Yet, the agile train charges on. A full 88% of the respondents said they were practicing some agile development. Over half of the respondents said they were using agile on a majority of their projects.

This suggests a gap between agile practices and the larger organizational culture. On the one hand, agile practices are widespread and used on many projects. On the other hand, most of the organization's culture seems to be opposed to agile. This causes a majority of agile initiatives to fail.

It is as if organizations are aware they have a problem and accept agile as a possible solution but don't like the taste of the medicine. This is one of the biggest challenges you should be aware of in attempting to change an organization to agile.

I go into some detail about agile practices, but I also try to give you a few examples of agile "choke" points. These are places where you will almost certainly run into trouble. If you are part of the 15% of projects that have the right culture, then you can gloss over these challenges, but this information is crucial for the other 85% who may struggle with agile projects.

Try to keep in mind that the practices in this book are only the first step. Please pay special attention to the "field notes" that show how these practices actually play out in organizations.

Chapter 2

Traditional Projects

For much of the 20th century, many projects worked just fine with a strategy of planning and control. Most of these projects were engineering pretty big things.

These early projects worked with iron, concrete, and hammers. They used physical objects that couldn't be deleted or remixed or easily reused.

These traditional projects typically had authoritative project managers who were an essential part of the project. They were large and in charge—a single source of accountability. Their job was to manage the project from start to finish.

In a traditional project, the project manager's work is *deterministic*. They help "determine" as many of the pieces of the project as they can. They try to create certainty. Each of the little project pieces is managed and catalogued.

They also divide the work into tasks. Then, they figure out how many people they need to complete these tasks. After that, they figure out how much it will cost to have these people work on the project. Finally, they determine the schedule for how long it will take each of these people to finish their work.

The project managers carefully control for the uncertainties and plan contingencies. Good project managers are judged on how well they plan the future and how well their project weathers the storms.

They use charts and reports that break down projects into smaller pieces. They use Gantt charts for their schedules and spreadsheets for the budgets.

This deterministic approach works very well for projects that can easily be *chunked* into smaller pieces. Rocket ships, highway systems, and skyscrapers in Chicago were all built using this approach.

This "chunking" is a type of science. It is about observing, guessing, and calculating. That is why it is often called scientific management. The project manager uses a scientific approach to divide the project into smaller pieces. Each of these pieces is catalogued and quantified.

The project manager overseeing one of these projects will use scientific management throughout the project. For example, the project manager will calculate that five people working eight hours a day can lay one yard of cement in four hours. That means in eight hours, 10 people can create four yards of a new highway. The person is one chunk and how long it takes that person to complete the task is another.

These are just two of the little deterministic chunks that a project manager might define. In a larger project, there might be hundreds or thousands of these deterministic chunks.

All of these identified chunks are then rolled back up into the three project categories—scope, budget, and schedule.

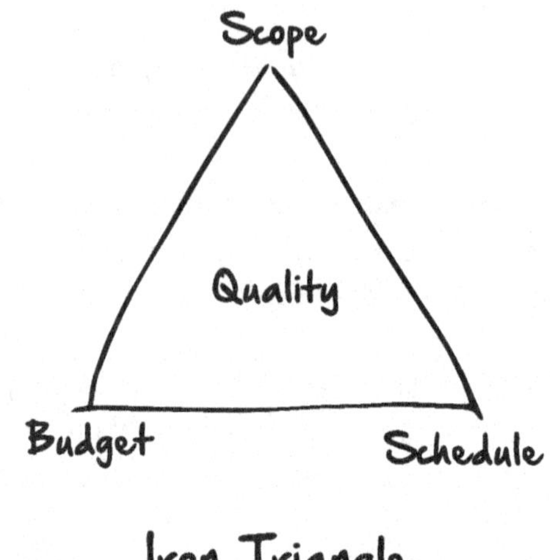

All the little pieces that the project needs to deliver are rolled up into the **scope**. The cost for all the people, places, and things is rolled up into the **budget**. How long it takes to complete each of the tasks is rolled up into the **schedule**.

These three categories are the project's key constraints. Each one is closely related to the other. For example, if you add more tasks, then you need to add either more people or more time. If you need more time, then you have to increase the budget or remove some of the work.

The scope, budget, and schedule give the project form and structure. It's what separates the project from just a bunch of people working.

These constraints rely on the fruit of all of the project manager's deterministic scientific planning. The scope is all the pieces the project needs to deliver. The schedule is all the tasks that need to be performed. Each of these is the sum of all the little pieces that the project manager gathers up about the project.

Pro Tip

The scope is what the project delivers. It is also what the project requires for delivery. This means the scope of a new bridge is both the bridge and the building of the bridge. The project team works with the customer to develop detailed requirements that chunk the scope into smaller deliverables.

This was the Iron Age of project management. Projects were ruled by the rigid "iron triangle." The scope, budget, and schedule each held a corner of the triangle. You couldn't change one without impacting the other two.

As the name implies, this rigid approach adds structure and inflexibility. Any changes require a rigorous change-control process. Each change impacts the other corners of the triangle. That means that each change request must be documented and balanced against the rest of the project.

The Project Management Institute

Many project managers recognized that although each project was different, many of the tools and techniques that they used were similar. The scope, budget, and schedule were the same constraints that affected every project. It made sense that each of the control processes for these constraints should have some common traits.

These project managers started to create a shared project management framework. This helped define project management as a discipline. Ideally, a project manager was the person who implemented the new project management framework.

One of the earliest contributors to this framework was the Project Management Institute (PMI). PMI formed in the late 1960s to foster professionalism in project management. Soon after it formed, PMI made an effort to standardize project management.

PMI developed and published *A Guide to the Project Management Body of Knowledge (PMBOK® Guide)*, which provides guidelines for managing individual projects and defines project management related concepts. The fifth edition of the *PMBOK® Guide* is comprised of 5 Project Management Process Groups, 10 Knowledge Areas, 47 processes, and 614 inputs, tools and techniques, and outputs.

Pro Tip

PMI never endorsed one project management approach. They simply tried to create a guidebook for all projects to follow. In practice, the PMI guidebook still encourages a structured, process-heavy view of the project. You can't use 614 inputs, tools and techniques, and outputs without some structure and process.

The *PMBOK® Guide* views a project like a complex machine with many moving parts. Project managers use common tools to manage the machine. They use the 614 tools and outputs like buttons, levers, and switches to manipulate their project machine.

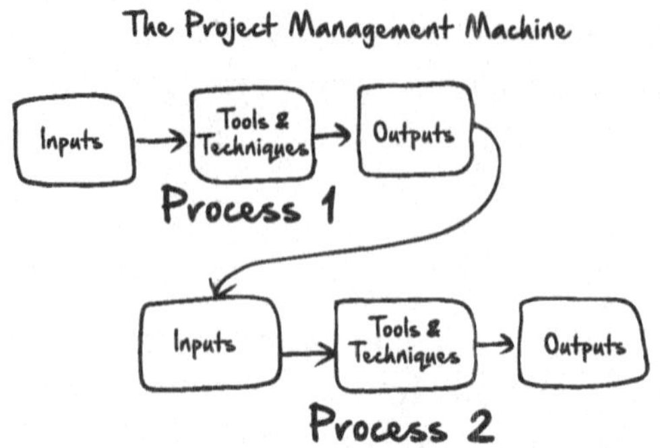

The tools and the machine help to manage the project's iron triangle. The more you understand the processes and tools, the more likely your project will succeed.

That is why there are more than half a million Project Management Professional (PMP)® certification holders. They work like project machinists to keep the project running smoothly.

Waterfall

The *PMBOK® Guide* closely follows a traditional engineering approach. These projects use a big-design-upfront or waterfall-style approach. The waterfall approach is still a popular way for engineering projects to work within the three constraints.

The idea behind the waterfall approach is that you have to spend a good deal of time at the beginning trying to understand all the pieces of the project. Only after you've planned the project from beginning to end should the team start working on the deliverable.

From an engineering perspective, it certainly makes sense to understand where the road is going before you lay cement. These assumptions heavily influenced traditional project management and were the reason behind waterfall's widespread adoption.

The waterfall approach breaks the project down into sequential phases. Each phase leads to the next. In each phase, there is a carefully designed set of control processes. First, you **plan** a project, then you **design** it, then you **execute** it, then you **test** it, and then you are **done**.

Even if you don't recognize the term *waterfall*, you'll probably be familiar with this approach. The top of the waterfall is the planning phase. This is when the project team does most of the deterministic project planning. They try to identify all the little pieces of their project.

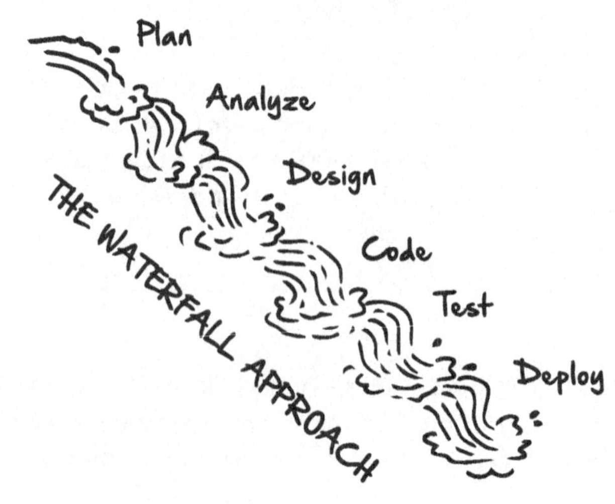

The planning phase is very challenging. The manager has to predict the project's pieces before any of the work begins. As you can imagine, this usually takes a lot of legwork and educated guesses.

Bonus Fact

Winston Royce is credited with connecting waterfall and its engineering approach to the world of software development. In the 1970s, he delivered a paper titled "Managing the Development of Large Software Systems." In it, he described the waterfall approach and how it was being used to develop software.

The paper was far from a full-throated endorsement of this approach. It opens, "I believe in this concept, but the implementation described above is risky and invites failure."

He also recommended that projects pass through the waterfall at least a few times. It wasn't intended as a model for projects from beginning to end.

At the end of the planning phase, the project will have a list of requirements. These requirements are the pieces of the scope that need to be delivered in order for the project to be successful. From this scope, the project manager can then determine the schedule and budget.

After the planning phase, the team starts to work on the deliverable. This is the execution phase. Soon after, the team will probably receive its first round of change requests.

When the team receives these requests for changes, they go back and update the requirements. Then they rebalance the three constraints (scope, budget, and schedule) and re-plan the project. Most projects can't predict everything that will happen, so there are usually at least a few rounds of change requests.

With the waterfall approach, the project plan becomes an effort unto itself. The planning can even overshadow the time it takes to *execute* the work. This investment makes it very difficult to accept new changes. Everyone on the team knows that too many changes slow down the project.

Changes are usually seen as a challenge to overcome and not as welcome feedback. A rigorous change-control process is like a lock on the gate of innovation. It doesn't leave much room for new ideas and customizations.

Failed Projects

The iron triangle and the waterfall approach gave projects their needed structure. The flipside is that they also gave projects a lot of rigidity. When the customer came up with a new idea, the team would have to go through a difficult change-control process to apply the idea to the project.

When the customer came up with a *lot* of new ideas, then it would increase the scope or exceed the project's budget. Project managers called this **scope creep**. It is one of the most common challenges with the iron triangle and the waterfall approach.

If one of the project's constraints slips too far outside of the predictions, then the project will have failed.

PMI defines a successful project as having delivered the agreed-upon project scope, to the agreed quality, within the agreed time frame and within budget. That means a successful project is able to balance all the corners of the iron triangle. A project fails when it is not delivered on time or on budget or is abandoned completely.

Unfortunately, this is what happens with most projects. They either fail outright or exceed their scope, budget, or schedule. There is something about software projects that don't seem to work well with the waterfall approach.

Many project managers dealt with these challenges by increasing their level of orthodoxy. They followed the waterfall approach with even greater diligence. They would guard the plan and remind others, "If it's not in the plan, then it's not in the project."

Other project managers would add buffers and variances to their project. They would give the waterfall approach a little needed flexibility in areas where it should adapt. But even this approach only got you so far. Why spend all that time planning when a good variance is plus or minus 10%?

The challenge with these newer software projects is that it is very difficult to determine all the little pieces before you start. The deterministic approach breaks down when it comes to software.

A software project is more exploratory. In a software project, you really don't know everything that might be required to deliver the project until you start working. The developers might find a new way of making things work. A new vendor might make part of the project easier to implement.

In many ways, a software project is like building a bridge to a destination hidden in the clouds. The challenges really only become clear once you get closer to your destination.

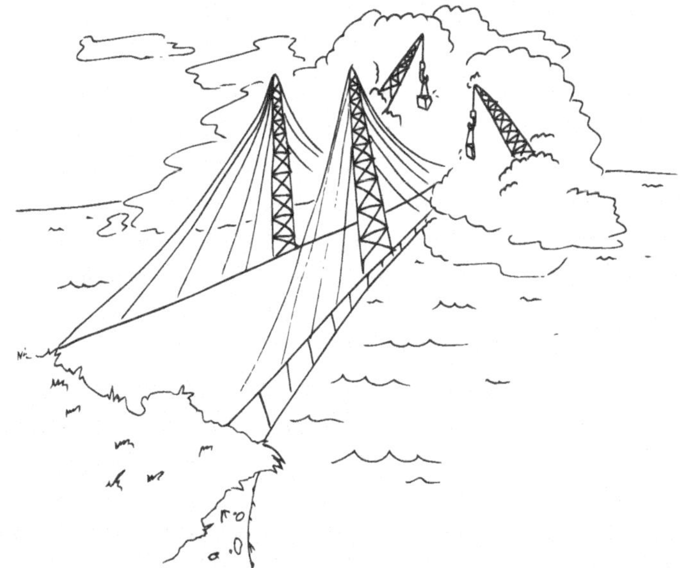

Software projects require a closer link between planning and adapting. Ideally, the developers can learn and adapt their work in real time. Then they can immediately apply these improvements to the new plan.

With the waterfall approach, this cycle is very difficult to create. In software development, there are simply too many changes and these changes happen far too often. Waterfall's phased approach doesn't allow for this type of flexibility.

As time has gone on, software projects have only increased in complexity. They have started to have even less in common with traditional engineering projects. Newer technologies have come and gone. Open source projects have started to solve many common software challenges.

A modern software project will usually depend on outside developers. There may be some open source projects and even other organizations involved in some fashion. Each one of these groups will relate to one another. They will react to changes in the whole system.

A vendor may update their software product. The open source software will react to the update. All of these changes will take time and their relationships are nearly impossible to predict.

The environment that these projects exist in has become increasingly *chaotic*. A multiyear software project might rely on a technology that will completely change by the time the software is delivered.

This is a whole new system for software projects. Software exists in a world of rapid change and invention. This environment has started to look more and more like a complex adaptive system.

Complex Adaptive Systems

Complex adaptive systems have been studied for over 20 years. They are systems that can't be simplified or reduced. They are beyond the reach of a project's deterministic tools. There is no scientific approach to breaking everything down into smaller pieces.

Some examples of complex adaptive systems are global weather patterns, the stock market, and even the Internet. These are large systems that change often, but still have some structure.

Think about the stock market. The market performs at a consistent rate when it's viewed over decades. This is true even though individual stocks go up and down in unpredictable patterns.

The climate patterns on the earth change all the time. One area may have a drought and another area may have a flood. But globally, the earth stays within that remarkably slim margin where life can flourish.

If you look at these systems as a collection of individual events, then they may seem unpredictable. When they're viewed as a *system*, then they are structured and consistent.

Bonus Fact

You can think of a complex adaptive system as the middle ground between chaos and structure. The close-up view of the system is chaotic because it's difficult to predict. The big-picture view has structure. There is an overall order to the system.

To work within a complex adaptive system, you have to give up the notion of planning and control. Instead, you have to focus on shifting and adapting. There are too many changes and too many interdependencies to predict what will happen from day to day. The system has too many moving parts.

The relationships in a complex adaptive system are not just the external groups. Often, your most unpredictable relationships are the ones with your customers. Sometimes your customer doesn't like the traditional project mantra of "put in the change request." They may want to make a last-minute change and still expect your project to deliver.

They also expect you to deliver these products much more quickly. For many projects, the time from idea to completion is shorter. That means there are a lot of benefits to getting your best ideas to market as soon as possible.

Your customer's best ideas might happen in the middle of your project. It's a key competitive advantage if that team can turn on a dime and deliver the best product.

When customers change their mind, an agile team can still accept these new ideas. This has made agile of particular interest to newer creative teams. Even though most agile teams are still developing software, there are now more diverse industries interested in the approach.

Pro Tip

In a complex adaptive system, there is much less value in sticking with a well-defined plan. There's too much uncertainty and any useful plan will require an enormous amount of replanning. Once you've spent this effort, there is still a very good chance that the system will adapt in ways that you couldn't have imagined.

It makes sense that the waterfall approach would break down in a complex adaptive system. It is too much of a departure from traditional engineering. When rocket scientists figure out a better way to design a rocket, they have to wait for the next project to begin. They can't redesign a rocket while it's being built.

The challenge then is figuring out a new approach. This new approach needs to be flexible and adaptive. It needs to react to the changes that constantly occur in a complex adaptive system. These are the key tenets of agile. It's about creating a lightweight strategy for working in a complex adaptive system.

Field Notes

Many years ago, I worked at Spiegel. At the time, it was one of the largest women's clothing catalogs.

The fashion industry is a large complex adaptive system. Each year, there are many trends that ripple through the entire fashion industry. No one person controls "fashion." Instead, "agents" start trends that might catch on for the entire system.

Field Notes (continued)

When I worked there, one of the most influential agents was the popular television show *Friends*. On the show, when Rachel wore a trendy sweater, it would impact the whole system.

The clothing buyers for the catalog had to learn to adapt quickly to stay in fashion. They couldn't plan each outfit from year to year. Instead, they kept their ear to the ground and tried to adapt to the latest trends.

A buyer might order sweaters, and then at the last minute change from V-necks to turtlenecks. They didn't buy everything at once. Instead, they had short buying periods all the time. These shorter periods allowed them to take advantage of quick-moving fashion trends.

In this complex adaptive system, it wasn't any one individual who drove the changes. Instead, it was the relationships between people that caused the system to change.

A few people will start to do something, and then based on their relationship, the rest of the group may follow. Their influence may start to spark larger influence.

Chapter 3

A New Lightweight Approach

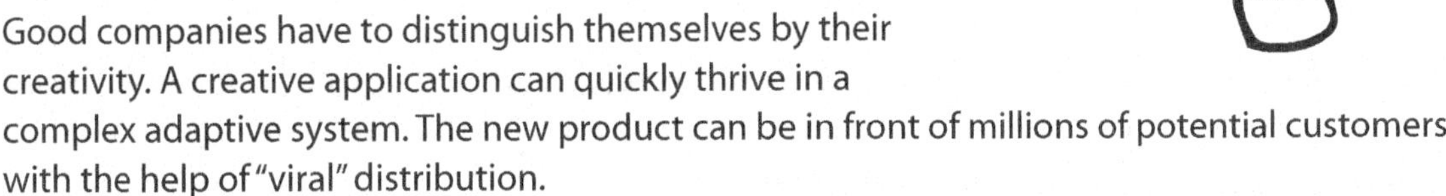

A typical software project might depend on several extremely complex adaptive systems that all interrelate. These are the hardware, software, and data components that have increased in capacity and complexity over the past few decades.

There's also been a leveling of the overhead that you need to deliver products to a large marketplace. If you're developing a mobile application, then it's fairly trivial to upload your application to a massive marketplace. Only a few decades ago, releasing software to a massive market was limited to well-heeled mega-companies.

Good companies have to distinguish themselves by their creativity. A creative application can quickly thrive in a complex adaptive system. The new product can be in front of millions of potential customers with the help of "viral" distribution.

When creativity is the most valuable currency, you need a team that's not afraid to make sweeping changes and last-minute optimizations.

These widespread changes have forced many organizations to think about adopting some version of agile methods. Even companies that have top-down, planning-heavy processes are starting to explore the idea that there might be a new, more efficient way of working.

Many teams adopt agile because they think it's new and, therefore, better. It's like the next version of work—work 2.0. But agile isn't a newer version of what you're doing now. Instead, it's a different way to think about working together. That's why you'll commonly hear new teams talk about agile as a change in mindset.

This mindset is not necessarily easy to accept. Most teams have spent the majority of their career working with a group that was not agile. It's very common for new teams to start the agile practices and create the reports but still hold onto the old way of thinking about work.

To begin to *think* like an agile team, it is often helpful to reflect on how you work. If you're more than a decade into your career, chances are you have some exposure to a traditional work environment.

Pro Tip

Much of what agile represents is not very complicated. The practices are intentionally simple and easy to learn. The agile "values" are listed and specific. What makes an agile transformation difficult is how different it is from how most people *think* about their work.

Most people work with the notion that they should spend a good deal of time planning and preparing. That way, they can eliminate the maximum amount of uncertainty. The thinking goes that a detailed plan will, at the very least, help with most unanticipated events.

This inflexible approach led to many failed software projects and unhappy managers. Software teams would have to hammer on the changes and work long hours to get working software out the door.

Some project managers thought a heavily prescriptive approach was too much of a burden. It didn't produce enough value for the effort. They envisioned "lightweight" frameworks that were more adaptive and less prescriptive.

The Agile Manifesto

These project managers called their approaches lightweight software development. These lightweight development frameworks included Scrum, Extreme Programming, Adaptive Software Development, Feature Driven Development, Crystal Clear, and the Dynamic Systems Development Method.

These frameworks were developed by different organizations all around the same time. Each of them represented a pocket of work in scattered organizations.

In 2001, 17 leaders from these lightweight teams met at a ski resort in Utah. They met to see if they could find a common thread running through what made their projects more successful.

The group didn't particularly like the name lightweight since being a lightweight team didn't have the appropriate heft for what they were trying to communicate. Their first order of business was to come up with a new name. They wanted a term that was adaptive, quick, and flexible. They settled on the term *agile* and called themselves the "agile alliance."

The language and terms that came out of this meeting were indicators of what they were trying to convey. They wanted to evoke drama and revolutionary zeal. They called themselves an alliance and not a work group. The document they created was called *The Agile Manifesto*.

The manifesto was an attempt to create a list of values that were common to all of their lightweight projects. The manifesto started by saying, "We are uncovering better ways of developing software by doing it and helping others do it." Then they created what they called the agile values.

The list of values was structured in a way so that the value on the left was more valuable. The lesser value was listed on the right.

They structured the manifesto this way because each value was both competitive and complementary. You can picture the two value columns as sides on a pendulum. The value on the left will pull resources away from the value on the right.

The list is short with only four values:

1. *Individuals and interactions over processes and tools*
2. *Working software over comprehensive documentation*
3. *Customer collaboration over contract negotiation*
4. *Responding to change over following a plan*

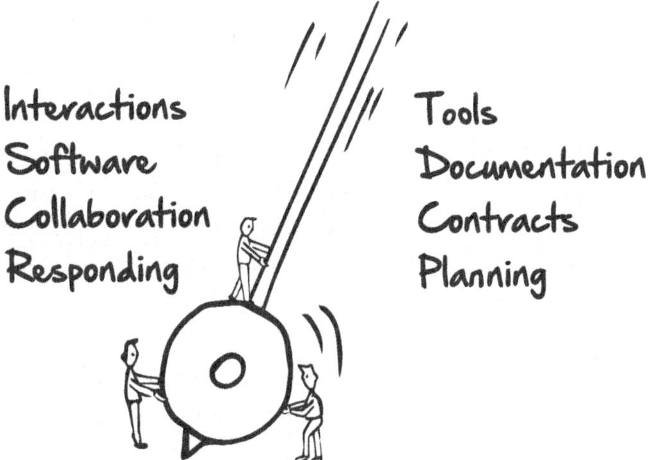

The alliance thought that too much emphasis was being given to the values on the right. They wanted to pull the pendulum back toward the opposing values on the left.

Now remember, the alliance is not saying that the values on the right should be ignored. A lot of agile project managers get particularly hung up on not following a plan. They assume that agile means no planning.

This list of values is not saying that. It is saying that responding to change is more important than following a plan. The alliance thought project managers were spending too much time planning and not enough time responding to change.

The list of values in the manifesto is the key to everything on your agile map and can be viewed as the four pillars of agile. Every agile process and practice should tie into one of these values. Even though these values are abstract, the agile team should always be thinking in these terms. They are guidelines for thinking like an agile team.

These values will go a long way to getting a team to think like an agile team. The ScrumMaster should list these values on the wall of your agile workspace. When the team is working, they should continuously check that they are in line with these core values.

Field Notes

I once worked on a project where the ScrumMaster spent the first month focusing solely on getting agile project management software installed. The ScrumMaster thought if the team would just start using this software, then they would be on their way to becoming more agile.

Even though the software was designed for agile teams, the ScrumMaster was ignoring a key value. The first responsibility of a ScrumMaster is to make sure that the team has a shared workspace. They need to focus on individuals and interactions. The software is a great agile tool, but it isn't as important as getting people to sit together.

Agile Is An Umbrella Term

The term *agile* is an umbrella term used to describe many different frameworks. A framework is "agile" when it supports the values and principals of The Agile Manifesto. The four agile frameworks you are most likely to see are Scrum, extreme programming, Kanban, and the Scaled Agile Framework (SAFe). Some of these are more prescriptive than others. A framework, like extreme programming, will have practices that you closely follow while another, like Kanban, might be more generalized.

These frameworks are like the differences between chess and poker. Chess has a clearly defined set of rules. Poker, on the other hand, is a more generalized framework with a lot of variation. Everyone agrees on how to play the game, but there is flexibility in how you bluff and bet. In agile, extreme programming and the Scaled Agile Framework (SAFe) are the closest that you get to chess. Kanban is more generalized like poker.

Pro Tip

Many of the agile frameworks borrow from one another as well. Scrum, in particular, will usually have key elements from extreme programming. Most managers might have a hard time distinguishing between Scrum and extreme programming teams. It is not clear by simply watching them work. For most organizations, Scrum seems to strike the best balance between structure and flexibility.

Sometimes agile is used to describe just one of these. At other times, the term *agile* is used for all of them together. You might see a Scrum team called agile. You will also see a team using Scrum, lean, or Kanban called agile.

Lean Software Development

One of the areas that contributed to the development of agile is lean manufacturing. The ideas and tools found in lean manufacturing led to the creation of lean software development.

The first lean manufacturing systems were used by Toyota as part of their Toyota production system (TPS). The Toyota system stressed the importance of eliminating waste, optimizing flow, and giving employees greater authority.

Lean manufacturing uses value-stream mapping. This maps all of the steps required from the beginning of production to the customer. This map separates activities that add value from those that are waste. Waste is considered anything that doesn't add customer value. This waste could even be something used to prepare for the more valuable activities.

Value-stream mapping is commonly used in quality control and is a part of the Six Sigma method of process improvement. Value-stream mapping is one of the ways this method streamlines business processes.

Lean manufacturing also used Kanban. This technique creates a signal card to regulate the flow of work through the system. Kanban cards create a "pull system" for just-in-time manufacturing. A pull system helps make sure that just enough items are produced as part of the manufacturing process.

Free Analogy

One way to think about a pull system is to imagine that you're having lunch in a Kanban cafeteria. It is a cold morning, so you decide that you're going to have a hot lunch. You get in line at the pasta bar and have the last helping of vegetarian lasagna. In Kanban language, you've exhausted the "initial demand point." You've had the last serving of the dish.

The cafeteria employee has a Kanban card with all the ingredients for vegetarian lasagna. They place the card in the empty tray. They then take the empty tray and put it in the warming oven underneath the serving area. The warming oven has one tray of ready-made lasagna set up to resupply the serving area. In Kanban language, the warming oven is called the "inventory control point."

Another employee goes through all the warming ovens looking for empty trays. When they find an empty tray, they go back to the kitchen and prepare another dish. They know the ingredients for the dish because of the cards left in the tray. In Kanban language, the kitchen is the "supplier."

This free analogy shows how the Kanban cafeteria would run if it were lean manufacturing all the meals.

In reality, most cafeterias produce all the food in advance. They make estimates based on what customers have ordered in the past. The problem with this approach is that they can always end up with too much or too little food. The inventory control system has to absorb a lot of uncertainty. When everyone has a salad, the cafeteria ends up with not enough salad and too much lasagna.

Most cafeterias supply everything up front using this *push* system. They're pushing the food out to the consumers and hoping their predictions are correct. The Kanban cafeteria is a pull system. They supply just as much lasagna as the customer demands. The customer *pulls* the product through the system.

The Kanban cafeteria also imposes constraints on the system. The kitchen only fills up one empty tray at a time. That way the kitchen can better organize their flow. They finish one tray and then move onto the next. They produce a steady flow of their supply.

Lean manufacturing also relies on an empowered workforce to optimize the value stream and regulate the flow through the system. In our Kanban cafeteria, there is less need for the role of an architect. No one needs to design a system that predicts the needs of its customers. There's no kitchen manager who says, "On cold mornings, make sure that we have double the trays of lasagna."

Instead, the employees focus on optimizing their flow. The employees try to eliminate all the waste to make sure that they can cook trays of food as quickly as possible. They optimize their work so they can increase the velocity of completed trays leaving the kitchen.

This gives the employees a lot of control over how they work. Since they're the ones running the system, it stands to reason that they're the authority on optimizing the process.

Lean manufacturing crossed over to the agile community in a few different ways. Mary and Tom Poppendieck published a book that mapped the principles of lean manufacturing to software development. David Anderson wrote a book that focused primarily on applying Kanban to software development. This book focused mostly on the theory of constraints and keeping a consistent software-development flow.

Finally, Ken Schwaber and Jeff Sutherland developed Scrum as a framework to apply lean to creating products. In software development, there are too many changes that may occur and these changes can impact one another within the whole system.

Schwaber and Sutherland thought the best hope to deliver products successfully was to have self-empowered teams that focused on delivering the highest-value items first. These teams would use cards as a way to regulate the flow of work coming out of the system.

They hoped that these lean principles would be a sound strategy for delivering software in a development environment that they viewed as being a complex adaptive system.

The Three Most Common Agile Frameworks

There are a number of frameworks that you can use when it comes to implementing agile in your company. Three of the most popular frameworks are Scrum, extreme programming, and the Scaled Agile Framework.

Scrum

Of all the agile frameworks, Scrum has enjoyed the most exposure and recognition. Schwaber and Sutherland presented a paper that first described Scrum in 1995. They used an early version of the framework while working together at the Easel Corporation.

A lot of the ideas behind Scrum were adapted from a Harvard business review article written in 1986 by Hirotaka Takeuchi and Ikujiro Nonaka. The paper described building a self-empowered team where everyone had a daily global view of the product.

The paper used rugby as an analogy and cited Scrum as an example of a holistic or all-at-once team. A rugby scrum tried to push to a destination without discrete roles but as a self-organized group.

The paper also introduced the idea of cross-functional teams. They described a cross-functional team as a group of organizational slices of sashimi. Different groups in the organization were all layered into one team. This means that customer representatives, testers, and graphic designers would all work as one team.

Scrum was one of the earliest frameworks, so many agile teams still use the Scrum language to describe agile roles. This is true even if the agile team decides not to adopt all of Scrum's processes.

Extreme Programming

In 1996, Kent Beck developed extreme programming (XP). He was hired to work on the Chrysler automotive comprehensive compensation system, or C3. Chrysler wanted to convert C3 to object-oriented software. Three years later, Kent Beck wrote a book on the best practices that he used on this project.

XP garnered a large following among developers. It was more prescriptive than Scrum, but it still gave developers much more freedom than the waterfall approach. Software projects were becoming larger and this prescriptive approach gave developers the ability to adapt.

Extreme programming was designed to develop software, so you are not going to be using XP if the agile project is for marketing. With that being said, XP is still one of the original "lightweight" frameworks. So a lot of its contemporaries, like Scrum, were heavily influenced by some of its methods.

Extreme programming usually practices test-driven development (TDD). Test-driven development is based on the idea that you should know exactly what your software is going to do before you start developing it. So with TDD, you actually develop a test to rate the functionality of the software before you develop the functionality.

With test-driven development, you usually have the test written by the same developer who is writing the function. Without test-driven development software, development teams would often have dedicated testers. These developers would create the test after the code has been written to stress test the application.

However, having dedicated testers proved to be much less efficient than having test specialists who work with the developers to try to improve the quality of the tests. Plus test-driven development improves the quality of the code by forcing the developers to think through how the software is going to play out before they start developing.

One of the main tenets of test-driven development is that it forces you to be disciplined about how you think of the solution. If you create a test before you create the function, you have to think about the problem in a simple straightforward way. What do you have to do for this specific function to work?

Free Analogy

Imagine you are going to create a test for something you need to build from scratch—for example, you need to build a fence in your backyard. The success criteria for your fence would be that it is high enough for privacy but low enough so that you still get some sun. Also, the fence has to be thick enough to withstand weather and the elements but not so thick that it sinks into the ground.

So, you create a series of tests to assert that each one of these criteria is met with success. You create a height test, a thickness test, and a sunlight test. Each one of these tests would be run against your fence to make sure that you have met your needs.

Now let's say that you have finished your fence but don't like the way a couple of the fence posts line up next to the trees. So you decide to improve or refactor part of your fence. Since you already established the success criteria, you could easily improve your fence and then run the same test against it to make sure that it is still designed properly.

Developers love to develop software, just like chefs love to prepare food and sculptors love to sculpt, but a problem can arise during software development that TDD helps to address.

When you have a team of developers and some of them leave, you can end up with code that is a work in progress. If you force the developer to create a test first, then they set up the success criteria before they start their solution. So it is much easier to see how the developer was thinking about developing the software.

The Scaled Agile Framework

In 2011, Dean Leffingwell created the initial version of the Scaled Agile Framework (SAFe). It's an implementation of many of the ideas that he introduced in the book *Agile Software Requirements*.

The idea behind SAFe is that larger organizations should take a Scrum model and upsize it to managers of big projects. These organizational players can use the same Scrum-style processes for big-picture strategy and budgeting.

Pro Tip

Many large organizations run a number of large projects simultaneously. That's why it's very common for these organizations to have a group of projects called a project portfolio. This project portfolio is then further subdivided into programs.

SAFe is a combination of lean, agile, and systems-level thinking. This gives SAFe a considerable advantage for agile transformations. Most organizations already have systems-level departments and processes in place. You can take the structure that's already in place and try to infuse it with some of the new lean and agile ideas.

SAFe divides a project into three levels: a team level, a program level, and a portfolio level. SAFe starts with a Scrum-style framework for the team level. The team level can also use hybrid frameworks, such as ScrumBan or AgileFall. They can even use a lean framework like Kanban.

These teams have a lot of the familiar Scrum players. They have a product owner, developers, and a ScrumMaster. Even though the names are the same, this is not a typical Scrum team.

The SAFe product owner is closer to a traditional business analyst and is not a true representation of the customer. Instead of the product owner setting the direction for the project, the program and portfolio levels set much of the direction. The product owner in SAFe mainly informs the team about this program-level direction.

In addition, the developers don't do as much estimating regarding the amount of work involved in the project as they do in other frameworks. The stories are already estimated at the program level.

At the program level, the managers use something called an Agile Release Train (ART). This train is very similar to a Kanban board. It's designed to be a pull system that represents the constraints of the team. Each train has a set capacity and the program-level managers negotiate which stories go into each car on the train.

The Dangers Of SAFe

SAFe has done a very good job of positioning itself as the "thinking man's" agile. It uses many of the practices that were designed to promote self-organized teams and upends them into something more top-down and management driven. It's agile grown up and ready for the enterprise.

In many ways, that's the point. SAFe is a reaction to parts of agile that are not seen as management friendly. The revolutionary language of *The Agile Manifesto* and the Agile Alliance doesn't appeal to many boardroom leaders who ultimately sponsor these projects.

Many of the creators of SAFe came from IBM's Rational Unified Process (RUP). This framework placed a good deal of emphasis on requirement gathering and portfolio management. This is the way that many organizations currently approach projects. For these organizations, SAFe will seem comfortable and familiar, like a well-worn pair of blue jeans.

Pro Tip

One key challenge to SAFe is the "Costco problem." If you've ever been to Costco you see that everything is big. If you buy salsa, then you can only buy it by the gallon. If you want to buy some apples, you have to get them by the bushel. That's fine if you're having a massive dinner party, but most people aren't having massive dinner parties. In Costco, you have to commit to too much to get anything.

The same is true with SAFe. It is a big framework and you'll have to commit to the whole thing to make it work well. Just like Costco, SAFe makes it easy and fun to go big. You can get a whole lot of process for your money. Still the question remains: How much process do you need?

This is especially true with new teams. Sometimes too much process is *too much process.*

Pro Tip (continued)

Fortunately, SAFe is a thorough and well-thought-out framework. It gives guidance to teams that are trying to shoehorn agile into a traditional organization. It provides many, many answers. For some, this will be welcome and helpful.

The key value in SAFe is that organizations are shoehorning agile into their companies every day. Many organizations are already trying many "SAFelike" things even if they don't know about SAFe.

They are trying to make agile fit their organizations. Often, these organizations are filled with departments and processes that can't be changed overnight. SAFe is a good guide to making these organizations more agile. In that goal, it is not much different from this book.

Chapter 4

Starting Agile In Your Organization

On December 27, 1831, the British naval vessel the HMS *Beagle* left port with Charles Darwin as part of her crew. The voyage was a terrific opportunity for the young biologist to travel and observe the principles of botany, geology, and zoology.

Through hands-on research, he started to formulate what would later become his theory of evolution. In his travels, he observed that many organisms thrived while others would die off through a process of natural selection.

On the distant shores of the Galapagos Archipelago, he watched colonies of land-loving iguanas dart into the water and feed on marine algae. He noted that in no other place on earth did iguanas swim in the water. These Galapagos iguanas thrived in the water, diving as deep as 90 feet.

It's commonly believed that the lizard's ancestors floated from South America on downed trees. When they arrived, they had nothing to eat. The Galapagos presented these iguanas with a unique challenge. Learn to swim or starve on the shore.

When those first iguanas arrived, it wasn't the smartest or the biggest that survived. The survivors were the ones that adapted to their new circumstances—the ones that were the most *agile*. This key trait made all the difference. It was a key factor in their success. Those were the ancestors of the modern Galapagos black iguanas.

Darwin argued that life was reinventing itself. When environments changed, organisms had to change to survive.

The agile team takes the same approach. The environment that you work in is not fixed. Many projects no longer live in a world of certainty and self-determination. Instead, these projects rely on many moving parts. These parts are outside of any one group's control. For a project to survive, it has to work well within a complex adaptive system. It has to be able to cope with many groups and many changes.

In traditional projects, you might find yourself whisked up in your own storm of uncertainty. You might find that the things that you depended on are now gone. Even more likely, you'll find that things that you never imagined are now the focus of all your efforts.

Like the iguanas, the best hope for survival is to be nimble and to adapt. As the system becomes more complex, it becomes increasingly difficult to create a detailed action plan. The plan itself becomes a monumental effort. The more complexity you have, the more detail you need in your plan.

In a modern project, the complexity can become overwhelming. All of the details that you put into the plan make it cumbersome and inflexible. If all of your effort is going into replanning, then it might be time to consider a new approach.

Agile teams rely on adapting and not planning. When a software vendor is six months late, an agile team will quickly adapt to this new reality. When a project gets defunded, an agile team can still deliver something of value.

The iguanas couldn't control the weather, their luck, or their food supply. Instead, they saw the patterns and adapted. The first iguanas wandered into the water and came out with a mouthful of seaweed. Then the others saw the pattern and followed close behind. Each one followed the next. They built a survival strategy—one green bite at a time.

The agile team is pretty much the same. When you see the patterns, try to adapt and even thrive on the new changes. Changes in your project can be great opportunities to produce a better deliverable.

Identifying Current Challenges

The activity around agile is a bit like the frenzy around a major league sport. A lot of people are talking about agile. Some people are writing about agile. Many teams try agile. But only a few teams play agile at a professional level.

An agile transformation is a major change from business as usual. To start, you need to prepare for significant challenges. To play like a pro, your team needs to practice and make a strong commitment to change. Becoming a professional agile team means re-engineering the way the team thinks and works.

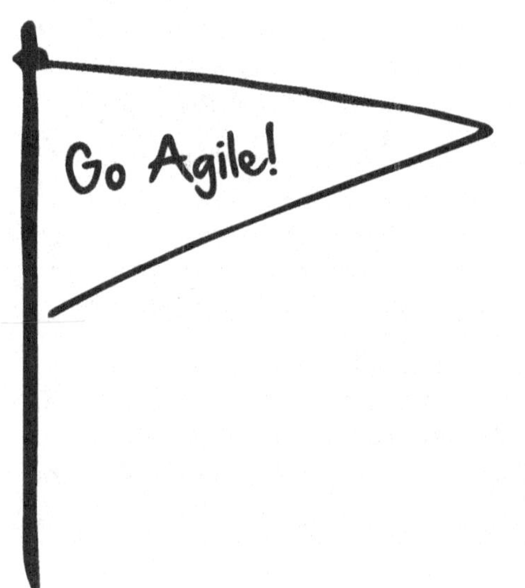

Agile teams will continuously improve and tighten their cycle of innovation and adaptation. They will strip away low-value activities and deliver products every few weeks.

To add fuel to the desire for change, traditional projects usually stumble for the same reasons. This is true even if you have a different team or a new project. This would suggest that there is something wrong with the process.

When you start introducing agile, you want to identify why the organization needs to change. This will help you build a foundation that will sustain your organization for the long haul.

Pro Tip

Agility is a skill that can be improved, but not perfected. Your team will always be on their agile journey. There is no "we're agile" pizza party or "agile complete" memo. There is no "finished agile" box you can check.

This makes agile particularly difficult to start in organizations. There's a long ramp-up period. It requires people to think differently and there's an unclear timeline. In a sense, it's a never-ending process of improvement.

Under normal circumstances, a transformation like this would have little hope of starting. Fortunately, most projects don't run very well and it's not hard for managers to imagine that there could be a better way.

Don't start by promising immediate results. That type of expectation is almost sure to fizzle. Instead, start by listing the challenges you have with your current projects, then see if you can get everyone to agree that there is a need for change.

Your list of challenges will probably look a lot like this:

Our projects have bad requirements. Not enough work is done at the beginning of a project to make sure that all the unknowns have been accounted for. After the project starts, the manager fills in the missing pieces to make sure the project works.

Our projects have unrealistic deadlines. Your stakeholder or sales team has trouble creating realistic timelines.

Our projects have changing priorities. After you start a project, it will often begin to transform into something unrecognizable from the initial plan. The project morphs to accommodate the new priority and begins to spiral out of control.

Our projects lack vision. A project will often begin before everyone really understands the deliverables. Some people on the team will try to compensate for this by instituting their vision for the project, which may not match the vision of the stakeholders.

Our projects lack communication with the stakeholders. Some stakeholders like to just throw an idea over the wall and see what comes back. They are not available to the manager or the team, and it is a long time before any feedback is given.

Our projects lack any quality assurance. As soon as a project starts to look like it can be shipped, it is sent out.

Our project manager is working on several projects simultaneously. A multitasking project manager can be a challenge not only for the project manager but also for the team.

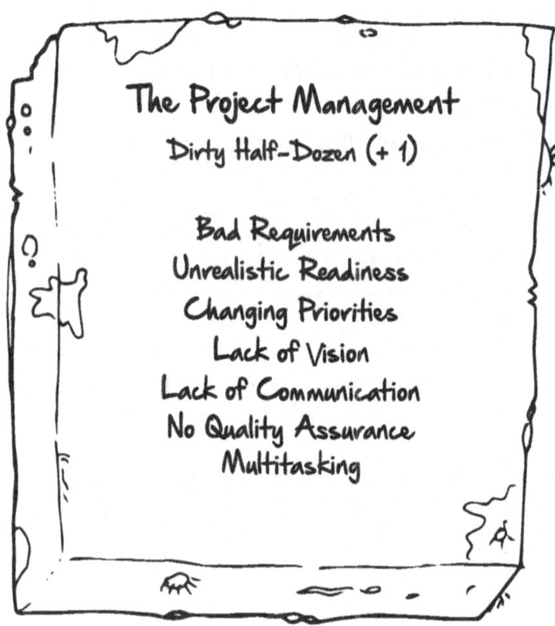

Feel free to use this list as a starting point for your agile transformation. It'll be much easier to start agile if everyone first agrees that there is a problem that needs to be solved.

A lot of organizations get stuck because they have too much invested in the status quo even though they realize the need to change. You'll want to start by listing what's wrong with the status quo as a way to motivate your organization to move forward.

Once everyone agrees that these are problems that need to be fixed, then you can start on the path of your agile transformation. If you can't get consensus that these problems exist, then you should wait before starting.

Pro Tip

It's very common for everyone to agree that these problems exist, but they still may not be ready for transformative change. They think the old system will work fine with just a few improvements. If that's the case, the agile transformation is unlikely to get off the ground.

You want to take time at the beginning of your attempt to implement agile to build a strong case for change. As with any change, there will always be a strong headwind to keep things the same. You need to have everybody onboard with the idea that this is going to be a long haul. If this isn't tied down, then your agile effort will end before it begins.

Shoring Up Management

There are many different ways to start promoting agile within your organization. Often you'll need to convince several different groups of stakeholders. The two groups of stakeholders you'll usually have are the executive sponsors and the development managers.

When you're starting agile in your organization, these groups are interested in very different things, and they'll listen for solutions to their own set of challenges.

Pro Tip

Executives will be more interested in predictability and delivery. This group is usually looking for ways to get teams to commit to delivery dates. Some executives talk about plans in terms of years, but will usually settle for predictable work over months. To bring an executive on board, you'll want to describe agile as a regimented and predictable delivery framework.

Most executives are not concerned about the way you run your agile activities. They will have little interest in terms such as standups, planning, or retrospectives. Don't focus on the particulars of the change. Just equate agile with predictability and delivery.

Development managers will have very different interests. These managers do not like directionless, high-pressure work. Software development is about solving problems in an elegant way. It's a craft. Developers do not like customer representatives standing over their shoulder trying to push things out the door. These managers will look for clear tasks and feedback in two-week chunks. Be sure to talk about agile as a way to define their tasks and regulate their work.

Once you've identified the groups that you need to bring on board, you can start laying the groundwork for your agile transformation.

If your stakeholders are unfamiliar with agile, you might want to start with some basic terms and definitions. Begin by defining agile as the ability to move "quickly and gracefully while at the same time being resourceful and adaptable." To be agile means having the ability to move quickly while balancing flexibility and stability.[3]

[3] *Agile Project Management: Creating Innovative Products* by Jim Highsmith (2002)

There are a few key terms in this definition that you should focus on while defining agile. The first is *quickly*. In most industries, lost time is expensive. Agile teams get working software in front of customers as soon as possible.

The second key term is *adaptability*. Agile teams give up a lot of up-front planning in favor of being able to adapt and change. The team will make estimations based on experience, but in the end, everyone on the team needs to be flexible and adapt to the "unknown unknowns."

You may also want to mention a bit about *agile methods*. Agile methods are simply the team's activities and new practices. These methods are the agile-driving processes which are combined into an *agile framework*, such as Scrum, Kanban, extreme programming, or the Scaled Agile Framework.

It's very important to get the language and terms down early in the process. Often agile transformations will start because managers hear bits and pieces of what other organizations are doing. They'll recommend their groups look into the techniques that other organizations are using, but they might not connect that all of these different efforts are under the same agile umbrella. If this has happened in your organization, make sure your executives recognize that all of these frameworks are related.

Field Notes

I once worked for an organization where the tech support team was using Kanban for workflow. Another group of software developers was using Scrum. And yet another group was experimenting with extreme programming.

When I met with their executive sponsors, they didn't realize that all of these different frameworks were agile. Parts of their organization had already started an agile transformation without any executive oversight.

After your audience is familiar with the terms, you should communicate both the benefits and challenges of your agile transformation. It's important to not oversell an agile transformation. Like any organizational change, it will take time to have productivity gains.

When you promote agile as an overnight productivity boost, the executives will soon question the results.

Pro Tip

It's equally important to lay out what you lose in agile transformation. If you don't lay this out early, then you could easily derail your later efforts. Agile will eliminate a lot of your team's up-front planning. This means that your team won't produce a lot of familiar artifacts, such as Gantt charts, Microsoft project reports, and budgets tied to milestones.

You want to communicate that loss very early. It can be very frustrating for a team to start an agile transformation only to have an executive asking about the missing Gantt charts.

Try not to sell the agile "sizzle." It's tempting when you get very interested in agile to try and oversell the benefits and undersell the pain. A true agile transformation will require everybody to think about work in a different way. That will take a lot of time and frustration.

Once you've educated management about agile, the best way to end your presentation is to recommend that the executive sponsor fund a small team for the agile pilot. Ideally, the project should not have a lot of interdependencies with other projects. It's also much better to go small than go large. Try to keep the team to fewer than seven people.

Agile Is Predictable

When you first think about agile, it doesn't seem like it would have much executive appeal. Many executives come from a management background, so you wouldn't think that they'd embrace the idea of a self-organized team. It's a tough sell for someone who is a leader and a manager to accept that teams do better without leaders and managers.

You would also think that they'd dislike the idea of having very little up-front planning since executives are often pressured to produce three-year and five-year plans. They need to establish long-term budgets and milestones. Why embrace a framework that specifically upends those goals?

So what do executives want from the agile framework? The short answer is that they want *predictability*. Usually by the time managers have become executives, they've realized that a plan is not always a great predictor.

Executives may plan for three to five years, but they worry in business quarters. An agile project builds up working software every two weeks. That gives executives a working, valuable deliverable. They can rely on a finished product.

Think about what executives are afraid of. They're given a finite budget to create increased business value. They don't want to have a big chunk of that budget placed in jeopardy.

Imagine you're an executive and you've convinced your supervisors that they need a new software product by the end of the year. Then you're given a large sum of money to deliver that project. You get a plan from the development team about how they intend to deliver the software. The plan shows that by the end of the year you'll have working software within that budget.

What often happens with these plans is that they don't turn out to be reliable. The software takes more time, more money, or both. Milestones disappear and commitments go unmet. This may not happen with every project, but it happens enough to be a problem.

So at the end of the year, you might have a tough meeting to schedule. You'll need to go to your supervisors and say, "Remember when I said I'd give you this great software for that money you gave me? Well, it's a funny story. . . ."

This is an outcome that most executives try to avoid.

Now the supervisors have to make a couple of tough decisions. Should they double down on the project and add more money? Or should they accept a business quarter of wasted effort and abandon the project? Either one of these is a tough call.

Many executives realize that planning and predictability aren't the same thing. They may plan on getting something really valuable at the end of the year, but if they depend on that plan, then they could end up in trouble.

Now imagine if you had sponsored an agile team for the software. Instead of a detailed plan from the team, you'll just establish a deadline. The product owner would coordinate with the executive team and create the software.

The team may run into the same challenges. There will be changes. The team might rely on software vendors that don't deliver. Agile doesn't promise to eliminate all of the unknown blocks that can crush a project. Instead, an agile team builds up working software in little bits over time. The project might not deliver everything, but it will deliver *something* and that something will work.

That makes a big difference for the executive at the end of the year. The executive will have working software, not just an unfulfilled promise. The agile software might not have all of the features and functions, but the executive won't have to settle for an IOU.

Now imagine your meeting at the end of the year after an agile project. You can now say, "Thank you for all that money. Here's the software we created. It may not do everything that was discussed, but it's still valuable."

Now the executives have a much easier conversation. Should they keep on building up the software? Or should they just keep the software as it is and invest somewhere else?

It's important to keep these pain points in mind when thinking about your executive sponsor. You should always use the language of predictability and delivery. This is especially true if you're trying to convince an executive to sponsor your agile project.

Self-Organized Teams

Another area where executives may be expected to have trouble with agile is in how teams are run. Agile is a significant change from traditional projects. The members of the team are not managed by a traditional project manager. Ingrained in the framework is the assumption that a self-organized team will create high-quality products. It's based on the belief that an orchestra filled with professionals doesn't need a conductor to create beautiful music.

Pro Tip

There is no secret sauce to becoming a self-organized team. The transition to self-organizing is often slow and difficult. If anyone on the team is unproductive, the team will struggle to self-correct. Just because you're agile doesn't mean the team will magically function like a well-oiled machine.

A lot of patience goes into getting the team to "gel." That is why project managers are not always a natural choice for agile transformations. You're forcing them to abandon skills that they've spent years developing. Someone who considers themselves a strong leader might be tempted to take control of the project if they feel the team is struggling.

Often, it is difficult for project managers to let go of their leadership over the team. If agile represents a bold new world of self-organized teams, it will probably be the project managers that will have the toughest time living in it. We will look at self-organizing teams in more detail later on in this book.

Pro Tip

Many organizations will have a well-established project management office, or PMO. The PMO will often have expectations around how a project manager should manage the project. This can make the project manager's role difficult. Even if the project manager accepts self-organizing, the PMO office might expect their leadership.

Defining The Agile Team Roles

In order to transform your company into an agile one, you will also need to define the new roles that are created as a result of becoming agile. The roles and responsibilities are different than in a traditional setting and everyone needs to understand and commit to these new roles.

In a Scrum team, there are three formal roles: the product owner, the developers, and the ScrumMaster. The Scrum team doesn't usually distinguish among testers, graphic designers, and programmers. They're all called developers.

ScrumMaster

The role that usually gets the most attention is the ScrumMaster. This role is often mistaken for a traditional manager who masters the team. The role is really intended to be a combination of an agile administrator, coach, and trainer. The "master" in the title is intended to show that this person masters the Scrum framework.

The equivalent role in extreme programming is called the agile coach. This title is a much better description of what this person should be doing, but people seem to prefer ScrumMaster.

ScrumMasters will spend most of their time removing obstacles for the team and ensuring they have a great work environment.

Pro Tip

The impressive-sounding term *ScrumMaster* has been a boon for Scrum certifications. The reality is that no one wants to be a certified agile facilitator. A certified ScrumMaster sounds like a role filled with panache. It has gravitas like Master Builder or Jedi Master.

In reality, the ScrumMaster's role is much more administrative.

Product Owner

The Scrum product owner is the true seat of power for the team. The product owner is the customer representative. Product owners typically work for the customer and ensure that the team is working on delivering the highest-value features.

The product owner should have a direct line of communication with all the customer stakeholders and will work closely with the final users of the product. The product owner will also gather up the work for the rest of the team.

The product owner will primarily work on maintaining the product backlog—the ranked list of all the functions and features that the customer would like to see in the final product.

The key challenge for the product owner is ranking this list. As you can imagine, not all customers agree on what should be the highest-priority work, but the product owner has the final say in what gets done first. They will have to deliver the software in a way that makes everyone happy. Their role can be viewed as being similar to the steady parent cutting the cake at their four-year-old child's birthday party.

Developers

In Scrum, the developers are the knowledge pool for the team. A key part of self-organization is that the developers estimate their own work, and then they commit to delivery.

The developers should have a good mix of skills because in a Scrum development team everyone in the rowboat rows. That means if the team is behind in testing, the programmers stop what they're doing and write test cases. There is a shared responsibility for the team to produce. No single team member should wait for others if they have the ability to help. That means there's always a drive for Scrum developers to pick up new skills and share their skills with the rest of the team.

Confusing Roles

Just because you're starting something new doesn't mean you're starting with a new team. That's just a normal part of how organizations operate. No one would want to work for an organization where new people were brought in after every change.

This is also true when you start using agile. Most of your team will likely be long-term employees trying something new. There'll be the same developers, project managers, and business analysts you've always worked with. Each of these people will have habits that they've formed from their previous experiences.

These habits can be difficult to break. Most of the team may accept that they're working on an agile project, but the day-to-day impact of the change is harder to fathom. If they've never worked with agile before, then they'll likely have legacy habits.

Pro Tip

Developers usually have a lot of habits clustered around accountability. They may be used to less accountability for project delivery. They'll have worked off detailed requirements and may have provided best-guess estimates.

In traditional project management, the project manager takes responsibility for delivery and the business analysts will communicate with the customer. Often the developer will not be involved until all these meetings are complete. They'll look to the project manager and business analyst to sort this out, so they can focus on development.

This creates an accountability buffer zone between the developers and the customer. The developers will shrug their shoulders and do their best with what they have. Channels to gather more information aren't available.

Agile breaks up this arrangement. The developers are expected to interact directly with the product owner. The developers will break down high-value items into daily tasks. They will also create estimates for their own work. The developers don't need to satisfy management—they need to focus on delivery.

These changes may be a challenge when a developer has spent years working behind the scenes.

Alternate Universe

I once worked on a project where developers wouldn't start until they got their detailed requirements. Over the years, they learned that no work was better than rework. So they waited until they had their paperwork in hand.

It was a very difficult habit to break. In agile, the people who do the work also task out the work. If the developers have a question, then they are responsible for interacting with the product owner. The team is on the hot seat. There is no document they can point to and say, "We're just doing what this says."

If your developers are having a tough time shaking these habits, there are a few things to keep in mind. The first thing is the Spider-Man rule of management, "With great power, comes great responsibility." Make sure that there's nothing blocking the team from self-organizing. You need to communicate to the team that they are the ones responsible for delivering the project.

Self-organization and accountability go hand in hand. If your developers are not accepting responsibility, then make sure that they are not being directed by a rogue manager.

Rogue managers are managers who have some authority over one or more members of the team. They're okay with self-organization, but they still like to pull off "their" employee every once in a while to help out on another project. Sometimes, this is also called an executive *peel off*. Someone with authority is trying to peel off a member of the team.

Legacy Habits

You are not responsible for delivery

You need to manage the project

Agile

Traditional

ScrumMaster (Former Project Manager)

You are responsible for delivery

You need to wait for clear requirements

Agile

Traditional

Developers (Former Waterfall)

The second thing to keep in mind is that it is okay for the team to have a failed sprint. The team will learn a lot more from a failed sprint than they will from a failed project.

Many organizations have mechanisms that spring into action at the first whiff of failure. Sometimes, it's best for the team to accept the consequences of failure. Many developers have never endured the wrath of an angry customer. A nasty meeting with the product owner might help illustrate that there is no buffer zone between them and the customer.

Pro Tip

ScrumMasters with a project management background might cringe at the idea of open failure. To them, it might look like a train wreck in slow motion: something they can easily prevent with good project management.

This is a habit that the ScrumMaster needs to break. A ScrumMaster is not responsible for delivery. A ScrumMaster is responsible for making sure the team follows the agile framework.

The ScrumMaster will show the team how to make proper estimates. If the team flounders, the team members should self-correct. If that doesn't work, then the ScrumMaster might set up a meeting between the product owner and the team.

There is a stark contrast between managing the project and enforcing the framework. It is not the ScrumMaster's role to keep the team moving.

There are a few things to look for if you think the ScrumMaster is having trouble shaking old habits. The first is to look at your ScrumMaster's "pain points." Do they focus on delivery or do they focus on the team? Do they worry about meeting deadlines or do they worry about training? You want them to focus on the team and training.

The project manager to ScrumMaster transformation is one of the most difficult to accept. The best way to stay out of trouble is to make sure that the organization sees the ScrumMaster role as intended. That can be a challenge when it's the same person in a different role.

The ScrumMaster needs to ensure that everyone understands their role and responsibilities. It's hard to imagine going agile if the ScrumMaster is having trouble finding his or her own way. If your ScrumMaster is a former project manager, make sure you spend time at the beginning to delineate the ScrumMaster's role to avoid any confusion.

Individual roles are not the only areas where you might run into trouble. It can also be difficult to make agile fit into a company with a lot of established processes.

Working With The PMO

An agile transformation may put the company's project management office (PMO) in an awkward position. The role of a project management office is to oversee all the projects in an organization. They will usually create project portfolios, which are essentially groups of related projects. The PMO will have established several practices and processes to oversee all of these projects. To transition to agile, the PMO will have to change many of their established norms.

When you start an agile project, the relationship with the project management office will be extremely important. The project management office will usually determine the success or failure of your agile transformation. In larger organizations, the PMO will be a powerful group. If your PMO is hostile toward agile, then your project will likely never get off the ground.

This can be a real challenge for agile projects. The PMO is usually heavily invested in traditional project management and many of the PMO's reports are not easily re-created in agile.

That usually means that the PMO will either have to change the type of reports that are required or ask the agile team to change their work. Convincing a PMO to change their reports is a significant challenge. Many PMOs see their role as defending project standards. These standards are almost always based on traditional project management.

Field Notes

I once worked for an organization where the PMO created an executive weekly status report. The report was a list of project milestones, and each milestone had a description as well as a real-time status update.

When I met with the PMO director, I mentioned that agile doesn't use milestones. Instead, the work is prioritized in the product backlog. The backlog could change based on the product owner's highest-value items.

The project manager could create milestones, but they'd be little more than a snapshot. They'd be based on an ever-changing product backlog. The product owner might have a meeting the next day and change the priority.

The director found this frustrating. Their work depended on stability in the project timeline. They needed to know when the project would be 25% complete, 50% complete, and 100% complete. The budget was closely tied to the milestones. When the project was 50% complete, then the budget should be down by 50%.

An agile project cannot be shoehorned to work in the traditional way with milestones connected to the budget. The agile project had a release, but it wasn't divided by dates and milestones. To divide the work, you'd need to know up front everything the project was going to deliver. The PMO didn't ask for it, but they still needed a project plan. When working with the PMO, the members of the PMO may not explicitly state that you need a detailed plan, they'll just ask for artifacts from the plan. They'll want to take a look at a Gantt chart or a project timeline. It's like the promise from Henry Ford that "any customer can have a car painted any color so long as it is black."

The problem with these reports is that they lead to increasingly creative works of fiction. You might find yourself struggling to create milestones tied to sprints. Or you might create a project plan with a schedule for the PMO and a product backlog for your agile team. The project manager will be working off this set of plans and the product owner will be working off another.

This could add a lot of confusion and instability to your project. The team will be working in agile, but the project manager and the PMO will be reporting the project as if it were a waterfall project.

Pro Tip

When faced with these challenges, it is important to respect the work of the PMO. The members of the PMO have a role to play. If your team tries to circumvent that role, they will run into avoidable obstacles.

Avoiding The Agile "Rowboat"

One tactic to develop a positive relationship with the PMO is to try to enlist the PMO into running and maintaining your agile training. Training is often an innocuous way to try and elicit changes in an organization. If the PMO takes responsibility for agile training, then they might become one of your strongest change advocates.

Another tactic is to try and elicit the help of your team's project manager. Often the team's project manager will have a much closer relationship with the PMO. Project managers could use their knowledge of the PMO to try and bridge the difference between the agile project and the expectations from the PMO office.

It is best if the project manager can interact with the PMO, but sometimes the PMO is not very interested in your agile transformation. The office might be overloaded with dozens of projects or your project might be too small to attract any attention.

This also may happen if the PMO is not very interested in making changes to their processes. Instead, they may set your team loose to run your project disconnected from the organization.

They may put your project in an agile rowboat. The team will be on its own like a little rowboat trailing behind the PMO cruise ship. They might expect some very high-level reporting, but not much more.

The challenge with a rowboat project is that your work will always be seen as a novelty. It might be fine for your team, but it usually means agile will not be adopted by the rest the organization. If your project is in an agile rowboat, then chances are when the project is complete, the organization will go back to traditional project management.

Spend a lot of time early in your project developing a good relationship with your PMO. It will be a determining factor in how well they embrace agile. If the PMO doesn't like agile or ignores your efforts, then you'll be in for a significant uphill effort. If you respect their role, they can be a boost for your agile transformation.

Renaming Over Retooling

Renaming instead of retooling can cause a number of problems. It will lead to a lot of confusion about what an actual agile transformation looks like. It will also deplete a lot of goodwill that you might have toward making an actual change. And it may prohibit your organization from ever adopting agile in the future. They will reject the framework without ever really having tried it.

Field Notes

I once worked for an organization that started every morning with an hour-long status meeting. The portfolio manager would show a multicolored spreadsheet on a large projector screen.

On the left were the names of each department. The columns were the milestones. Each cell had a date. If the milestone was on track, the cell was green. If it was red, then the milestone was behind.

The portfolio manager went around the table asking every project manager for a status update. In between sips from giant coffee mugs, they'd explain why their milestones turned yellow or worse.

Field Notes (continued)

This organization had a legacy in construction. The milestones, the status, and the table were all familiar pieces of a project. This was the same meeting they had when they were building condominiums. It was the expected rhythm of delivering a complex project.

When the organization started developing software, the executives suggested they try agile.

Agile would be a difficult change for this organization. They were heavily invested in their current processes. All the project managers followed milestones, big designs, and managed groups. The organization went through several rounds of training, but still wouldn't accept key agile concepts.

The portfolio managers didn't want to reject agile, so instead they renamed their current processes using agile language.

The meeting around the table was now a daily standup activity. The same project managers were now ScrumMasters. The milestones were now dated sprint releases. The language changed, but none of the activities changed.

This led to a lot of confusion. No one stood during the daily standup. They also created new agile roles. Now there was a *super ScrumMaster* instead of a portfolio manager and an *agile team lead* for the senior developers.

In the end, the organization didn't get any benefit from the changes. Instead, they just frustrated their administrators with endless renaming and rescheduling. They were asking questions like "Are you the super ScrumMaster or just the ScrumMaster for this project?"

Because of all the confusion, the managers reported back that agile was not ready for enterprise-level projects. Then everything changed back to the way it was before the confusion.

This renaming over retooling usually happens when an organization doesn't want to change. It's much easier to use agile language than to have teams go through a difficult transformation.

There are some things to look for if you think your organization might be renaming over retooling.

The first thing is the easiest to spot. After your transformation, are you doing the same thing, at the same time, with the same people, in the same place?

It might sound silly, but many teams underestimate the effort it takes to change. A successful agile transformation requires long-term commitment. If the teams don't change, they will soon settle back into the way they've always done things.

Do your agile team activities seem familiar? Then chances are you haven't changed.

The second thing to look for is support from the executive level. It is very difficult to make meaningful changes if the executives don't invest their time and resources into that change. Renaming over retooling is an easy out for middle managers. It is a penny's worth of change for a penny's worth of investment.

The third thing to watch for is whether you're trying to change agile to fit the organization. This is particularly true with new agile roles. If you're changing agile, it usually means that you're not changing your team. You're fighting the framework when you create roles like *super ScrumMasters* or *agile development leads*. Before creating any new roles, ask yourself if this new role will help or prevent a change.

Finally, take an objective look at your organization. What does your organization do? Are your executives all former construction engineers? Then your organization might not embrace less planning. Do you have a lot of project managers? Then your organization might have trouble with self-organized teams. Try to predict the trouble spots in your organization.

Some organizations will have an easier time embracing agile. For organizations that might have difficulty, it's important to commit to the change. If you try to force agile on an organization that isn't ready, it will just lead to confusion. In the words of Jedi Master Yoda from *Star Wars*, "Either do or do not, there is no try."

Setting The Stage

Ensuring people understand what agile means and how it works are not the only difficulties you will have to deal with when transforming your company to agile. You will also have to deal with the actual space where the work occurs.

If you come from a technology background, then you may have heard of the Bell Labs facility in New Jersey. This laboratory was responsible for much of the technology innovation that happened in the 1960s and 1970s. The building was filled with academics, engineers, designers, and technology experts.

If you look at the pictures of the old building, you'll see that each office let out into a long hallway. If you ever left your office, you would certainly run into someone. Many of Bell Labs, unplanned technology innovations came out of spontaneous face-to-face conversations.

Thirty years later, when the late CEO of Apple Computers Steve Jobs helped design the building for Pixar, he designed the building so that each office flowed into an open atrium. When the employees moved from their old building, they ran into team members they hadn't seen in months.

What these companies knew is that innovation is not created by voicemail and email—innovation is the product of real-time, face-to-face collaboration.

Compare that to many modern office environments. In a modern office, you're more likely to see rows of cubicles. People sit in cubicle clusters based on their role. The software developers will be clustered in one area, the designers will be clustered in another area, and the project's sponsor might even be on a different floor or building.

This modern environment is designed to inhibit collaboration. It gives everyone their own private space to work on their own specific tasks. It's also designed to divide the work. One group will work on one set of tasks and then pass it on to the next group.

This is the opposite of what you want for your agile team. An agile team should have cross-functional communication and real-time collaboration.

This is why it's extremely important for an agile team to be in a shared workspace. If someone in a team has a great idea, they can walk over for an immediate chat.

Pro Tip

Encouraging face-to-face communication is a theme that will work its way through the entire agile project.[4] The customer will get face-to-face demonstrations and the team members should discuss things in a face-to-face setting.

When it comes to your agile projects, try to think of email, memos, and voicemail as a way to schedule activities. Think of face-to-face communication as a way to actually collaborate.

If you rely on electronic communication, you'll quickly discover how little information is actually communicated. Think about how many times you've talked with someone after several email messages. You can usually clear up any confusion pretty quickly.

The ScrumMaster is primarily responsible for making sure that the team is in a shared workspace. In some organizations, this might be an easy fix. There are also a number of organizations that will battle this change every step of the way.

This is a battle that the ScrumMaster should fight to win, but in many organizations, it just won't happen. In these cases, you should seriously reconsider if agile is a good fit. If you decide to press on with agile, then try to ensure that at least two things happen.

First, try to make sure that the product owner sits next to some members of the team. The team wants to know what will make the project successful. That's the information they get from the product owner. The product owner will have certain expectations whether they tell you or not. They will be the best insight you have into the customer's expectations.[5]

[4] *The Agile Manifesto* Principle 6 expands on the value of customer collaboration. The principle states, "The most efficient and effective method of conveying information to and within the development team is face-to-face conversation."
[5] *The Agile Manifesto* Principle 4 expands on the value of customer collaboration. This principle says, "Business people and developers must work together daily throughout the project."

Second, the ScrumMaster should at least try to have some dedicated space for the team to meet. This can be a Scrum room or an open space next to the cubicles. The hope is that after the daily standup (a short team activity), many team members may stay in the space to collaborate. It is a way to get some shared work time.

Even with these fixes, you should still invest considerable energy in getting a full-time, dedicated shared workspace. These decaffeinated fixes will only give you a fraction of the benefit that you get from the real thing.

A shared workspace will give you the most bang for your buck in your agile transformation. Just this one simple change will increase your team's collaboration and communication.

Also, if the team is working in cubicles, it's very difficult to convince them that agile is different. It will be difficult to communicate to your team that agile is a big change if they are sitting in the same place with the same people in the same way. A simple move will be a big win and go a long way in communicating the organization's dedication to agile.

Chapter 5

Thinking Like An Agile Team

By now you should have a good understanding of some of the challenges you will face when trying to convince your company to implement agile. Once your company has agreed to take the plunge, the people within the agile team need to start working differently. They need to give up the old roles and start taking on new roles and responsibilities as part of a team.

The developers, the product owners, and the ScrumMasters are simply called the team. This makes sense because Scrum is a bit more abstract than extreme programming. Team members may also include marketing specialists and sales analysts. In extreme programming, the developers are primarily software developers and testers.

Since the developers are responsible for estimating and completing the work, it is usually a good idea to have a development team with a generalized skill set. This will create a team that doesn't have to be overly dependent on resources that are outside the team.

If no one on the team knows anything about setting up computer servers, it would be very risky to create an estimate about how long it would take to install a web server. If the team is more generalized, they will be able to create accurate estimates for a much wider range of tasks. It is also better to keep all of the work inside the team. If there are outside contractors, then the team becomes disconnected from their work. The team will still have accountability but no ability to complete the project.

Don't Depend On Superheroes

In the 1940s, there was a very popular radio show called *Superman*. Invariably, someone in the show would be in a dangerous situation. Lois Lane or Eddy would be caught up in some sort of trap with little hope of escape. Then the radio announcer would start, "Look up in the air! It's a bird! It's a plane! No, it's Superman!" Then in a flash, Superman would swoop in and save the day.

As strange as it may sound, that's not much different from how many organizations view their projects. They will try to hire their own superheroes for the team. Typically these superheroes

will have some knowledge or experience that is meant to save the day. Instead of lifting locomotives, they work long hours. Instead of leaping tall buildings, they leap milestones. The superhero is the developer who will drive the team to deliver the project.

There are a few challenges with this approach. The first challenge is that when one superhero drives the work, it becomes increasingly difficult to maintain the product. The second challenge is that if one person is responsible for more of the work, then that person becomes a bottleneck for the rest of the team.

Agile tries to break away from this superhero model. For the project to succeed, the responsibility for the delivery of the product is distributed to the entire team. There is less need to find one person to drive and deliver the product. An agile team should try to share knowledge and share responsibility.

That's why agile places so much emphasis on communication and collaboration. One of the best descriptions of how an agile team works comes from the world of extreme programming.

Extreme programming is one of the earliest agile frameworks. The framework preceded The Agile Manifesto, so it started out with its own list of values. These values were designed to help an agile team work in harmony.

The five core values are communication, simplicity, feedback, courage, and respect. These might sound like the refrain of a country-western song, but when viewed as a whole, you can see agile work patterns.

Communication: Agile puts a high premium on communication. This is the reason behind the use of a shared workspace, user stories, pair programming, collective code ownership, and daily standups. The team has a dedicated ScrumMaster whose job is to notice when people aren't communicating.

Simplicity: Agile teams put a lot of emphasis on simplicity. The output should be the simplest solution for the job. Over-engineering can be a big problem in software projects. The team should "do the simplest thing that could possibly work" (DTSTTCPW principle), or "keep it simple" (KISS). You might hear an agile team use the term YAGNI or "you ain't gonna need it." An agile team will try to deliver the simplest solution and improve it over time.

Feedback: This core value is really a subset of communication. The team needs to give feedback to one another. The product owner should give feedback to the team. The team should collaborate with the product owner and make changes. There should always be someone giving you feedback or getting feedback from you.

All this feedback requires a lot of communication. When the team is working, it should be quietly active. A good agile workspace should have the feel of a newsroom and not a library.

Courage: In a way, this value gives insight into how an agile team interacts. It takes courage to communicate and accept feedback. Many developers have spent most of their career solving problems on their own. It takes a lot of courage to solve problems in a group setting.

They also need the courage to improve working code.[6] Agile teams build and improve products a little at a time. Not all the daily work makes it into the final product. The developers need courage to throw away working code. That means that the small simple solution created earlier might have to be redone or improved. This is called software refactoring and is a continuous effort by the team.

Respect: This value was added a few years after the first four. It means respect for one another and respect for your own work. This is the anti-superhero value. Every team will have varying degrees of experience and expertise. The developers will know more than the customer. Some of the developers will be more experienced than others.

For the team to work well, the team needs to share their knowledge and respect their coworkers. They need to accept that there is no one superhero and that the entire team deserves respect.

An agile team will always strive to have greater transparency. In many projects, there is a steep penalty for making mistakes. There's a lot of incentive for developers to hide and quietly cover up their errors. Agile developers need to have respect for their own work. They should only deliver clean working code. If the code is ugly or buggy, they need to share that challenge with the rest of the team.

Good training in agile will help ensure that your team does not have any "supermen" and that everyone is focused on working together to deliver the software.

Training The Agile Team

Ideally, the training should happen before the work begins and should have two main goals. The first goal is to give everybody a good understanding of the rules surrounding agile. Team members need to understand the new roles and expectations. The team should also know how to participate in the activities and how to make estimates and plans within the agile framework.

[6] *The Agile Manifesto* Principle 9 states that "Continuous attention to technical excellence and good design enhances agility."

Field Notes

I once worked for an organization where the developers wrote most of the user stories (the stories written from the user's perspective that describe what the product does). In agile, the product owner writes the user stories. I asked how this practice started and traced it back to a misunderstood exercise in the agile training. The core team went to agile training and spread this incorrect information to the rest of the organization.

Once that practice was solidified, it was almost impossible to purge the misinformation from the organization. The retraining took way longer than it would've taken to more carefully explain the first exercise. That's why the core group is usually the most important group to go through training.

The second goal is to try and give the team a forum to discuss their doubts and concerns. An agile transformation is a big undertaking. It's a journey the team shouldn't take lightly. Many organizations aren't ready for this transformation. If the organization isn't ready, it will come out in the training.

There are also organizations where agile is not the best fit. The training shouldn't present agile as a sort of magic dust that you can sprinkle on your projects to make everything better. It shouldn't be an agile sales pitch complete with promises and sizzle. Instead, the trainers should present how agile can improve the team, and then discuss how this might work for the organization.

One way to avoid this sales pitch is to make sure that your trainer is not the same person who is selling other agile products. A good salesperson will never want an open forum to discuss whether the product is a good idea.

Instead, try to find agile trainers from a local university. You can also find certified agile trainers on certification websites like the Scrum Alliance. A good trainer shouldn't be afraid of challenging questions.

Often, agile transformations are the result of top-down organizational changes. Many times, executives in the organization are the only people who can drive significant change. The downside is that not everyone in the team has a sense of why the change is happening. Then, before you know it, everybody's working on the change without understanding the benefits.

The trainer should understand this and should set aside enough time for everyone to express their views. This doesn't mean that the training should start to look like a town hall meeting, but there should be enough time for the team to talk to one another about what they're doing and why they're doing it.

If possible, you should try to have everyone on the team attend training at the same time. This is especially true for product owners. Often a product owner is the last person identified. That doesn't mean that they should miss out on the training. In fact, product owners are usually one of the greatest beneficiaries of the training, since they may be the least familiar with agile.

Letting The Team Self-Organize

Think about the majority of jobs in the early 20th century. They were the autoworker, retailer, and construction worker jobs. People used to migrate to the great hiring centers like Chicago, New York, and Detroit.

Today, these show-up-and-work jobs are increasingly difficult to find and even more difficult to hold.

Most of these early jobs followed a clear hierarchy. There were employees and managers. The managers would *manage* the employees. And the employees, if they wanted to stay employed, listened closely to their managers.

Most workers at that time were hardworking, but replaceable. They were not always hired for what they knew, but for their ability to put in a hard day's work. The managers were the ones with the skills. They were the ones being groomed and developed.

Now fast-forward to a modern agile project. An agile team may have graphic designers, developers, and database engineers. The team will have members who have spent years developing their skills.

The designers will have attended design school and have access to sophisticated software. The developers usually have engineering degrees and will have mastered several programming languages. The database engineers will have certifications from Oracle or Microsoft.

A manager cannot be expected to have this level of expertise. They can't have all the team's degrees, the knowledge of dozens of software packages, or the understanding of multiple programming languages.

This makes it difficult to manage these employees in the same way managers did 50 years ago. The team usually has a lot more knowledge than their managers.

Because of this reality, an agile team is best qualified to make many of the decisions for the project. That's why an agile team is self-organizing.

Self-organization is a loaded term for project managers who have spent their careers managing teams. It often conjures up images of unicorns sliding down rainbows.

They often see self-organizing as an unfulfilled promise like self-cleaning ovens or self-watering plants. They will think self-organizing is all happy talk. At some point, you are going to have to clean your oven or water your plants.

But self-organizing is not about taking the manager out of the team. Instead, it's about making the people who are *doing* the work responsible for scheduling the work.

Alternate Universe

When I used to work as a project manager, I would have a scheduling dance at the beginning of every project. I would first set up a meeting with the team to see how long it will take to complete the project. They would always say I forgot to invite the one person who can make this determination. Then I would reschedule the meeting with that missing person. The team would say there's not enough information for an estimate. I would say of course there's not enough information, that's why it's an estimate. They would insist on more information but grudgingly give me a date.

I knew the date was double what they actually thought it would take to finish the work. They were right. They did need more information. But I would put that bloated date into the schedule and we'd have our timeline. As a project manager, I would then commit to delivering within that timeline.

The self-organizing team takes on a lot of the responsibility that was previously left to the project managers. In an agile project, the team does the estimating. The team breaks the work down into chunks and works to improve their performance.

Agile recognizes that the estimation dance puts project managers in an unfair position. They're responsible for the outcome even though they have little knowledge of what's going into the estimate. Project managers can thump everyone's desk, but they can't write the software and they can't design the graphics.

Self-organizing isn't about taking authority from the project manager. Instead, it's about breaking down the inefficiency of being responsible for the team's work. This problem is only increasing as teams get more skilled and the work becomes more complex.

Despite this, self-organization is still one of the hardest obstacles to overcome with the team. It's just not how teams are used to working. Managers are used to managing teams. Teams are used to being managed by managers.

Of the two, it's usually much easier to get the team to accept responsibility for delivery. Managers usually have a much more difficult time accepting the idea that the team doesn't need to be managed.

Pro Tip

If you're the ScrumMaster for the team, you should try to protect the team from being managed. If there's a project manager on the team, make sure that the manager understands that this is not a traditional team. It's not the project manager's role to create estimates and drive the work.

The ScrumMaster might also be an impediment to self-organization. This is especially true if the ScrumMaster comes from a management background. Sometimes it's hard to get rid of old habits.

If you're a ScrumMaster with a management background, then you need to be keenly self-aware when you try to manage the team.

Delivering Like An Agile Team

In traditional projects, there is often a rift between the team responsible for delivery and the customers using the product. This rift makes it difficult to see how the customer views the product.

Many projects create very detailed specifications. The problem with this approach is that not every customer knows everything they want before the project begins. This is especially true with software projects.

Agile addresses this challenge by changing the way the customer views the deliverable. The product owner doesn't try to know everything about the project. Instead, they focus on the highest-value items first, which get ranked in the product backlog (a list of items and functions to be developed). This product backlog is always being updated by the product owner.

The hunt for agile value is part of a story that started a century ago. An Italian economist named Vilfredo Pareto was getting peas from his garden when he noticed that roughly 20% of his pea plants produced about 80% of his peas. That meant that 20% of his pea plants produced 80% of his overall pea harvest. This 80/20 rule stuck with him.

He later noticed the same distribution when he looked at economic data. He saw that around 80% of the land was owned by 20% of the people. Modern project managers have found the 80/20 rule to be true in a lot of scenarios. Managers often refer to this as the 80/20 rule or the Pareto rule: Eighty percent of your value comes from 20% of your product.

20% of your effort
gives you 80%
of your value

Pareto would never have guessed that, years later, his rule would also prove true for software. In 2002, the Standish Group published a chart that showed how functions and features broke down in software products.

This chart showed that, on average, customers never used 45% of the functions and features delivered in software, 19% of the functions and features were sometimes used, 16% were rarely used, 13% were often used, and finally 7% were always used.

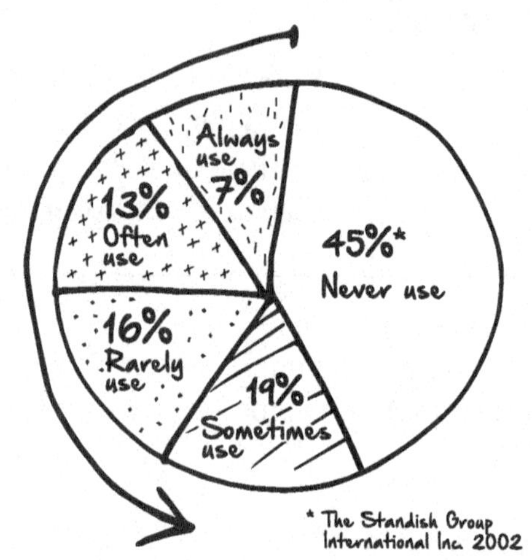

FEATURES AND FUNCTIONS USAGE

If you look closely at the chart, you'll see Pareto's rule. Only 20% of the software was often or always used. The customers were primarily using 20% of the same functions and features. This was very interesting when you consider that they were paying for 100% of the software.

Agile projects take advantage of this Pareto rule. If only 20% of your effort is giving you 80% of your value, then the product owner has a responsibility to deliver that value first.

So if you were the product owner, where would you start development?

With an agile project, you always start with the 7% of functions and features that the customers will always use. Then after that 7% is finished, you start working on the 13% of functions and features the customer will often use.

Once those high-value functions and features are complete, you can start working on the lower-value items. These are the functions and features that are sometimes used.

If you think about it, the Pareto rule will probably hold true for you as well. Think about the software products you use. How many different features do you use on your smartphone? There are probably some features you'll never use.

Now, imagine that you are a CEO of a software-development company and you have a limited budget to create smartphone software. Where would you start? You would probably start by hiring a product owner who understands smartphone software. That product owner would work closely with the customer to see what they always use on their smartphone.

Pro Tip

In agile, finding the highest-value items and making them the highest priority is a mission and not a goal. The product owner will always be working to prioritize the highest-value items and marking them down in the product backlog. Each change will have a cascading effect that re-ranks the items in the product backlog, which will alter how the work is done.

Say the new smartphone comes out and it has a really terrific feature. You, as a product owner, might push to have this feature included in your software project.

That is why ranking of the items in the product backlog is not a goal to meet. Instead, it's a mindset that will dictate how the work is delivered. Working the ranked list from the top down is an ongoing part of an agile project.

A traditional project forces the customer to do all of the planning before the team starts developing. The stakeholders need to know exactly what the software will look like before a single line of code is written.

Think about how you would approach receiving a long list of work. A very natural tendency is to start with the work that you know how to do. You may also start with the items that you think you can quickly finish. If you know everything up front, you're delivering software based on your ability to finish the product. That could mean that the customer will have to wait until the entire project is finished before they can start to use the software.

The role of the product owner is to keep this from happening. The team starts work on what the product owner ranks highest and not on what's easiest for the team to deliver. This change forces the team to finish the 20% before any other work begins.

Staying Agile With The ScrumMaster

Few roles are as misunderstood as the agile ScrumMaster. Many organizations look to ScrumMasters as their senior managers responsible for the agile transformation. They see them as a throat to choke if things go wrong with the agile project.

An agile team is self-organizing, so thinking of the ScrumMaster as a manager removes the shared responsibility from the team. It is important to remember that the ScrumMaster is responsible for managing the agile framework—not for managing the team. A ScrumMaster administers the project, creates reports, eliminates obstacles, and removes distractions.

But names matter. And any role with *master* in the title is almost certain to inherit management responsibility. That means ScrumMasters are often placed in an awkward position of trying to reduce their own scope of authority. A good ScrumMaster stands behind the team, not in front of them. ScrumMasters have to stay in the background to ensure the team is self-organizing.

Field Notes

I once worked for a project where the senior managers simply changed their title to ScrumMasters when they started agile. They assumed that anything with *master* in the title would be appropriate for a senior manager. Unfortunately, these managers just continued to operate the same way they always had. They drove the project, communicated with stakeholders, and ran the meetings.

These overzealous ScrumMasters ended up slowing the agile transformation and confusing the teams. To succeed, the ScrumMasters had to unlearn the skills they'd spent their career developing. Instead of driving the team, they learned to coach the team. Instead of running the meetings, they started to facilitate the agile activities. They started to spend less time talking and more time listening.

It was a culture shock at first. But after a few months, most of the ex-managers decided that this was what they had always wanted. They could encourage the team without taking responsibility for all of the team's work.

The ScrumMaster's job is to facilitate most of the agile activities, so it's important to understand the difference between facilitating and managing. If a ScrumMaster starts by asking everyone for status updates, then they are managing and not facilitating the activity. That's why it's often best for ScrumMasters to sit off to the side in these activities. They shouldn't communicate management authority.

If two developers start discussing a challenge at the daily standup, then it's the ScrumMaster's responsibility to interrupt them and keep the activity on topic. Again, they are responsible for making sure that the activity follows the agile framework. They are not responsible for the team's productivity.

The ScrumMaster will also create charts showing features completed in a two-week sprint, or a chart to show whether the estimates were accurate.

These reports are not about shame and blame. A ScrumMaster would never put up a chart that says, "Team member of the month." That is not about the process. That would be about congratulating individual team members and, therefore, outside of their role.

Finally, a ScrumMaster should act as the project's obstacle remover. If a team member highlights an obstacle, then the ScrumMaster takes responsibility for that obstacle. This could mean ensuring that the computers arrive on time or having an awkward conversation with a team member about talking too loudly on the phone.

They will remove barriers that keep the team from reaching peak productivity. This may include finding the team a better workspace or making sure that the customer is involved with the team. It may also include mundane tasks such as making sure that the team has pizza for the pizza party.

Pro Tip

The ScrumMaster is the team's *servant leader* and needs to be very knowledgeable about agile. The ScrumMaster's authority comes from showing the team how to correctly follow the framework.

There are also several soft skills that ScrumMasters need to develop. An obstacle might not simply be stale coffee or bad office space. It can also be hurt feelings and misunderstandings. For example, someone on the team might feel slighted by less experienced team members. The ScrumMaster needs to be emotionally intelligent about these issues and suggest a resolution.

One way to think about the ScrumMaster is to think of them as the team's sweeper on a curling team. If you have cold winters, you've probably seen the sport of curling. It also shows up every four years in the Winter Olympics. Curling is a bit like playing checkers on a massive sheet of ice. A player will slide a massive stone across the sheet of ice to a target on the other side. They hope to land on the target and knock the other player's stone off their spot.

Each team will have a thrower, the one who sends the stone down the glistening sheet. Once the thrower releases the stone, it is up to the sweepers to remove all obstacles that could slow the stone down. The sweeper will frantically dust away everything in the stone's path. They can't touch the stone, but they can keep everything else out of its way.

The sweeper is a good image for the ScrumMaster. They keep the stone moving forward by sweeping away anything that might slow the momentum. If you ever see an Olympic sweeper, you'll see that it takes a lot of effort to keep those obstacles away.

Your ScrumMaster will sweep away miscommunication and barriers to change. These are the obstacles that can keep an agile team from moving forward.

Gathering Work With The Product Owner

An agile team maintains a close connection between the customer and the developers. The customer is not seen as someone outside of the team. Instead, the customer is seen as a crucial driver of the team. The customer is the one who directs the team to deliver high-value features every two weeks.

Alternate Universe

With agile, customers are extremely involved in the project's outcome—they share the hot seat. They have real skin in the game, and if the project fails, they will shoulder their share of the blame.

This is a significant departure from how most organizations currently deliver products. There is usually a separation between the customer's department and the group responsible for delivery. In a traditional project, the customer usually throws the request over the wall and waits for something to come back.

The agile approach to delivery is much different. A customer representative sits full-time with the team and works to deliver the project.

As mentioned earlier, this representative is the product owner. In extreme programming, this role is called the customer representative. It is the product owner's responsibility to help create the product vision by helping to develop and monitor the product backlog.

The product owner will maintain the product backlog throughout the entire project and will adjust the backlog if there are new items to rank or if the developers cannot finish a task within a two-week sprint.

This makes the product owner the "North Star" for the project. Product owners keep the team focused and on track to deliver the highest-value items.

The product owner also creates the acceptance criteria. This keeps the developers from guessing what will make the project sponsor happy. The product owner says, "Here's what makes the customer the happiest, now let's do it."

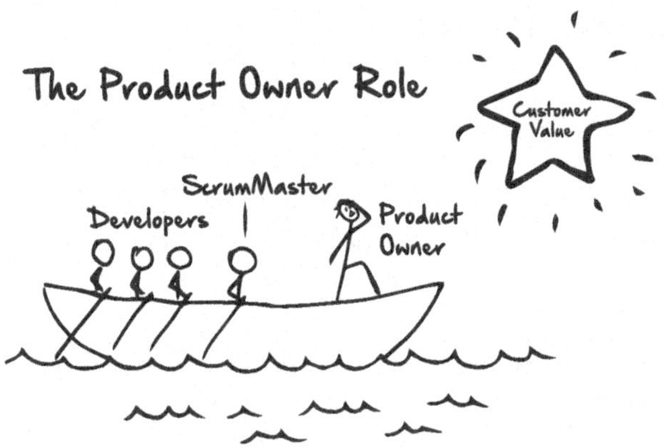

When developers pull things off the top of the product backlog, this ensures that they are developing the most important parts of the project first.

Ideally, the product owner will have a direct connection to the project's sponsor—the person who is funding the project. The sponsor is usually the final word on the project's deliverable. The product owner will ideally be part of the sponsor's department. Practically, that is very difficult to do because it is a full-time job and the sponsor doesn't always want to dedicate a full-time subject-matter expert to a project.

Pro Tip

It's important to remember that the product owner needs to be fully integrated into the team. It's better to have someone with less expertise and more availability. You don't necessarily need an expert, but you need someone who will talk to the experts and make real-time decisions.

The product owner is the best resource for mining the talent in the organization. They will be responsible for tapping domain experts and making sure that all the organization's knowledge is available to the team.

The product owner is often referred to as the most challenging role in a Scrum team. They *own* the product.

The product owner, in conjunction with the product sponsor, will come up with a high-priority task list. The developers take that information and do their best to estimate the effort required to complete the tasks on the list. After the developers create the estimate, it is their responsibility to commit to that estimate and to commit to completing specific tasks within a specific sprint. If the task is too large to fit into one sprint, the developers may go back to the product owner and ask that the task be broken up into smaller subtasks so that the new tasks can be completed in one sprint.

As always, it is the developers' responsibility to make sure that they are communicating to the product owner what work they will complete within a two-week sprint. It is essential that the developers go back and forth with the product owner to make sure that everybody understands what tasks are to be completed within each sprint.

Protecting The Team With The Project Manager

The project manager plays a central role in traditional project management. When you think about it, this makes a lot of sense. In traditional project management, a lot of emphasis goes into creating the plan. In an ideal project, all the work will closely follow the plan. Project managers are the people who help execute the plan. They don't usually do the work, but they make sure that everyone doing the work is proceeding according to the plan.

In an agile project, there is no detailed plan to follow. The work is not completely planned out at the beginning. The plan simply emerges over time.

The role of the project manager isn't clearly defined in any of the agile frameworks. Understandably, this causes some friction with many project managers. It's hard to motivate managers to embrace agile if they feel their role is less than essential. Also, project management has several structural challenges that make it difficult for many of them to see the path to follow when it comes to using agile.

One challenge is the variability that can be found within the concept of project management. Project management means different things to different organizations. Some organizations see a project manager as the key driver. They secure the funding, communicate with the sponsors, and closely manage the team. Other organizations see the project manager as an accountant or coordinator. They'll spend most of their time balancing constraints in tools like Microsoft Project.

This variability makes it difficult to make any widespread changes to project management. Unfortunately, any meaningful agile transformation will require these widespread changes.

Also, many organizations see project managers as a talent feeder into positions with greater responsibility. As a result, many project managers are ambitious and well connected. There are also many directors or senior managers who started out as project managers. They will tend to see the organization from that perspective. This will make changes even more difficult and uncertain.

It takes a very open-minded project manager to accept some of the key tenets of agile. The self-organized team, the product backlog, and the role of the ScrumMaster are all significant departures from traditional project management.

Despite these challenges, it is still possible for project managers to add value to agile.

There are usually two routes that project managers can take. They can travel upstream to the portfolio level or they can continue to work at the team level.

Portfolio project managers don't work on any one project. Instead, they work with a group of projects, or a *project portfolio*. Instead of enforcing any single project plan, they work on a group of projects to make sure that the projects all coordinate with one another.

Let's say that a company is making a web application and a mobile application. A portfolio manager might make sure that both of these applications have a similar design and color scheme. They won't do the work, but they might recommend that each project use the same designer.

If possible, it is much better for project managers to travel upstream to the portfolio level. The Scaled Agile Framework, or SAFe, is a useful method to help facilitate this transition to the portfolio level. SAFe is designed to introduce agile to larger organizations. This framework has a lot of roles that will be familiar to project managers.

In SAFe, many project managers become portfolio managers. They'll own the relationship with stakeholders and work with a familiar release schedule. Then they'll coordinate this work into an agile release train.

But not every project manager has the ability to self-promote to the portfolio level. Also, not every organization has a project management office. It's far more common for project managers to continue to work with the team. This requires a lot more effort to change. Project managers need to rethink the way they approach projects.

Project managers can help the team by translating agile work into something that's digestible to a traditional enterprise. That usually means working with the team to create milestones. They can also take the agile reports and charts and convert them into more traditional weekly status reports and schedules.

In this new role, the project manager will be protecting the team from sliding back into traditional project management. It will take a high degree of professionalism to work against what many project managers have done their entire career. It's almost like when a company hires a computer hacker to be its security expert.

To be effective, project managers will have to see a lot of value in agile. They'll have to drink the Kool-Aid and keep others from spiking the punch. For many project managers, this is a long journey.

There are a few things that project managers need to keep in mind during the transition to agile. The first and foremost thing to remember is that agile is a significant departure from traditional project management. It's all too easy to see new things as "more of the same with a new name."

Many project managers don't accept that agile is a significant change. They'll say that two-week sprints are just project phases. They'll say that they've never micromanaged and so have experience with self-organized teams.

Field Notes

I once worked with a project manager who described himself as "tool agnostic." He said he didn't care whether we used agile, waterfall, or whatever. He said he was just interested in getting the job done. He would say, "As long as I can get everybody on the same page and doing the right work, then I don't care how we get there."

It was very difficult to get him working with the agile team because "getting everybody doing the right work" was inconsistent with self-organizing.

He was also asking the team for Gantt charts and milestones. He needed these reports to "get everybody on the same page." The problem was the agile team wasn't creating schedules; they were using a product backlog.

It certainly wasn't his intention to stifle the team, but his expectations were not in line with agile. He didn't realize that his perceived tool-agnostic approach was actually a career's worth of expectations and norms.

If you're a project manager and you're working with an agile team, it should feel very different. It's like starting out with yoga. If it doesn't feel uncomfortable, then you're not doing the move correctly. Try to accept that agile is a significant change. Then you can decide to work for or against agile in your organization.

Spreading Agile

The best way to start agile in your organization is to start small. Begin with a small core agile team and make sure they follow the framework. If you work for a smaller organization, that team could have as few as four people.

Then you can expand it in your organization through conversion-by-contagion. The conversion is successfully converting one team. The contagion is getting that team to sing the praises of agile to the rest of the organization. To get there, you need to focus on the team and make sure they're well trained.

Work closely with the team to make sure they know what they're doing. Try to keep this core team as happy as possible. If they like agile, then they'll be your strongest advocates for change. This small team will be the ones talking in the lunchroom with the rest of the organization.

Give them time to be successful. They should see the benefits of the change. Don't spend a lot of time trying to sell agile to the team. Instead, put all of your energy into making agile work well.

To get the team to work well, you need to work with your optimists and your skeptics. There is an old story about a drill sergeant who marched his troops for miles. They would plead with him to finish and the sergeant would yell back, "We'll be done when the slowest one finishes." Your first agile team will be the same way. It won't be finished until the entire team is agile. This will include the team members who were excited right from the beginning and the ones who were very skeptical.

This core team will be your ambassadors for agile, so you need to make sure they are correctly following the framework. If the first team doesn't understand agile, then they will likely spread a lot of misinformation. In an organization, misinformation is usually much harder to stamp out than facts. A well-trained core team will keep you from having to do a lot of retraining in the future.

Chapter 6

Working Like An Agile Team

Once you have established and trained your team, it is time to begin working. One of the first things you need to do is create a project charter. Remember that just because you are doing agile does not mean that there is no planning. It's just that the planning is different from the planning that goes on in a traditional project.

Creating A Project Charter

Agile does not mean that there is no need to develop a project charter, but you need to remember that an agile charter is an agreement, not a plan. It should list what every party wants from the project. That doesn't mean that things won't change. What it does record is what everyone was thinking at the time the project started.

Field Notes

I once worked for an organization on a large agile project. The project had started about six months earlier. After I arrived, I asked to see all the project documentation. I figured that the documentation would be a good way to see the overall direction of the project.

I was handed a large, white three-ring binder. In the binder, there were three printouts of slide presentations. One slide printout was introducing the project name and direction. The other was selling the benefits of the technology. The final page was a bulleted list requesting funding.

One thing I immediately noticed was that the criteria to determine the successful completion of the project weren't written down. I also noticed that there wasn't an overall mission. I asked about this and the ScrumMaster said as long as they keep delivering value, the team would be successful.

In some ways, the ScrumMaster in my story was right. A key tenet of agile is adapting to deliver value, not predicting the value before you begin.

But there is a difference between the team's success and the project meeting its vision. I am not suggesting that the team should build a charter to control the value. The customer should be the one to create a charter. The charter will set the initial direction and record the project's reason for starting.

Setting up a good project charter is an essential part of closing out the project. At some point, the product backlog will be exhausted. The project will either run out of money or deliver all the value the customer requested. At that time, the team will hold their final retrospective. This is when they look at the whole project from beginning to end and record the lessons learned.

It's then that the team and the customer can decide if the project delivered on its initial promise. There are many successful teams that work on projects that ultimately fall short of their vision. It will be important for the team to see what, if anything, they could've done differently.

A good agile project charter should be one page or less, and it should have three main sections: **project vision**, **mission,** and **success criteria**.[7]

The project vision should answer one question. Why are we doing this project? You can answer this question by thinking about the project's purpose—the reason everyone started the project.

The project's mission is what everyone will do to accomplish the vision. How do you see the project playing out? How will it meet its vision?

The success criteria are the most practical of the three criteria. These will be simple one-sentence tests to make sure that the project accomplished its mission.

Let's think about a ridesharing application. A good vision statement for a ridesharing application might be the following:

Help people save money, share resources, live simply, and connect with others by sharing rides to and from their place of work.

Notice how this vision doesn't talk about the technology. It talks about the initial idea. Even if the technology changes, the idea might stay the same. Think of it as the light bulb over the customer's head. It's that initial spark of inspiration that led to the project.

The project mission is much more nuts and bolts oriented. A mission statement for the rideshare application might sound like this:

Create a cutting-edge technology platform that combines a website, a smartphone application, and location awareness with all the customers including guests, rideshare seekers, and rideshare providers.

[7] Based on work by Gil Broza

This part of the charter creates overall goals. From it, you can see the various user stories that will be needed. (Remember, user stories are the stories from the user's perspective, which describe what the application does.) The project should have web development user stories, mobile application user stories, as well as some user roles.

The product owner could start developing user roles by thinking about guests, rideshare seekers, and rideshare providers.

The final section is the project's success criteria. Be careful not to confuse the project charter's success criteria with functional success. The smartphone application might have all the functionality described in the mission statement, but it might be too expensive, too ugly, or counterintuitive. The application might functionally be a success, but it won't help accomplish the project vision if people don't use it in order to connect with others.

For our ridesharing application, a few success criteria might be the following:

- *Sign up 10,000 users within three months of initial version*
- *Sign up 100,000 users in the first year*
- *Connect 5,000 rideshare seekers to providers within the first year*
- *Have 99.999% uptime the first year*
- *Get endorsed by a major metropolitan area*
- *Create premium edition with $125,000 revenue in second year*

The success criteria have nothing to do with the application's functionality. Instead, they set out clear tests for how well the application succeeds in delivering its vision.

Writing Your Release Plan

Having a scheduled product release date might seem counter to agile, given that the product owner reprioritizes the work every sprint. If the product owner can't define the deliverable, then it is difficult to imagine a scheduled release date. How can the team commit to delivery when the customer can't define the product?

Remember that in agile, teams will release working software at the end of every sprint. [8] Some teams even sooner. It's not like a typical planned unveiling in traditional projects because it doesn't depend on everything coming together in the end. In every sprint, the product is built up bit by bit, getting better and better. New features are rolled in as the product owner defines improvements.

[8] *The Agile Manifesto* Principle 1 states, "Our highest priority is to satisfy the customer through early and continuous delivery of valuable software."

But this doesn't mean that you can't plan on bundles of value being delivered over time. In many organizations, it's still important to align your agile delivery with other projects. There'll be tradeshows and accounting pressures that may need to be addressed by the organization.

The way an agile team works is not always consistent with what an organization demands. Agile projects don't have milestones. There's no scope. There's nothing to split into quarters, months, or weeks. This difference between how an agile team delivers and what an organization demands creates an expectations gap—but there are a few ways you can fill this gap.

Instead of milestones, agile has groups of stories called epics. These epics should represent a large chunk of the customer's value. You can use these epics to create a rough order of value, or ROVe. This means that you can plan to deliver these groups of epics over time.

ROVe Release

Agile tries to ensure that the deliverable is the highest-value product. That product might change during development, and ROVe planning helps keep everyone's eye on the ball. It is not based on what the product does. Instead, it is a commitment to give a rough order of value on a certain day.

To come up with a realistic release plan, you will be required to do some old-fashioned horse trading. In the past, a horse was one of the most valuable possessions you could own. Horses were your car, truck, bulldozer, and generator. That's why bartering for horses was a serious business. There were festivals for the special event. There were even professions created to deal with quality assurance. Special whisperers would even coax out a horse's previous history.

Buyers and sellers would gather near the stables and trade different horses. They could swap two old ones for one young one. Maybe they'd trade three small ones for one large one. This event was commonly known as horse trading.

Centuries later, you still see groups of people horse trading valuables. Politicians will horse trade votes. Major league sports will horse trade contracts between different cities.

Today, horse trading pretty much works the same way. You have a large group of people in a room making trade-offs in real time. You'll still see the same compromises. Maybe you'll get two small ones for a big one. Or maybe you'll put off three less important ones and think about them later.

To create a release plan, you can assemble all the stakeholders and do some real-time horse trading. To develop an agile release plan, the ScrumMaster puts all of the epics, or groups of stories, on a trading board. Each of these epics will have an estimate of the amount of effort it takes to deliver the stories. The team will have created these estimates and assigned story points to these stories in their planning poker session (more about this later).

The team's velocity (the set number of stories that they can deliver in each sprint) might be 50 story points. This means that every two weeks the team can complete 50 story points. One epic might have five stories that are estimated at two story points each. That epic would have a total of 10 story points. This means that the team could deliver this epic and another 40 points for the sprint. The agile horse traders need to decide which epic to deliver. It could be a big one for 40 points or maybe two small ones that have 20 points each.

The ScrumMaster will place the epics into each sprint. The customer will decide the rough order of value of these epics. Maybe three sprints will have a ROVe to deliver the website. Maybe 10 sprints will have the ROVe for the website in the mobile application.

It's important to keep the customer talking about value instead of milestones. If they think in milestones, then they'll think about scheduled commitments. That's not part of the agile plan. The product owner might decide after three sprints that they want to add more value to the website. That's perfectly acceptable. But adding value to the website might delay delivery of the mobile application. The product owner should know that too many changes would impact the rough order of value.

Let's see how this horse trading might work in the release plan for our rideshare application. The rideshare application could have created dozens of epics for its initial release. Let's say that five of these epics were:

(10) Create rideshare provider search
(20) Create rideshare provider profile
(30) Create rideshare seeker login
(40) Design landing page for website
(50) Create map page with rideshare providers

Now imagine that each of these epics was filled with estimated stories. From top to bottom, the total story points were 10 points, 20 points, 30 points, 40 points, and 50 points.

On the trading board, each of these epics would have this number written underneath them. So *create rideshare seeker login* would have the number 30 written under it.

The Scrum team has a velocity of 50. The team needs to fill up the sprint so that the total number of story points equals 50.

This is where the horse trading begins. Does the customer want to start with the second and third epics? Or does the customer want to start with the last epic because it's the most important?

Let's say the customer doesn't care as much about creating the landing page for the website. Instead, they decide to start with epics two and three for the first sprint. Then deliver epics one and four in the second sprint.

The team now has a release plan for the first month. The two sprints will amount to four weeks of work. The four epics will give you a rough order of value. At the end of that month, the website should have a rideshare-provider search profile, a rideshare-seeker login, and a map page with rideshare providers. The product owner could change the priority in the second sprint, but if they do, the value delivered at that time might change.

With ROVe planning, your focus is on the value the product provides. The release is not about the features—it is about the value.

The SAFe Way

The Scale Agile Framework, or SAFe, has a similar release-planning activity. Although this activity is designed for several Scrum teams, these teams will align their efforts into a joint agile release train.

The Scaled Agile Framework creates three sets of backlogs. There is the portfolio backlog, the program backlog, and the team backlog. With each set of backlogs, the customer is expected to give up some flexibility.

When the product management team moves from the program backlog into the team backlog, they are expected to freeze their features. The flexibility is locked down even further with the team backlog. When they move into the team backlog, the items are nearly set.

This is a workable compromise as long as the program backlog represents a short period of time. In SAFe that is typically 8–10 weeks. If the program backlog starts to take more than two months, then you are usually giving up too much flexibility. The role of the product owner starts to look a lot more like that of a business analyst. They don't have the flexibility to reprioritize. Instead, they are helping create a defined set of requirements.

The team may come to view the sprint as one large release. When this happens, the team may stop prioritizing the value over a two-week timebox. If you know the highest-value features over months, there is no reason to reshuffle every two weeks.

If the product owner becomes a business analyst, then they may not collocate with the team. The product owner will deliver a team backlog much like a set of business requirements, then head back to the office and wait for the result. Your agile project will start looking a lot more like a traditional project.

It's important to remember that a program backlog is a slippery slope back to waterfall. If you respect the danger, then you can certainly get value from the additional alignment. If you embrace a program backlog with too much enthusiasm, then you might find yourself running a traditional project.

Pro Tip

If you're the ScrumMaster, you should watch the Team backlog very carefully. Keep everyone aware of the dangers and always engage with your product owner. You need to sound the alarm bells if product owners start delivering requirements and then return to their desk.

Delivering Without Scope

In traditional projects, the scope is the *what* and the *how* of your product. It's the constraint that keeps you from over-delivering. Let's say your project is delivering a hot stack of pancakes. The *what* would be the stack of pancakes, and the *how* would be all the work that goes into preparing a stack of pancakes. The hot griddle, the flour, and the eggs are all part of the scope of the project.

The scope is a very important constraint. It defines your project. That's why in traditional projects you'll often hear the phrase, "if it's not in the scope, it's not in the project."

Traditional projects create the scope before they create a schedule and budget. If the scope increases, the project manager will go back and ask for more time or money.

This is the iron triangle that we talked about earlier. The scope, budget, and schedule are all locked together. If you change one, you have to change the other two. A change in scope will lead to a change in the schedule and budget.

The iron triangle doesn't work very well for an agile project. In an agile project, the scope is variable. You start by defining the schedule and the cost. The sponsors define *when* they want the finished product, then they decide *how much* they're willing to pay. The team fills up the scope based on the budget and schedule.

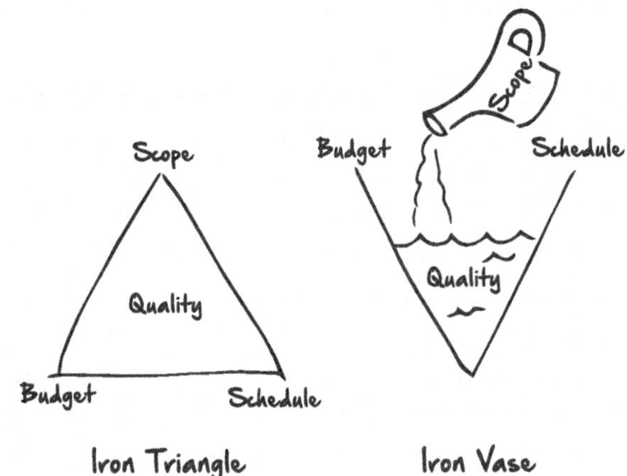

The budget and schedule still remain constant throughout the project. The scope can change based on what the product owner sees as the highest-value items.

There is no release date, or one set date, for the completed scope. Instead, the sponsor will get all the scope they paid for within the original delivery constraints. What they eventually get is what the product owner prioritized as the highest value.

In agile, the quality and value are not outside the scope. An agile team cannot deliver low-quality products. It wouldn't fit with the agile definition of *done*. That means that when you fill up your vase, the quality in agile is included. It is "baked into" the scope.

Instead of using an iron triangle, remove the base of the triangle and flip it upside down. Think of this as an agile iron vase. The two remaining sides still represent the cost and schedule, but instead of a set scope, you fill up the vase with as much scope as the schedule and cost allow.

To see the difference between the iron triangle and the iron vase, try to imagine two projects. One of these projects will use the iron triangle and the other will use the iron vase.

Both of these projects want to create a mobile application to find the closest place to buy a good burrito. One application is helpfully called Traditional Burrito and the other application is called Agile Burrito.

The sponsor for the Traditional Burrito application wants to create a detailed project plan. They define everything that the application will do before any work begins. The scope, cost, and schedule are all constant at the very beginning.

The Traditional Burrito application spends about a third of the project planning out the work—with most of the work going into defining the scope. The project sponsor decides that they want the customer to be able to look up all burrito shops within a one-mile radius. The sponsor will monetize the application by charging for advertising and prioritizing some burrito places.

Now let's look at the other project. The Agile Burrito project defines very quickly the cost and schedule. The sponsor for this project says they want a burrito application in six months with an appropriate budget.

Because they don't have to define the scope, the Agile Burrito project starts developing immediately. The team starts filling up the iron vase with the highest-value items within the defined schedule. The product owner prioritizes finding quality burritos. The second-highest priority is calculating the distance between the burrito shop and the consumer.

Soon after starting, the Agile Burrito product owner finds out about the competing application. So the product owner decides to reprioritize the project scope. They change the application to Burrito Beacon. Instead of looking for burrito shops, the customer leaves the application running and burrito sellers send them coupons when nearby. Because the scope isn't fixed, the product owner can pivot very quickly and reprioritize the work. The application is still delivered on time, but the product is very different from the original vision.

The Traditional Burrito team will have a much more difficult time making this change. A good deal of the project's cost and schedule has been consumed defining the scope. The sponsor would have to abandon the plan after a sizable initial investment.

The Traditional Burrito team would have to restart with a new scope with a new cost and a new schedule.

It's certainly possible to deliver a successful project using the iron triangle. The sponsor just needs to know that they're giving up flexibility for more planning and insight. That's why projects with a well-defined scope do better with fewer changes.

Software development projects have a tendency to be volatile and subject to change. That's why it's usually easier to deliver these projects without a defined scope. The iron vase still leaves two constraints, but the team has the flexibility to fill the scope with the highest-priority items.

Planning With Agile User Stories

Agile does involve planning. You have to learn how to develop user roles, make estimates, and write user stories as well as a number of items before your agile project can take off.

Planning Incremental Delivery

Agile usually uses short durations of work called iterations.[9] In Scrum, these are commonly called sprints. A sprint is a short completed deliverable that can be improved over time. This is very different from a traditional project. In a waterfall project, there is one final product released at the end.

Based on work by Henrik Kniberg

[9] *The Agile Manifesto* Principle 3 states, "Deliver working software frequently, from a couple of weeks to a couple of months, with a preference for the shorter timescale."

This might sound like a subtle difference, but they're actually two different ways of working. One way is creating something bit-by-bit and improving it over time.[10] The other is incomplete work finished in phases and delivered at the end.

To see the difference, imagine you hired a team to build a vegetable garden. You want to have three planters, each with vegetables. The first planter would have tomatoes. The second planter would have peppers. The final planter would have zucchini.

Each planter needs to have soil, a special fertilizer, and seeds. You get proposals from two different gardening teams to help you with your project.

The first team, following the waterfall approach, recommends that you finish the work in three phases. In the first phase, all three planters will be filled with soil. In the second phase, all three planters would be filled with the correct fertilizer. In the final phase, all three planters get seeded with each vegetable.

The second team, following the agile approach, recommends that you finish your garden bit-by-bit over three sprints. This team will start with whichever vegetable is most valuable to you. Tomatoes are your favorite vegetable, so you ask them to start with this planter. For sprint one, they add soil, fertilizer, and tomato seeds to one planter. For sprint two, they add soil, fertilizer, and pepper seeds to the second planter. For sprint three, they add soil, fertilizer, and zucchini seeds to the final planter.

If you think about it, the agile team would have a lot of advantages over the first. The first advantage is that you get a completed planter every two weeks. Your favorite plant will be delivered first. It will start growing after the first two weeks. If you went with the waterfall team, you would have to wait for six weeks before anything started growing.

Garden Team 1
Traditional Project
Phase 1
Phase 2
Phase 3
Tomato
Tomato
Tomato
Pepper
Pepper
Pepper
Zucchini
Zucchini
Zucchini

You'd also have a lot more flexibility with the agile team. Let's say after two weeks your tomato plants really take off. So you decide to cancel your pepper and zucchini plants. Instead, you ask the second team to plant tomatoes in all three. There is a good chance that you won't have much rework. At worst you just have to redo one whole planter.

With the waterfall team, you'd had to wait until the project was complete. Then you might notice that

[10] "Small deeds done are better than great deeds planned." – Peter Marshall

Garden Team 2

Agile Project

Sprint 1 | Sprint 2 | Sprint 3

the tomato seeds are really growing. But by that time, it would be too late. You would have to redo the entire project if you wanted three planters of tomatoes.

What would happen if you ran out of money before the project was complete? If you went with the agile team, you won't have a full garden but you'd at least have one planter. It would also be your favorite vegetable. If you went with the waterfall team, you'd have three planters filled with soil and maybe some fertilizer. Not really anything of value. You'd have just a few half-filled planters without any seeds.

The more uncertainty there is with the project, the easier it is to deliver in sprints. You wouldn't be able to deliver the project with the waterfall team if the customer was fickle about their plants.

Now what if you didn't want to hire any garden teams? Let's say you're a do-it-yourselfer and wanted to create your own garden. How would you approach the work? Would you completely finish one planter at a time, bit-by-bit? Or would you do the more phased approach? First, you get them all filled up with soil. Then go back and do the fertilizer. Then, finally, you'll finish them all at once.

Chances are you would do the waterfall approach. You would most likely deliver the project in phases like the first team. That's just how most people think about work. They try to finish one big thing first then go onto the next big thing, finally wrapping it all up at the end.

Pro Tip

One of the biggest challenges with agile teams is breaking away from this phased mindset. Many agile teams struggle with this idea of delivering the project bit by bit over time. Often what they wind up doing is just renaming phases to sprints. Then they'll come up with a big unfinished deliverable at the end.

The product owner should always be driving the team to incrementally produce valuable deliverables. They may be knocking the team off track if they start running sprints like traditional phases. It's not that difficult to spot when this is happening because the deliverable will start to sound like an IOU.

In the garden project, imagine if the product owner had just changed the phases into sprints. They might create a sprint deliverable like "three pots filled with soil." Or even something worse like, "three pots ready to be seeded." The ScrumMaster should recognize that these are not real sprints. The stakeholders don't have a finished deliverable at the end. A finished deliverable would be one pot filled with soil and fertilizer with seeds ready to go.

It's very common for an organization that has a lot of experience with traditional project management to struggle with this difference. Incremental delivery is not just a way to divide up work. It's an alternative way to *think* about work. Keep your eye out for these renamed phases. They will almost certainly pop up if you work for an organization with a lot of traditional project management approaches.

Planning Starts As Estimates

Projects are unique by definition. There will always be something in your project that is new. Maybe the team has never worked together. Maybe the project is working with new hardware or software. Either way, there will be a degree of uncertainty.

Usually the greater the uncertainty, the more trouble you'll have with traditional project planning. Traditional projects depend on a lot of up-front planning. If you have a lot of uncertainty, then you'll have a lot of guesses in your plan. If your guesses are wrong, it will create a lot of instability. Traditional projects work much smoother if your predictions are accurate.

Think about a typical project. The longer the project runs, the more you know about how to finish. That's usually because you're learning a lot from actually doing the work and you don't have to rely as much on predictions. Unfortunately, the more you work, the more expensive it is to make changes.

Think about a mobile application project. Let's say you wanted to create an application that can identify birds just by taking their picture. You call the application the Mobile Bird Finder.

There are several things you won't know about the application. For example, you won't know the number of bird pictures you'll need to make a match. You can make a pretty good guess, but you'll never really know until you build the application. Also, you won't know how long it will take for the application to match a picture to a bird. Again, you can guess, but you won't know until the application is near complete.

Now let's say that halfway through the application it becomes clear that the number of pictures you need to make a match is far too large. The only way to get the application to work is by splitting it into several regions. Now you're calling the application, Mobile Bird Finder – North American Edition.

Because the application is halfway finished, the cost of the change is now much greater. You'll have to rename all the files. The designers will probably have to redesign the application. There'll be a lot of rework. The cost would have been much less if the project had originally started with the application split by region.

This is called the project's cone of uncertainty. It's when you're forced to make all the predictions at the time when you have the least information. If you look at the chart, you can see that projects are the most uncertain before they start. This was true with our mobile bird finder application. You didn't know how many pictures you'd need until after the work began.

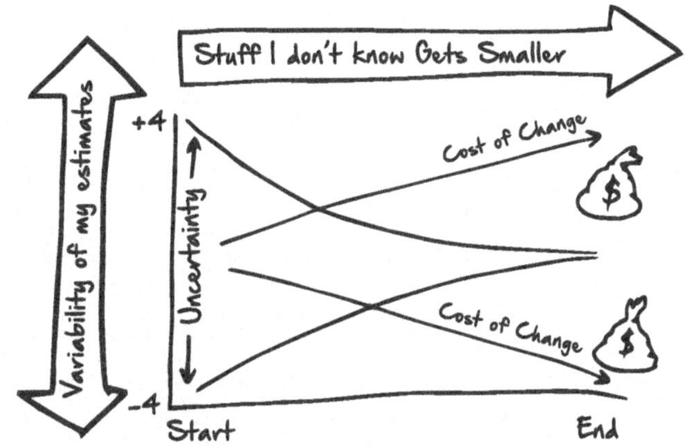

THE CONE OF UNCERTAINTY

As the project moves forward through time, you can see that it is more expensive to make changes. These are the two arrows pointing to the money to show these costs increasing over time. The cone of uncertainty narrows, but the cost of making changes increases.

The cone of uncertainty is one of the big challenges with trying to design everything up front. This is the reason why project managers working on traditional projects will often complain about bad requirements. They're usually not happy with the project's predictions. Often the plan doesn't even identify the problems.

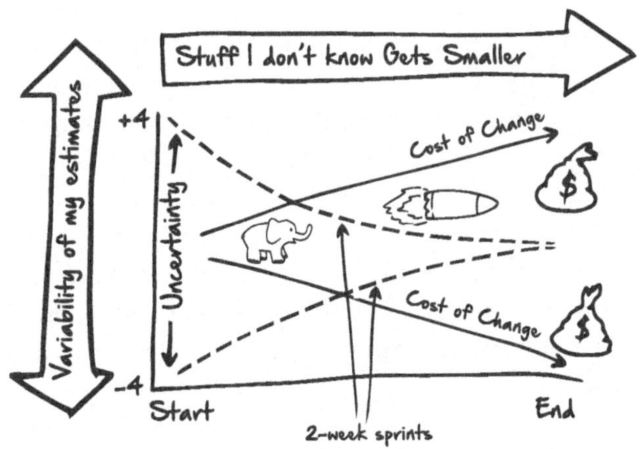

THE CONE OF UNCERTAINTY WITH AGILE

The agile approach to the cone of uncertainty is quite different. In many ways, the framework sees too much up-front planning as a waste of time. It's too difficult to make worthwhile predictions for the whole project and there's no reason to try.

For agile, it's like the joke about eating an elephant. The only way to eat an elephant is by taking one bite at a time. You shouldn't try to swallow everything up front[11] in one big plan. Instead, agile breaks it down bit-by-bit over time. These are the iterations of the project, or the sprints.

The team will also start with the highest-value items first. It's not just about eating bites of elephant—it's also about eating the highest-value items first. If you're eating an elephant, you'll want to start with the tastiest parts. I've never eaten an elephant, but I'm guessing that would be the trunk.[12]

The team should work like a heat-seeking missile. From the very beginning, the team will be working on the tastiest parts. Then they'll move through the project until they get to the tail.

Each sprint should have a stakeholder checkup at the finish line. The product owner will present the deliverable to the stakeholders to make sure they're building the right thing. In a sense, each finishing line is the team asking, "Am I building the right thing?" If the answer is yes, then they move on to the next sprint. The team will use this rhythm to complete the project.

For our bird finder application, the team would've created a small bit of the larger project. Perhaps for the first sprint they would have just created an application that took a picture of a bird. And then during the next sprint they would have an application that took a picture of a bird and matched it against two or three photographs.

The project would continue that way, bit-by-bit, until the stakeholders agreed that all of the functionality was complete.

A traditional project will always be working on the whole elephant. The only way to divide up the work is by the amount of time and effort. The team will be working on the items they predict will take up the most time. Project managers often call this the *long pole in the tent*. It's the biggest piece of the elephant from head to tail.

In our bird application, it is likely that the team would be gathering up thousands of photographs to test out the matching feature. The more time the team works on gathering

[11] "It is a mistake to look too far ahead. Only one link in the chain of destiny can be handled at a time."
– Winston Churchill to the House of Commons, February 27, 1945

[12] Please do not attempt to eat an elephant. They are majestic creatures that have been poached to near extinction.

the photographs, the more difficult it will be to later make changes to the project. If nothing changes, that will be fine. If there is a change, then it usually means there will be a lot of rework.

Starting With User Roles

Agile projects don't use traditional project requirements. Instead, the product owner maintains a set of user stories for the project. The user story is a conversation vehicle. It's a short story from the users' perspectives about what they find valuable in the product.

The product owner, as the maintainer of these user stories, is a very important person on an agile project. They're the team's North Star. They're the light that represents the customer's value. They may know a little bit about what it takes to deliver the project, but they won't create the kind of detailed technical specifications you need for a traditional project. Instead, the product owner will always speak the customer's language.

Pro Tip

This customer's language is much different from what you'd see in a traditional project. It focuses on the users' experiences and not on what goes into creating those experiences.

Let's go back to our ridesharing application. In a traditional project, you would create a plan to finish the website. In that plan, you might have milestones. Maybe after three months the project would have a milestone to complete the server installation. You might call this milestone *infrastructure complete*.

Now you'd go back to your customer and say, "the infrastructure will be complete after three months." The customer who's sponsoring the website is probably not technical, so the customer would need to learn what infrastructure means. Then the customer would have to figure out how that helps with their website. At best, it would be a large learning curve if the customer wanted to prioritize the work. You usually wouldn't have a customer who says, "Well, why don't we use virtual machines?"

Let's take that same website and use our agile product owner. The product owner will also have limited technical knowledge. How can they prioritize when the infrastructure should be complete? Why do they need to know what the server does when all they want is a website?

Instead, the product owner will prioritize the work based on their view of the product. They don't view it as a technical achievement. The product owner will view it as a means to an end. The easiest way for a product owner to do this is to create user roles. A user role is not a person. Instead, think of it as a bundle of user experiences.

For our ridesharing website, there could be many user roles. There might be a user role called rideshare visitor. This is someone who lands on the site but isn't logged in. For a user who logs in, you could create another role called rideshare customer. You could then divide these into other roles, such as rideshare seeker or rideshare provider.

If you come from traditional project management, you might be tempted to confuse user roles with stakeholders. Stakeholders are often viewed as people. They could be customers or the nonprofit that runs the site.

Agile user roles are a bundle of user experiences. Someone might enter the website as a rideshare visitor. Then they'll register on the site and become a rideshare customer. Once they're a customer, they might decide to be a rideshare seeker. So in this case, you have one person who actually went through three distinct user roles. They had three different bundles of experiences based on what they were doing with the site.

Usually, product owners will create all the user roles for the project. It can be a real challenge for product owners to come up with these bundles. They have to really think through how someone will interact with the final product. They'll have to decide what makes a visitor different from a customer. Another decision will be whether to divide user roles into those who are seeking rides and those who are giving rides. These are the tough questions product owners will have to sort out early.

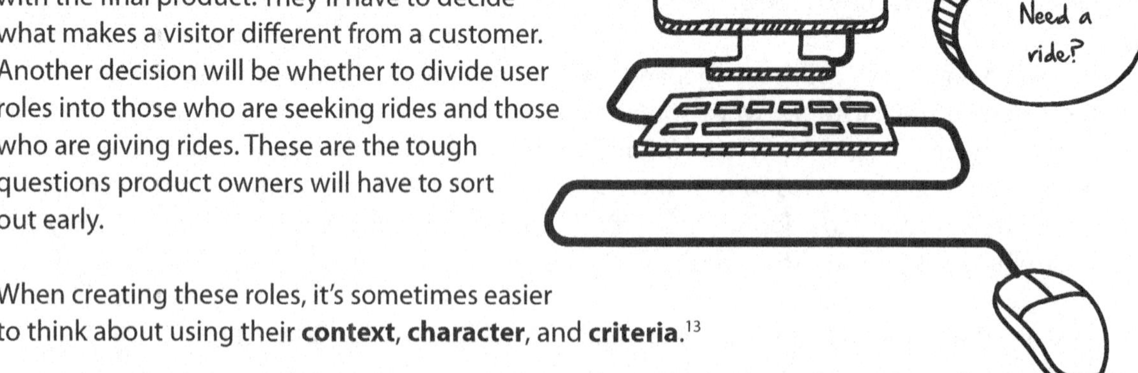

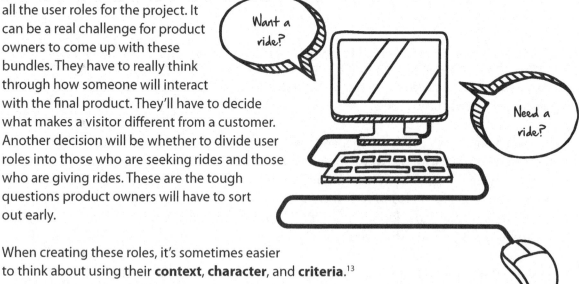

When creating these roles, it's sometimes easier to think about using their **context**, **character**, and **criteria**.[13]

[13] Based on work by Larry Constantine

The **context** is the bundle of experiences the person will have based on where they are in your product. In the ridesharing website, the product owner will probably separate rideshare visitors from rideshare customers. The rideshare visitor will have a different context. They'll probably expect some basic information about the site and maybe a place to create a new account. They probably won't expect the first page of the website to be a login and password box.

The **character** is a little bit of insight into the experience a user might expect when interacting with your product. A rideshare visitor might be more curious about who runs the website. A rideshare seeker might be more curious about who they are connecting with for a rideshare.

Customers
Quick Seeker
Standard Seeker

Finally, product owners might create new user roles based on a person's **criteria**. They can create a role based on someone's expected outcome. There might be a quick-rideshare-seeker role that is separate from the regular-rideshare-seeker user role. The quick-rideshare-seeker role might have an immediate need to find a ride. For this person, the criteria are getting hooked up with a rideshare quickly and without too much difficulty.

If you're just starting to create user roles, it is easier to start broadly, and then create subgroups of experiences within those larger roles. With the rideshare site, the product owner could start with customers and then break down the role into different subroles. Try to use the context, character, and criteria of the role to break down the bundle further.

Creating User Stories

User stories are a great way to have conversations between developers and the product owner. That's usually a good thing. In software projects, developers need to spend time making sure they're developing the right thing. If you don't have these conversations, then you could end up with unnecessary rework.

Free Analogy

I was traveling through a large airport once, and I didn't have much time so I stepped into a fast food restaurant. There was a big sign that welcomed me at the door. On the sign it said "supersize everything for a dollar."

While I waited in line I was wondering whether I should supersize my fries. I wasn't interested in supersizing my drink. That's always a bad idea before a long flight. The problem was I was a little bit confused about how to order. Would they supersize everything for a dollar? Then I would get a huge soda and fries. Or did I have the option to supersize anything on the menu? Then I could pick and choose what I wanted supersized and for each supersizing event, I'd pay a dollar.

When I got to the front of the line, I placed my order. Before I had a chance to clarify, the person asked me very quickly, "Would you like to supersize anything on your order?" Just a little snippet of conversation cleared up all my confusion.

Anyway, it was too late. By that time, I had decided it was a bad idea to eat a big pile of fries.

When planning a project, many people assume that when you write something down, it becomes much clearer. Project requirements strive to be written in clear direct language. What could be clearer than "supersize everything for a dollar."

It's usually when you turn this clear language into work that you realize there's a lot of room for misinterpretation. Unfortunately, it's almost impossible to predict how each person will interpret your language. I'm sure hundreds, if not thousands, of people walk by that fast food sign with little confusion. Often, a quick conversation is the only way to make sure that everyone knows the work.

Creating user stories begins with the creation of the user role. This is the bundle of user experiences that a product owner defines before creating user stories. The following format is a common format for creating a user story.

As a <user role>, I <want/need/can/etc.> <goal> so that <reason>[14]

Now the product owner takes this bundle and attaches some value to it.

With our ridesharing web application, you might want to create a user role called rideshare seeker. Now you need to attach some business value to that role.

[14] Based on work by Mike Cohn

For this story, you might say:
"As a rideshare seeker, I want to see a list of rideshare providers within my zip code, so that I can coordinate a ride with someone close to my house."

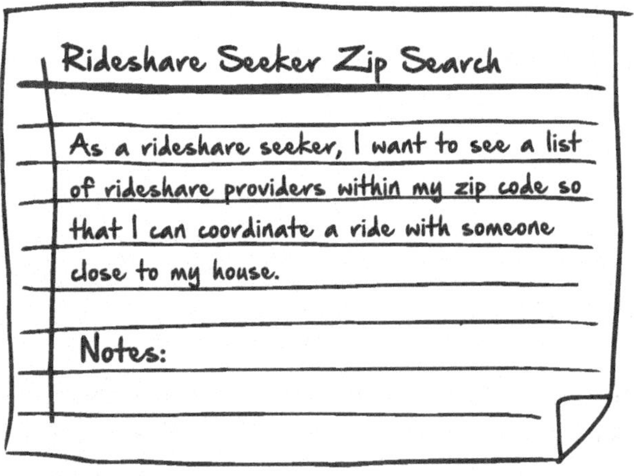

This user story accomplishes two things. First, it uses the customer's language. The product owner doesn't need to know how the application is going to search for a zip code. There's no talk about how the website will work.

The story is only about the *what* and the *why*. This will be much easier for the product owner to understand and prioritize.

The story format is important because of what it *doesn't* say. It leaves the technical decisions up to the team. It's very important for the product owner to not swim in the developer's pool. They need to leave the *how* to the development team.

Second, the story is immediately linked to some business value. You could tell from the story that what the rideshare seeker really wants is to find rideshare providers near his or her house. Maybe there's a better way to do this? The product owner might not know about other options to track the user's location.

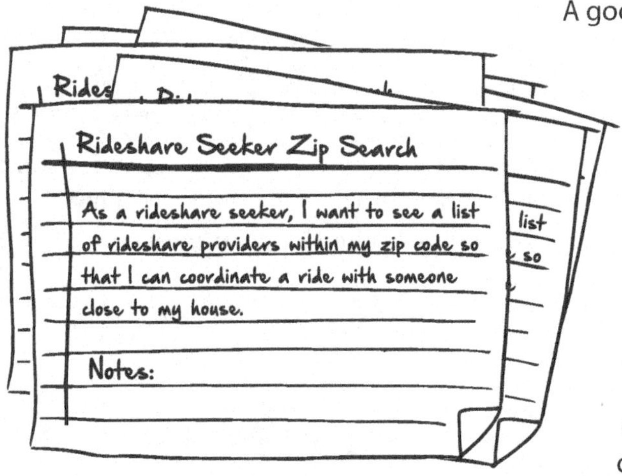

A good way to create user stories is to think about the three Cs. This comes from the world of extreme programming and stands for **card**, **conversation,** and **confirmation**.[15]

User stories are best recorded on a 3 × 5-inch index **card**. Many product owners are tempted to create a user-story spreadsheet, but if you try this, what you'll find is that it's more difficult to communicate about individual stories. You don't want to overwhelm the group with lists of information.

[15] Created by Ron Jeffries

Instead, you want to have a group conversation. Many times when an agile team is starting out, they're very focused on the format of the user story. They make sure every story starts with the "as a user role" and ends with the "value goal." What they forget is that a user story is a means to an end. It's not about the format. It's about having a back-and-forth **conversation** between the developers and the product owner.

You will have many more natural conversations if you have a stack of cards in the middle of a large table. You'll be able to slide the card back and forth as the developers come up with new questions.

The final part is the acceptance criteria. This is the **confirmation** that everyone knows how to produce the required deliverable. This is typically written on the back of the card. In the language of extreme programming, this will be the "definition of done."

It's very important that the acceptance criteria closely match the user story on the front of the card. The acceptance criteria should be the result of a conversation with the development team and will go into much greater detail regarding how the developers will deliver the requirements to address the user story.

The acceptance criteria are a good way to keep the user story from being too convoluted. You can add a lot of details to the acceptance criteria without putting it on the front of the card. For this story, you could sort out the details, like whether you want to use five-digit or nine-digit zip codes. This would add too much bulk to the user story, but it's fine to add this to the acceptance criteria.

Writing Effective Stories

When you first start having these conversations about your user stories, you will probably realize that they are not very good. It will be like picking up a trumpet for the first time. There'll be a horrible screeching sound instead of music. But that's okay. Creating user stories is a skill. And like any skill, you usually get better over time. The good news is that even small projects require dozens, if not hundreds, of user stories. So you'll get a lot of practice.

The real challenge will be figuring out just why your user stories are so awful. When you figure that out, then you can start to make them better. Thankfully, there is a good way to figure out the challenges you will face writing user stories. You should use the acronym **INVEST**, which stands for

independent, negotiable, valuable, estimable, small, and testable.[16] This is a list of common challenges you will have to deal with when creating your user stories.

Independent: It's important to remember that independent doesn't mean your stories are functionally independent. It means they are independently *valued*.

Let's look at the rideshare application again. The product owner could create two stories: One story would be to create a list of the closest rideshare seekers and another would be to sort the list closest to furthest.

These two stories are functionally dependent on each other. The team can't sort the list without first displaying the result. But they can be independently valued. The product owner might not place a very high value on sorting the list. Maybe the product owner wants the first list to be based on the rideshare provider's feedback and not distance.

The product owner also might not be interested in sorting the list until the next version of the application. It's important for the product owner to try and create user stories with these small bits of independent value.

Negotiable: You want your development team to negotiate with the product owner. The developers should be the ones to decide the best way to deliver the value in the story.

In a traditional project, the developers would get a list of detailed requirements. User stories are different. They are small narratives about customer value, and they are written from the customer's perspective. The product owner shouldn't create user stories that focus too much on how to deliver their request.

For the rideshare application, you wouldn't want to create a user story that says, "In the same database query, return a list with a metric that enables sorting." A user story like this isn't focused on what the customer wants. Most customers don't care how you sort the list—they just want it sorted. You'll get these directive-style user stories when the product owner has too much technical knowledge.

Valuable: Customer value is the most important part of the user story. Without it, the product owner can't prioritize the backlog and there's no way to complete the story.

It's very common for product owners to struggle with value when they've come from traditional project management. What often happens is that they'll see user stories as rewritten requirements on index cards. They may even create a requirements document and then break it down into users' stories.

16 Created by Bill Wake

Typically when this happens, you will get user stories that have little or no customer value. Something like, "as a rideshare seeker, I want the search method tested so that I know it works." That's just a restatement of a testing task in a traditional waterfall process.

These challenges also come up when product owners neglect their responsibility to create good stories. They'll ask the developers to create their own stories for the project. Then the developers will just create index cards that break down the project into functional chunks.

Estimable: When developers can't estimate the work required to address the user story, it usually means it's too big or not clearly described. Usually, the smaller the user story, the clearer the description. If you're the product owner and you see the developers struggling to provide an estimate for a user story, then you may need to go back and break it down further.

Small: A user story should be delivered within a two-week sprint. That means the size is closely related to whether the team can make estimates about the user story. When the story is too big for developers, they can't predict everything that will go into delivering the value. In general, the smaller the story, the easier it is for the team to understand everything it entails. That makes it much easier for the team to estimate the tasks required.

Testable: Think about a user story like, "as a rideshare seeker, I want to see the list of rideshare providers *quickly* so I can share my ride." This might be a true statement of customer value. The rideshare seeker will certainly want the application to work quickly and easily.

Danger Zone!

The problem with this story is that it's not testable. What is quick for one customer might be slow for another. How do you test the concept *quickly*? Will the product owner be the one who decides what is quick?

Watch out for these adjectives and adverbs in your user stories. Words like *simply*, *clean*, *easily*, *fast*, or *nice*. These will only make it more difficult to estimate.

Instead, focus on customer value, and if necessary, use the acceptance criteria on the back of the card. On the back of the card, the product owner might put, "the list will come back with 10 records at a time, and so the rideshare seeker can scroll through them in batches."

Grouping With Themes Or Epics

A theme or epic is a way to organize stories into groups. It's inevitable that most user stories start their lives as epics. The product owner usually creates a large value statement instead of several smaller stories. That's okay. That's just the way that most people think. Most people think about what they want. Then later they break it down into valuable little details.

It's important to remember that these are large, vague epics and not actionable stories. They are naturally grouped together and need to be split up. It's like being given a whole orange to eat. Once you have the orange, you need to go through the process of splitting it into edible segments.

Epic splitting isn't an easy task. There are many different ways to split your epics into more stories, and splitting stories often leads to further splitting. This means that you could end up with completely different stories depending on how you split them.

It's like any ordered division. Think about splitting a bag of candy by weight and then by color. You'd end up with different groups than if you split the candy by color and then by weight.

That's why it's important to know some of the common ways to split your stories.[17] That way you can have some control over the final grouping, and you can split the epic using the same criteria each time.

There are several common ways to split your stories. These are the eight most common that I've seen on agile projects. The best way to remember these groups is by thinking of the acronym FEEDBACK, which stands for flow, effort, entry, data operations, business rules, alternatives, complexity, and knowledge.

[17] Based on work by Richard Lawrence

Let's start with a user story we might use for our rideshare application.

"As a rideshare seeker, I want to see a list of rideshare providers within my zip code so that I can coordinate a ride with someone close to my house."

This user story could easily be an epic. Let's try to break it down into groups using our FEEDBACK splitter.

F E E D B A C K

Flow: This is how the story might step through the application's workflow. You can split this epic into a few more stories.

"As a rideshare seeker, I want to see a list of rideshare providers within my zip code so that I can coordinate a ride with someone close to my house *when I'm on my smartphone*," and "... *from my GPS watch*."

Effort: You might decide to break the epic down based on the developer's level of effort.

"As a rideshare seeker, I want to see a list of *highly rated* rideshare providers within my zip code so that I can coordinate a ride with someone close to my house," and "*highly rated rideshare providers* within my zip code...."

The developers will need to spend most of their time creating the list of rideshare providers based on the zip code. It should be trivial to add more selective criteria like "highly rated" and "superstar" providers. But it will still give the product owner an opportunity to prioritize the work.

Entry: Sometimes, the team might want to break down the epic by how the customer enters the data.

"As a rideshare seeker, I want to see a *sorted list* of rideshare providers within my zip code so that I can coordinate a ride with someone close to my house," and "a *reverse-sorted list* of rideshare providers...."

This is how your customer will see the data. You can break it down based on their entry and view.

Data Operations: You may want to break up your epic based on common data operations like read, update, and delete.

"As a rideshare seeker, I want to *read a list* of rideshare providers within my zip code so that I can coordinate a ride with someone close to my house," and "*update that list with my information.*"

Business Rules: Sometimes there's a lot of complex value in the epic. When that happens, you may want to break down the epic into business rules.

"As a rideshare seeker, I want to see a list of rideshare providers within my zip code and *4-digit extension* so that I can coordinate a ride with someone close to my house." And "*within my GPS coordinate range* so that I can...."

Alternatives: Some epics can easily be broken into stories with alternative criteria. This story uses a zip code. You can create many stories based on alternatives.

"As a rideshare seeker, I want to see a list of rideshare providers within my *street address* so that I can coordinate a ride with someone close to my house," and "*within my city*," or "*within my county*."

Complexity: Many epics are just the beginning. When product owners start thinking about user stories, they may find greater and greater value. User stories can be like a diamond mine with a few scattered pieces off the top that hint at the treasure below. When that happens, the epic is just a simple start. Then you can break it down into stories with increasing complexity.

"As a rideshare seeker, I want to see a list of all *new rideshares* within my zip code so that I can coordinate a ride with someone close to my house," and "*a list of all recommended rideshares* within my zip code...."

Knowledge: Sometimes the product owner will present the epic and the team will need more knowledge. They have to research the epic to break it down into stories.

When this happens, the developers will create *spikes*. These story spikes have secondhand value since they answer questions that are needed to deliver the main user story.

In this epic, the real value is finding rideshare providers that live or work near the customer. There might be a better way to deliver this value. Maybe modern web browsers can deliver the customer's location. A smartphone user might have their GPS coordinates available.

When this happens, the developers might create spikes like "*investigate location services for most web browsers*." They might create another spike for "*investigate GPS services on smartphones*."

Story spikes aren't stories, but they *lead to stories*. They're an IOU for the product owner. The developers just need to answer a few questions.

Using Relative Estimation

Early humans had a pretty tough time. They must've lived in near constant fear of being eaten. They were also in danger of not getting enough to eat. Throughout their life they went through a process of relative estimating. "If it's big like a bear, I need to run from it. If it's small like a fish, I might be able to eat it."

It wasn't until much later that humans developed metrics. "If it's taller than a meter, I should probably run from it. If it's less than five pounds, I might be able to eat it."

Now let's fast-forward thousands of years to an office park. All the project planning is in hours, days, and weeks. In these meetings, you'll go around the room and ask for time estimates. Often the metric is more precise than the team's ability to understand the work. So they'll end up giving you a range. They'll say, "It could take one to three days."

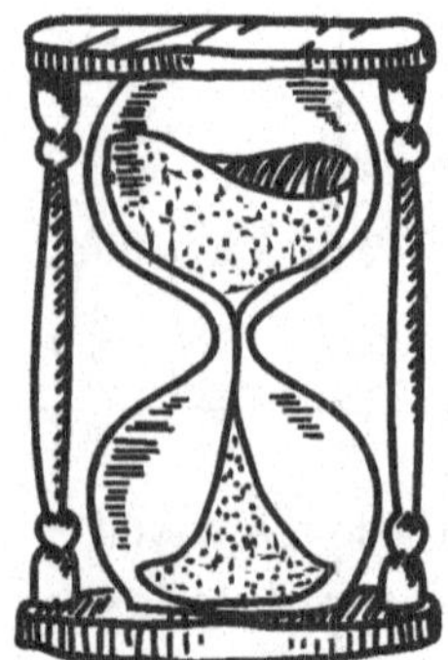

The project manager gathers up all these ranges and creates one big estimate. Maybe they've decided it can take anywhere from four to six weeks. Then they add project buffers just to be sure. The number might seem precise because it's in weeks or months. But it's still just a range in disguise. What's worse is that it took hours of meetings to come up with these questionable results.

Pro Tip

Agile doesn't fix how bad teams are at estimating. Instead, the team spends much less time on this activity. From an agile perspective, *not* doing something is the fastest way to getting it done.[18]

An agile team goes back to the technique used by our early ancestors. The team won't think in hours, days, or weeks. They'll think in relative sizing. Is this user story bigger than a bear? Maybe it's smaller than a fish.

Relative estimating compares what you *don't* know against what you *do* know. You might not be able to guess how much a truck weighs. But if you saw the truck you can probably guess how many cars equal a truck. You might not know how much a lion weighs. But you can guess that it may be three or four dogs.

Now dogs, lions, trucks, and cars all have different weights. This estimation is not designed to be precise. But that doesn't mean it's useless. Instead, it gives you a starting point—a way to start the discussion on what it takes to deliver your stories.

Agile teams use this relative estimating for two reasons. The first reason is that it takes away the false comfort of precision. The team is accepting the fact that the estimates will be imprecise. So they use a simple method to make a best guess. Everyone knows it's a guess and the team's not going to get hammered for getting it wrong.

Assigning a date to guesses always makes them seem more concrete. It forces developers into a world of precision, even when they don't have enough information to be precise. That's when you find yourself in a bizarro world where developers take a half hour to decide if something will take five or six hours.

Relative estimating gives these teams freedom to abandon this false precision. It's a way to say, "It's okay that you don't know. Now it's time to guess." That way we can start talking about what it takes to deliver the story.

[18] "Simplicity – the art of maximizing the amount of work not done – is essential."
– from *The Agile Manifesto*

The second reason agile uses relative estimating is that it keeps the team from confusing **estimates** and **commitments**.

Think about your drive home from work. Some days, it may take you up to an hour because of some construction. Other days, it seems like you might make record time and you'll be home in 10 minutes. If there's a snowstorm, then who knows when you'll get home. Despite all these unknowns, it still usually only takes you about 20 minutes.

Now imagine that you needed to get home for a deadline. Maybe your dryer is broken and the repairman will be there at 6:00. Or say you needed to be home for an early dinner.

In either case, you would probably commit to an hour to drive home. That way you can meet your deadline and might even be home early. You probably wouldn't commit to 20 minutes. That's a best-case scenario. If there's any traffic or any bad weather, you'll be sure to miss dinner.

Now imagine you needed to make an estimate. Let's say that a coworker lives near your house and asks you how long it takes for you to get to work. For that, you would probably say it usually takes you about 20 minutes. You're giving an honest estimate. You're not worried that your coworker will storm into your office if it takes more than 20 minutes.

An estimate is the useful information that you might give a coworker. A commitment is something that you usually give to a supervisor. An estimate is a best guess. A commitment is often a worst-case scenario.

That's why for agile planning you want estimates and not commitments. Let's say you needed to estimate how many hours you'd be commuting each week. You would probably guess it would be 20 minutes each way, which would be 40 minutes a day. Then you would multiply that by five workdays and have an estimate of a little over three hours.

The commitment would be much higher than the estimate. If your supervisor asked, you might say it took you an hour each way. That's two hours a day and ten hours a week.

Even with this simple task of driving to work, you have a range of three to 10 hours a week. That doesn't really help anyone with planning.

Playing Planning Poker

Planning poker helps the team get the best estimates with less-than-perfect information. The game assumes that everyone on the team is an expert. As experts, not everyone will agree on how long it takes to meet each user story. There is wisdom in the whole team. Planning poker gives everyone a voice.

One developer might decide the story is complex while another developer might think that the story will be finished before starting lunch. There's no way to tell which developer is right until after the work begins.

In agile, you're not estimating for individuals; you're estimating work for the entire team. Many different developers on the team will work on the same story. An agile team should be cross-functional and filled with many experts. That's why it's important that each team member makes estimates. Everyone should have a say when you're all working together to deliver the work.

Planning poker is not just about creating an estimate. In many ways, the estimate is a by-product of the game. The activity is really about combating **groupthink**. There should be a consensus on what's involved in delivering each story.

Groupthink is the way that people tend to agree with the most popular idea. The loudest voices will drown out any disagreement. Without any disagreement, the group then assumes that they must be right.

You may have been in a groupthink meeting. The few people who are not on board are easily dismissed or ignored. Then the group endorses the most popular idea even if it's wrong. This is especially true if one of the opinions is a HIPPO, that is, the highest-paid person's opinion.

Planning poker tries to combat this tendency. Each team member makes an estimate before they're told what to think.

Planning poker is simple to play and accurate enough for agile planning. Each team member will make a relative estimate for all of the stories. They will use story points as an estimate of the relative size. Remember that this is a relative estimate. If you're the ScrumMaster for the team, try to make sure that everyone thinks in story points and not hours, days, or weeks.

Each developer will have a deck of planning poker cards which will have an exponential number sequence, something like: 0, ½, 1, 2, 4, 8, and 16. Many cards use the Fibonacci sequence of 1, 2, 3, 5, 8, and 13. These are the points for each story.

The Fibonacci sequence often works better because it gives more options at the bottom. It's easier to estimate with 1, 2, 3, and 5 than 0, ½, 1, or 2. The *teens* are almost always a sign that a team member doesn't understand what it takes to deliver the story.

There is also a coffee card and a question mark card. The coffee card is a request for the whole team to take a break. Sometimes, the debate is too unproductive. Other times, people just stop thinking clearly.

The question mark is a way for someone to skip the first round of estimates. It usually means the developer wants to hear the first round and then later add their estimate. This card should be used sparingly. It is best used when someone needs a little more information from the rest of the team to understand the story.

Pro Tip

Sometimes teams that come from traditional project management organizations will have trouble using story points. They'll think of the points as hours or days. When this happens, you might want to consider buying a bunch of cards with

Pro Tip (continued)

animals on them. It'll be much easier for the team to think about relative sizing with animals. A good set of animal cards will have a mouse, squirrel, cat, dog, horse, grizzly bear, and whale. You can usually find these cards at children's stores.

You could ask the team to think about the tasks with various animal sizes. Is the task the size of a mouse or a grizzly bear? Try to get the team to think in relative sizing.

To begin planning poker, the team identifies one of the smaller stories and assigns it a value of 2. This will be the estimation baseline. The baseline will be the first half of the relative estimate.

Think about our rideshare application. Let's say the story for the baseline estimate is: "As a rideshare seeker, I want a checkbox to save my username so I don't have to retype it every time I log into the site."

That would be the smallest story to deliver in the sprint. All the later stories would be a relative factor of that story. The team can think of it as: How many *checkbox stories* are there in each of the estimates? A larger story might be four times as large as the checkbox story.

The ScrumMaster will pull out the other stories in no particular order. The product owner also needs to be there to answer any questions the team might have about the story.

The story is read to the team either by the ScrumMaster, the product owner, or one of the developers. It's important that the team immediately start estimating. If you're the ScrumMaster for the team, make sure that there is no discussion about the story before the first estimate. Any discussion can lead to groupthink. You could lose ideas before you even begin playing.

"The relative estimate is a number that takes into account time, risk, and complexity.

Without any discussion, developers select a card from their deck that is the relative estimate for the story. They place the card face down on the table. Then all the cards are flipped over simultaneously. If everyone agrees on the number then the size is recorded and the team moves on to the next story.

When the estimates differ, the developers with the highest and lowest numbers defend their estimates to the rest of the team."

The ScrumMaster might ask the person with the highest estimate to explain why the story is so complex. They might also ask the person with the lowest assessment to explain why the story is so easy.

The group briefly debates with other members who have different estimates.

A new round of estimation starts and the process continues until the team reaches consensus and the ScrumMaster records the estimate.

The team will want to repeat this for each story. In the beginning, the team might need a lot of guidance from the ScrumMaster. Over time, the ScrumMaster should be able to sit in the background and simply record the final estimate.

Calculating Your Velocity

After points have been assigned to the user stories, the team needs to calculate the team's velocity. Velocity is the number of story points a team can complete in a 2-week sprint.

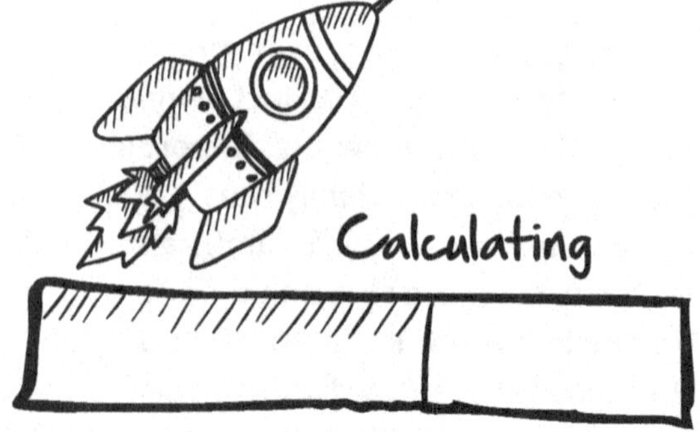

To calculate the team's **velocity**, the team will look at their own work history to determine their sustainable pace. They'll see how much they *have* worked in the past, and that will be how much work they commit to in the future.

Determining a team's velocity is not simply choosing how much work needs to be done, it also needs to take into account productivity and the number of hours in a workweek.

Bonus Fact

In 1914, Henry Ford noticed that his employees worked best when limited to eight hours a day. After eight hours, their productivity began to slow down. That's why the Ford Motor Company established the 40-hour workweek. The change increased their productivity and many companies soon followed. That's why the 40-hour week became standard.

In the 1980s, fewer people worked in manufacturing. They became desk workers and computer programmers. As a result, many employers felt that the 40-hour workweek was outdated. It only made sense in manufacturing. Working a 70-hour week became a badge of honor for desk-working go-getters.

Agile pushes back on the ever-expanding workweek and promotes the idea that people should go home at a reasonable hour. Every person should work within their 8-hour time box. Even though they're not building cars, developers have the same limits on their productivity. The team will have only a marginal increase in completed stories if they start working 10, 11, or 12 hours a day. They're much better off going home, then starting fresh the next day. Often developers will think more clearly when they are driving home or walking the dog.

An agile project should have a challenging pace but there shouldn't be any project crashes. A crash is when a project manager adds people or time to the project when it is clear that the team is behind schedule. The existing team will have to put in long hours or a group of new people will need to be brought up to speed. The team shouldn't have this flurry of activity at the end of the sprint. Agile projects should run like marathons. They should have a rigorous but consistent work pace. The team should have a predictable and practical workday.

The team will use the story points assigned during the planning poker sessions as a way to manage this sustainable pace. The product backlog will have all the user stories for the project. Most of these stories will have been given a relative estimate.

Typically, the ScrumMaster will calculate the team's velocity. They'll create the number based on the story points delivered in each sprint. Let's say at the end of the first sprint, the team completed six stories. Four of these stories were estimated at two points each and one story was estimated at three points. The last story was estimated at five points. That means that at the end of sprint, the team completed 16 story points.

Now the team knows that they have completed 16 story points in their first sprint. Let's say at the end of the second sprint, they completed 17 points, and at the end of the third sprint, they completed 15 story points.

Now the ScrumMaster has enough information to make a rough guess at the team's velocity. They'll average out the first three sprints. In this case, the average for the first three sprints is 16 story points. That will be the team's velocity.

Pro Tip

Velocity is a **rolling** average. That means that the velocity may increase or decrease depending on what happens with the team.

It's usually bad practice to add developers after the work has begun, but if you add a few developers, the velocity might increase. Let's say the team added a developer during sprint four. With the new help, the team was able to complete 24 story points. Then the average for the four sprints would be 18 story points. The team's velocity will go up by two points.

On the flipside, the velocity might also decrease. Let's say sprint four was in the middle of flu season. Too many people took time off. The team only delivered 12 story points at the end of the sprint. The team's velocity would slightly decrease to 15.

One of the challenges with velocity is that it is often misused. Senior managers will sometimes push the team to increase their velocity. They think that means the team is being more productive. But remember that story points are a relative estimate. The team assigns them in the planning poker session.

Field Notes

I once worked for an organization where a senior manager was pushing the team to "achieve greater velocity." They thought that increasing velocity meant the team was finishing more work. The team started out with a velocity of 15. Then the manager pushed the team to increase the velocity to 18, then to 25 and finally to 30.

The manager was delighted to see the team reaching these levels of hyper-productivity. The team was twice as productive as when they started.

In reality, the team was just reacting to the positive reinforcement. In planning poker, the team started estimating each story at two or three points. After the manager started to push the team, they started estimating the stories at three, five, and eight points.

The team wasn't really completing more work. They were just estimating the work with higher values. The five stories they completed in sprint one may have been worth 15 points. After the manager started pushing for an increased velocity, the same five stories would have been estimated to be worth 25 points.

It's important to keep this in mind when estimating velocity. These numbers are really created by the team for the team. When anyone outside the team tries to alter the numbers, they become much less useful.

Planning Your Sprints

Sprint planning is when the team takes stories out of the product backlog and puts them into the sprint. Some teams will create a separate sprint backlog. This backlog will only have the stories to be completed in that sprint.

Other teams will take stories from the backlog and place them on a large task board. This task board is usually a whiteboard with four columns. From left to right, the columns can be labeled *stories, to do, doing,* and *done* or something similar. The team will pull the stories from the backlog and place them into the first column.

It's more common for a team to just use the task board, although a sprint backlog works well if you want to keep track of what the team does over time as well.

Sprint planning involves the entire team and is usually timeboxed to four hours. Timeboxed simply means that a strict time limit is placed on the task. In this case, the team has four hours to complete the sprint planning.

The product owner begins by going through the product backlog and presenting what they want done in the sprint. The development team decides how much of what the product owner wants they can deliver. It should be a back-and-forth between what the product owner wants done and what can be done.

The Task Board

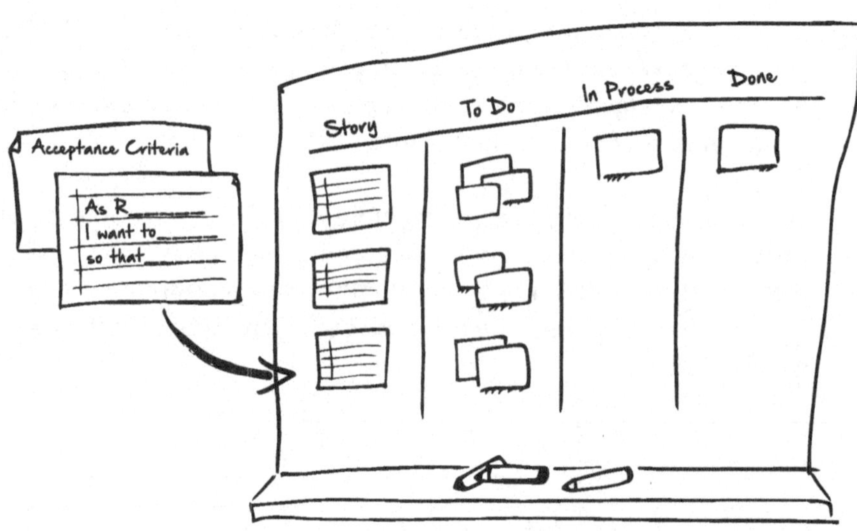

Often the details about the stories get resolved in sprint planning. Up until now, the stories have only been considered in the abstract. The product owner created the user stories. Maybe they were organized into large groups like epics. Then the development team estimated the work required to complete the user stories with a round of planning poker. This was all done at a very high level.

Now the team is very interested in what it takes to deliver the stories—what actually needs to be done. An abstract story suddenly needs to be implemented.

Once the product owner and the team have agreed on a group of stories to be delivered in this sprint, the development team will start to task out the story. Usually the team will be sitting around a large table. The ScrumMaster will provide a bunch of yellow sticky notes for the developers to write down their tasks. Each task should be one day of work per developer. That means that if the story has eight tasks, it will take eight developer days. That might mean four developers for two days or one developer for eight days.

You want to keep the task limited to one day so that the team can track their work easily. You don't want one sticky to represent one day of work and another to represent eight days of work.

Once the team decides what stories to deliver, they'll place them top to bottom under the *stories* column on the task board. Then next to each of the story cards, they'll place the tasks that are required to complete the story. All the tasks should be recorded on yellow sticky notes and placed in the *to do* column.

There are two ways for the team to decide how many stories they should deliver in the sprint. The first way is to deliver based on the team's **intuition**. The second way is to deliver based on the team's **velocity**. As mentioned earlier, velocity is how many stories the team has historically completed over time.

There are advantages and challenges to both methods of deciding on the number of tasks that will be addressed.

Rolling Average

Remember, the team's velocity is a rolling average. For example, let's say on average you received a hundred email messages a week. Does that mean you should plan each week to answer a hundred email messages? You probably shouldn't. One week you'll have three hundred email messages. Other weeks you may only have fifty.

For long-term planning, a hundred email messages a week are fine. You can probably guess how much storage space you'll need on your computer, but for week-to-week or day-to-day planning, you may run into problems.

That's the same challenge you'll run into when planning sprints using the team's velocity. The developers will see the velocity as the team's capacity. Even though there are times when the team thinks it will deliver more, they won't commit to more.

There is also a danger that the team will make their velocity self-fulfilling. [19] Let's say after four sprints, the team has a velocity of 15. From then on, the team uses 15 to plan the sprints. Over time, 15 solidifies as the team's only velocity.

Work expands to fill the time available for its completion – Parkinson's Law

On the flipside, it can also be dangerous to use the team's intuition. They might be wrong about what they can finish. When the team can't complete a story, it goes back into the backlog. That may be fine if it's just a few stories, but it gets to be a problem when there are many incomplete stories over several sprints.

Often the team will spend valuable time on the stories even if they're incomplete. That means a lot of half-completed stories get dumped back into the backlog. This could create a lot of confusion for the product owner. It also makes it more difficult for the team to predict their delivery and maintain a sustainable pace.

Pro Tip

To deal with these trade-offs, it's usually better to mix the two approaches. If you're the ScrumMaster for the team, you should start out having the team fill the sprint using their intuition. Then when you see their estimated story points leveling out, you can think about switching over to using their velocity. It usually takes at least six months for the team to have a sustainable velocity.

The advantage to mixing the approaches is that you get a more accurate velocity over time. The disadvantage is that you might have a bumpy six months before the team settles on a consistent number.

Chapter 7

Driving Productive Agile Activities

There are a number of agile activities that are necessary to keep your organization agile. A good understanding of these activities will help ensure that they are being conducted properly.

Staying Lightweight

The difference between an agile activity and a regular meeting is easy to spot. Like a bouncer in a nightclub, there are only five approved agile activities on the list. Anything else should be left at the door.

These five activities are the only ones necessary to support the framework. These are sometimes called the agile activities. These five activities are usually facilitated by the ScrumMaster.

The agile activities are scheduled, well-structured meetings and shouldn't be confused with the spontaneous discussions that come up as part of a shared workspace. Those impromptu chats are for when developers need to sort out problems or hammer out details about a task.

The shared workspace is intended to eliminate the need for scheduled meetings because in a sense, the agile team is always meeting.[20]

The shared workspace relies on osmotic communication—the ability to take in conversations in a crowded space. It's similar to dinner-party chatter. You can eavesdrop on conversations even when you're doing something else. You can focus on getting the last scoop of mashed potatoes and still hear someone in the other corner debate politics.

Osmotic communication has been fine-tuned over millennia. Your agile team should take advantage of this natural ability by prioritizing team collocation. Just sitting together in a shared workspace is enough for the team to get an idea of everyone's progress.

Human beings are naturally inclined to take in information from a shared space. Scheduled meetings try to make up for too much unnatural communication. Think of the times you've

[20] "Individuals and interactions over processes and tools," from *The Agile Manifesto*

had a face-to-face meeting and finally understood what someone was saying—even after they've sent dozens of email messages.

The combination of osmotic communication and a shared workspace should keep the team out of scheduled meetings.

Any scheduled meeting that is not one of the five activities is considered low-value work.

Bonus Fact

The famous management consultant Peter Drucker once said, "Meetings are . . . a concession . . . either meet or work . . . . [You] cannot do both at the same time."[21]

Agile views meetings that are not part of the framework the same way. It's not that these meetings are bad. It's just that they're not considered work. You can work on delivering your project or be in a meeting—not both.

This is particularly true of scheduled meetings for external groups. These are the meetings familiar to anyone who's worked in a large organization. It's usually a presenter using a slide projector to give a presentation to a midsized audience.

The challenge with these meetings is that they don't deliver value to the customer. Remember that agile emphasizes working software. Anything that's not working software is considered lower value.

In modern teams, working software requires some degree of internal collaboration. A slide presentation is not collaborative.

Presentation meetings are centered on one-way communication. The presenter is updating the audience. This is usually a status update, a budget request, or an executive summary. It's the meeting equivalent of comprehensive documentation. Instead of delivering a report, you're presenting a status meeting.

[21] *The Effective Executive* by Peter Drucker (1993)

It's not just the work lost during the meeting. It's also the work that goes into creating the material. If you have ever created a presentation, think about the time that went into tweaking your slides, then multiply that effort by the number of meetings you attend every two weeks.

Field Notes

I once worked for an organization that emphasized what they called "work socialization." It was the organizational equivalent of "you tell me what you're doing and I'll tell you what I'm doing." At these meetings, the agile team spent a lot of time presenting their work to other work groups.

These meetings took days out of the sprint. The team was socializing their work with five other work groups. Each work group had around five people so there were 300 new channels of communication. To fill these channels, each team spent several hours in meetings with every other work group.

It was a friendly exercise. Each team had a better sense of what the organization was doing. It gave the sense that everyone was working toward the same goal, and there were also a lot of other groups to sit with in the cafeteria. But from an agile perspective, it was a time waster. Each team produced about 20% less work per sprint.

Some of these meetings are deeply ingrained in an organization's culture. That means you'll have to pick your battles. One thing to keep in mind is that you should be completely transparent about the productivity the team is losing.

The agile team in the organization that emphasized work socialization decided to keep track of all the hours that they spent during each sprint in socializing their work. They simply kept track of the hours on a whiteboard. This allowed the product owner to do the simple math and figure out how much productivity was being lost.

If external meetings take up too much of the team's time, then the ScrumMaster might see these meetings as an obstacle that needs to be overcome.

Timeboxing

An agile project depends on scheduled, repeatable chunks of time called timeboxes. A timebox is intuitively named. It is a box of time that cannot expand. If you have an activity timeboxed for an hour, the activity cannot go more than an hour. When the hour's up, the activity ends.

THE AGILE TIMEBOX

The timebox is the building block on which all agile planning and scheduling depends. All the work in an agile project is broken down into the smallest possible timebox. Even the developers have their own timebox—they must work within their eight-hour day. Overtime and working weekends will interfere with the predictability of the schedule.

To understand the importance of a timebox, you have to look at an agile project as a whole.

An agile project has less up-front planning. Remember that agile is adaptive and not predictive. *The Agile Manifesto* values change more than planning.[22]

With agile, when you start the project, you don't know how it's going to finish. You start with a general notion of where you're going and make frequent improvements on how to get there. Agile is adaptive but not predictive. Much of the energy comes from these project changes.

In traditional project management, a plan has project milestones that lead to a delivery date. An agile project also needs a delivery date. You'll never have a successful project without delivery. No executive would ever accept a "you'll get it when it's done" delivery schedule.

This means an agile project needs a different method for creating delivery dates. The product backlog is always changing, so you can't use that to create milestones. The product owner has the freedom to change the deliverable throughout the project. The high-priority task created one month ago might become a lower priority the next month.

Even though your agile project has a flexible scope, the budget and time remain constant. So even though you might not know the full scope, you can still commit to the cost and the schedule. To do this, an agile project needs to build up the schedule with these immutable timeboxes. You'll build your deliverable one box at a time—like a LEGO project.

22 "Responding to change over following a plan," from *The Agile Manifesto*

Free Analogy

LEGO

Let's say you have a cardboard box filled with 500 LEGO blocks. Now let's say that each one of those LEGO blocks represents one unit of work. Over time, your team has found that they can complete 50 blocks of work every two weeks.

The timebox for your LEGO project would be two weeks. Let's call this the LEGO sprint. You know you should be able to build something with 50 LEGO blocks every LEGO sprint. That means your 500 LEGO blocks will be gone after 10 LEGO sprints.

After 10 LEGO sprints, or 20 weeks, you will have delivered an impressive structure with 500 blocks. It could be a house, a car, or a battleship—it's up to the product owner. All the team knows is that at the end of 10 LEGO sprints, they'll make something with 500 blocks.

Now let's say that the LEGO convention is in town and your entire team took the week off. They returned well rested but now face 50 LEGO blocks that need to be placed. The team decides to expand their LEGO sprint an extra week so they can finish the work—easy peasy.

The problem now is that they've broken their LEGO sprint. In 20 weeks, they will have placed only about 475 LEGO blocks. They will still have around 25 LEGO blocks left over. Maybe those 25 or so blocks are needed to complete the structure. They could be the roof of the LEGO house. Maybe your team has committed to finishing after 10 sprints and now the work is incomplete.

The team has undermined the predictability of 10 LEGO sprints placing 500 blocks. Now the project will deliver whatever, whenever, and that leads to an unhappy LEGO sponsor.

Conventions, sick days, and holidays are all part of any project. That means that the real trick is coming up with the number of blocks completed per LEGO sprint. Maybe for this project, a better number would've been 45 blocks per LEGO sprint. The team commits to their pace of work for the project. If there is a convention in town, they might only finish 30 blocks. Then 50 blocks the next LEGO sprint. That would average out to 45 blocks over time. For this project, we might call 45 blocks the team's LEGO velocity.

Since the timeboxes are always building up, it is important to maintain them for all your work and activities. The daily standup is usually timeboxed to 15 minutes. If it takes one hour one day and 10 minutes the next day, then you've introduced variability into your sprint.

This is true of the other activities as well. If the sprint-planning activity takes four hours one sprint and then two hours the next, one sprint will give the team an extra two hours of work.

It will be near impossible for the team to create a predictable pace if the timeboxes have no meaning. It is unfair to ask the team how much they can complete per sprint if they don't know how long they'll be in a standup, planning, or other activities.

The ScrumMaster on the team is responsible for making sure these timeboxes remain constant. It won't take long for the agile framework to break down when the team breaks the sprints or allows the activities to run too long.

Multitasking

If you started work at 9:00 in the morning and had three tasks which will take an hour to complete, how would you organize your schedule? When most people are asked this question, they will say that they would start one task at nine, begin another at 10:00 and start the last one at 11:00 in order to have everything finished by noon. They would start one task at a time and finish each one before starting the next one.

In reality, few people actually work that way. The way most people work is they start all three at 9:00 and do a little bit of each simultaneously. That way, they will have more time for all three. If something takes longer than an hour, they will still have time before noon.

This is commonly called multitasking.[23] Most organizations encourage that trait in their teams. That's why on job websites you'll often see "ability to multitask" near the top of the list. But multitasking comes at a heavy price. People can't work on a number of tasks divided into even slices of time. A person is not like a pizza where if you take two slices of task time, then you'll still have six slices left. No one works that way.

Think about the last time you were working on something important. Sometimes it takes a long time to get started. Then you'll get momentum. Maybe you've figured out how to finish a memo, or maybe you finally got a good idea about how to balance the budget.

Then somebody knocks on your door. Or there's a beep. You see an email with an exclamation point. You switch off what you were doing and focus on this new task. Then you have to switch back and restart what you were doing.

[23] "If you chase two rabbits, you will not catch either." – Russian proverb

This is called context switching. You go from what you were doing to doing something else. The impact of context switching is much greater than most people realize.

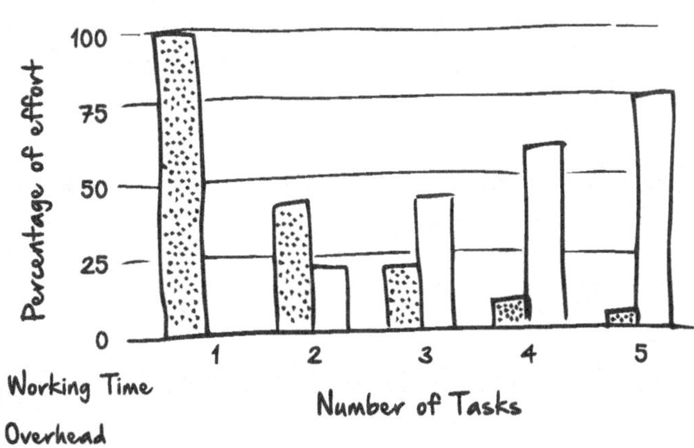

Most people think that if they have an hour, they can finish two 30-minute tasks. What's actually true is that when you work on two tasks, you really only have about 48 minutes of work time, not 60. The other 12 minutes are overhead from switching back and forth between the two. Overhead is the time when you say, "Okay, so where was I?" and then go back to work.

The more tasks you have, the greater the overhead—the time you need when switching between tasks increases with the workload. You can see by the bar chart,[24] that by the time you're working on three tasks, you've spent more time switching than working. The chart also shows that when you're working on more than five tasks, there is no reason to come into the office. Three-quarters of your time is spent just figuring out what you're doing. Instead, you can come into work for just one day and focus on a single task and have the same productivity.

Agile is designed to reduce this inefficiency. The whole team should be focused on the fewest number of tasks. All the activities are timeboxed. This forces the team to finish one thing and start another.

The agile activities (the five approved activities) should run the same way. Each activity is designed to build a finished artifact. The ScrumMaster needs to make sure that each timebox will create one thing. Maybe it's the plan for the next sprint or it could be a list of improvements after the retrospect.

[24] *Quality Software Management: Systems Thinking* by Gerald M. Weinberg (1991)

That means that at the end of the planning activity, there has to be a completed plan. You can't mix up this activity with something that you couldn't complete earlier. When the timeboxes are exhausted, the team has to work with whatever was finished. They can't schedule more time. They can't combine this activity with the next daily standup. This would create too much multitasking and cause all the work to slow down.

It also means that when everyone is focused on a team activity, they can't work on other tasks.

Field Notes

I once worked for an organization where it was common for people to bring their smartphones or laptops into meetings. You could hear people typing while other people were talking. They were answering email messages or finishing up a memo.

As the chart shows, there's really no reason to run a meeting that way.

There's no reason to have an hour-long meeting where people are working on several tasks. Instead, it's far more efficient to have a 15-minute meeting where everyone is focused on a single task. Then let everybody go answer their email or work on their memo.

Pro Tip

Most agile activities should be **unplugged**. There's no need for a laptop or smartphone in an agile activity. There's not enough time to do any research. There's no reason to communicate with anyone outside of the team. They'll start breaking their timeboxes if they multitask during activities.

It is easier to plan for the next two weeks when the team is participating and they are fully engaged. They're all working together to complete a single artifact. Everyone in the rowboat is rowing at the same pace to the same place. If you have people on the team multitasking, it will slow down the entire effort, and it will take longer than the two hours you are allowed for this activity.

As a ScrumMaster, this might be one area where you find yourself in conflict with the project manager. Often the project manager will like people multitasking. It is the human equivalent of a Gantt chart. You have people working on multiple concurrent streams of work. From their perspective, this makes sense. Traditional projects often depend on multitasking to meet the timeline.

These managers and project managers might require extra coaching. It's very hard to overcome the belief that working more doesn't always deliver more work. An agile team works harder by working more efficiently. Often, the only way to convince them is by running the agile project and over time showing an increase in productivity.

Running Agile Activities

The five agile activities that support the Scrum framework are standup, plan, refine, demo, and improve. Each of these activities should produce an outcome. Four of the five are limited to a maximum time limit. The activity is lightweight but has a tight agenda. If you're the ScrumMaster for the team, make sure you understand these activities and their results.

In the beginning, most of the ScrumMaster's time will be safeguarding these activities. The ScrumMaster should always be running interference for the team to keep from falling victim to *meeting creep*.

In traditional projects, there's a tendency to make sure everyone has a voice. When a project overlaps with a department, then you need to invite a representative of that department to join.

In agile, the activities should strive to become smaller and shorter. The five activities should have the fewest number of people possible, since everyone should be focused solely on achievable results. That's why the agenda for these activities is limited and should be closely followed.

The Daily Standup

The daily standup is a developer-led, 15-minute activity where developers tell one another what they're doing. It is the only agile activity the team performs every day.

Of all the agile activities, the daily standup is probably the most misused. It's like the ranch dressing of agile activities—widely accepted but also widely abused. Standups are often repurposed and may end up taking much longer than their scheduled time.

Pro Tip

It's important to remember that the standup is a developer-led activity. Everyone else should sit and listen. It is an activity for the team by the team and is about self-organizing.

The development team stands in a circle and updates everyone about what they're working on. It sounds simple enough, but that's not how most organizations operate.

Most meetings are driven by whoever called the meeting. A self-organized standup is contrary to how most people think of working. Most managers feel that a group left to stand and chat will continue to chat until someone starts the meeting.

The ScrumMaster and the project manager must fight the temptation to drive the standup. The team may start chatty, but they'll quickly become more disciplined. All you need is a few standups that end on time even though a few people didn't contribute. Most meetings will continue to run if there's unfinished work. Agile activities don't have that luxury. Agile activities end when the timebox ends.

You can also think of it this way. If the team can't self-organize a standup, then how will they ever deliver a working product?

The daily standup will be a good indicator of how the self-organized team is progressing. If you're the ScrumMaster, take a look at how the team interacts. Are they fumbling and unsure? Who are they looking at when they talk? These will be your clues about what the developers are thinking.

If they're looking at the ScrumMaster, it usually means they haven't embraced self-organization. Those developers might need some extra coaching. Try to encourage these developers to look at other members of the team. They need to understand that they're working for one another.

The standup is typically held at the beginning of every day. It's not first thing in the morning because the team usually needs a little time to settle. Most standups start at 9:30 in the morning. The team will stand in their shared workspace and form a circle. The team stands to keep the meeting shorter. If your team decides to sit down during a standup, then they may have a more difficult time finishing.

The Daily Standup

Some teams like to stand in front of the task board so they can point to their work. Other teams will stand wherever they're comfortable. Some aggregate around the team's coffee machine.

If you're not a developer, then you're a sitter in this activity. This usually means you'll sit off to the side taking notes. Only the developers should contribute to the standup. The ScrumMaster and the product owner can answer questions, but they shouldn't start conversations.

There is one daily standup for every team. You should never merge several teams into one standup. The timebox is never large enough to accommodate that many developers.

Pro Tip

Once the team is settled, they should take no more than **15 minutes** to answer three questions. What did I do yesterday? What am I doing today? Are there any obstacles in my way?

It's important to keep the standup moving. A midsized team of seven developers will have about 45 seconds per question. So when a developer talks about what they did yesterday, they need to talk about specific tasks. You don't want them to start knowledge sharing.

A good response to the question "*What did I do yesterday?*" is something like this: "Yesterday, I finished the username and password fields for the mobile customer login page. So I moved that task over to the done column."

Compare that to this response, "Yesterday, I finally found out why it's so difficult to login to the mobile login page. It turns out the new version of JavaScript isn't fully documented, and so I had to spend a lot of time searching the web. I went to a website called Java dev. Has anybody ever heard of that? Their information was really the most accurate."

Then they'll go on and on about the best way to find information about JavaScript. This response will quickly exhaust the timebox.

If this happens, the ScrumMaster should coach them on how to contribute within the timebox. The ScrumMaster should fight the urge to interject while the standup is taking place. This might mean a few failed standups, but it will be better in the long run to encourage self-organizing.

Many organizations have a really difficult time allowing teams to self-organize their standup. One warning sign is when the project manager drives the activity. They will go around and ask each developer, "What did you do yesterday? What are you doing today? Do you have any obstacles?"

This style of status update sends a clear message: "I'm going to organize this self-organized team."

This arrangement will always slow down development. It will send a mixed message of how the developers should work. For one, it confuses the role of the project manager. Developers might start to think that they work for the project manager. Then they'll approach the project manager with management questions. If the project manager answers those questions, you'll quickly transform into a traditional project. The project manager will manage the team. A closely managed team is not able to self-organize.

It may cause even bigger problems if the team also treats the ScrumMaster like a project manager. Then you'll have a traditional project manager and an agile project manager. That's two managers for your self-organized team. This type of arrangement is difficult in a traditional project—for an agile team, it's completely unworkable.

Creating The Product Backlog

The product backlog is a ranked list of user stories. These are often called your product backlog items, or PBIs. How the list is created isn't very important. It could be a spreadsheet, 3 × 5 cards, or even a simple Word document. What is important is how the team *uses* the list. The product backlog is the only way to add user stories for the team. The product owner has the sole authority to add work to the project. That includes all work, whether it's a change request, additional documentation, or a new feature.

Pro Tip

The best way to create your product backlog is by writing your first user stories. These stories will start out vague and unclear. They'll be a struggle to create. Chances are they'll be epics that you'll have to break down further into clearer stories. Your product backlog will start as a clumsy and confusing wish list. Then over time you'll refine the backlog. You'll make it clearer. Each updated version of the backlog will get better.

In a traditional project, the team relies on having complete requirements before the work begins. In agile, the product backlog replaces these requirements. The backlog doesn't try to capture all the work at the beginning of the project. Instead, it's an ever-changing document. Work goes into the backlog. The list gets reprioritized. The highest-value stories are reordered and pushed to the top.

A good way to think of your backlog is to think of it as your project's PEZ dispenser. A PEZ dispenser is a little candy case with the head of a famous character on top. When you push back the character's head, a tiny little candy brick spits out from under their neck. Each time you push back the head, another candy brick pops out. A PEZ dispenser will only produce one brick at a time. It goes from top to bottom. Each time you push back and a brick pops out, another one slides up to take its place.

The dispenser keeps you from having too much candy at one time. It acts as a constraint. The highest-value candy pops out from the top and the next brick slides up to take its place.

Occasionally, you'll take out more than you can eat in one sitting. All you have to do is open up the dispenser and reprioritize the extra brick. Maybe it's one of your favorite flavors, so you put it close to the top. Or it could be Wintergreen, and you'll want to put it near the bottom.

The project uses the product backlog the same way you go through these candy bricks. The backlog dispenses one story at a time from top to bottom. You finish the highest-priority item and then on to the next brick. The next story clicks in as the top one is pulled out. If it's too much, you open the dispenser. Then you can replace, relist, and reprioritize.

Not every organization will respect the product owner's authority over the product backlog. Some organizations that are new to agile might have managers who will throw work into the backlog. To work effectively, the product owner has to be the only person who manages the team's work.

Field Notes

I once worked for an organization that had a high-profile data-consolidation project. In these projects, you have a lot of different stakeholders. Each team was trying to get their data into the new data store.

Some of the managers would pull developers from the team and task them with working on only their data. It made the agile project very chaotic. There was no way for the product owner to prioritize the team's work. Senior managers wanted their developers to work on their highest-priority items. Unfortunately, this wasn't necessarily the same priority that the product owner used in the backlog.

The managers started peeling off developers one at a time. Instead of one project PEZ dispenser, each of the developers had their own list of work. The agile team started to disband. Each developer was working on their own manager's priorities. The product owner had no way to coordinate the entire project.

The ScrumMaster had to intervene and meet with all the managers. They had to agree that all the work had to go through the product owner. They explained that if each manager only works on their own list of priorities, the team would never finish the whole project.

Because the backlog is a ranked list of stories, there is no reason for the product owner to reject changes. It's a way to add work to the list without disrupting the team. This means that the product owner doesn't have to evaluate what goes into the list. They only assign the priority. That often makes it much easier to work with the project stakeholders. The product owner is not giving their work a simple yes or no; instead, the product owner is saying we'll get to it when we have time.

This doesn't mean that the product owner has an easy job. When the product owners prioritize the work, it usually means they have to de-prioritize other work. That can lead to some tricky conversations with their stakeholders. The product owners have to explain to stakeholders why their work is less important.

The product owner also has to work with the development team. Sometimes the highest-priority work is not the best way to develop the product. The development team might request that some lower-priority stories be grouped together to increase efficiency.

This is particularly true with software development. Sometimes it's easier to develop stories slightly out of order. The developers might request that they develop stories one, three, and five. It's not always as simple as developing stories from top to bottom—one, two, and three. When that happens, the developers need to make the case to the product owner. A little patience might mean more of the product gets delivered.

It'll be up to the product owner to decide what's fair. You need to balance the highest-value items against the functional realities of delivering software. This can usually be done without the development team leading the project off track.

Refining The Product Backlog

Backlog refinement is the most fluid of all the agile activities. All of the other activities have set times with set limits. The refinement of the product backlog happens as needed by the product owner. In this activity, the product owner will request a meeting to estimate any new items in the product backlog.

The product owner needs these estimates so the list can be prioritized. These meetings are the least structured. The product owner will go over the product backlog with the developers. Developers might make recommendations on how to organize the list. This may include breaking larger items into smaller items. They also may talk the product owner into removing some items from the list because of complexity or redundancy. The team will also make estimates on the new items, which usually means another round of planning poker.

In Scrum's early years, this was called *backlog grooming*. Most of the Scrum community later abandoned the term.[25] Instead, they settled on the more neutral term *backlog refinement*.

Whichever you call it, the activity is pretty much the same thing. You refine the backlog by adding, removing, or updating the backlog items.

In many ways, *refinement* is probably not the best word. In the beginning, you'll be adding a lot of new stories to the backlog. It doesn't seem like much of a refinement if your backlog

[25] In some countries, it refers to the potential mistreatment of children.

continues to grow. It's very common to have your backlog grow into a very large list. Then later, the product owner will prune down some of the items. It's better to think of the activity as *backlog preparation*.

The product owner should spend four to eight hours a week with the team on this activity. The backlog preparation should be timeboxed for two hours or less. Anything longer than that and the team will start to lose focus. The activity should be open and set up for discussion.

Typically, the activity starts with the product owner presenting a few user stories to the development team. The development team will try to understand the user stories at a high level. Remember that the development team doesn't task out the user story until sprint planning. The ScrumMaster should work hard to make sure that the team doesn't get too much into the weeds of how to deliver the story.

Once the team understands the story, they can go through a few rounds of planning poker. This will give the product owner a relative estimate of how much effort it takes to deliver the story. Then the product owner can go back and use this estimate to reprioritize the product backlog.

Usually, the biggest challenge with backlog preparation is how often to schedule the activity. The backlog represents the project's future. The question is how much of the present you sacrifice to prepare for the future.

Free Analogy

In many ways, backlog preparation is like the old challenge farmers have when planting their crops. If you are growing corn, you need to harvest all the corn you want to eat. You also need to set aside some of the best corn for next year's seed. Farmers typically call this their seed corn. In lean years, it takes a lot of effort for the farmers to set aside enough corn for the next year. You give up a few more meals today to ensure you have enough to eat tomorrow.

The team runs into a similar problem with the backlog. If you spend too much time planning for the future, then you won't have enough time to finish what you need today. If you ignore the future, then it will take up too much of your time tomorrow. You have to set aside just enough seed corn to ensure the project keeps growing, but not so much that the team stops working on what they need today.

The team might spend as much as one full day each sprint preparing the product backlog. That might seem like a lot of time to tie up the entire team, but remember that this activity takes the place of more traditional project requirements. In traditional projects, it is certainly not uncommon to take one month to plan a one-year project. For many organizations, that would be much too quick. Agile spreads out this planning over the entire course of the project.

Still, it might be tempting to cut back on product-backlog preparation. It'll be up to the ScrumMaster to ensure that the product owner is getting the time needed to plan for the future.

A good way to remember the agenda is to think of the acronym DEEP. This acronym was created by Mike Cohn and is a good starting point for backlog refinement.

In this activity, the stories should be **detailed** appropriately. The highest-value user stories should be well understood so they can be completed in the next sprint. Distant stories can be described with less detail.

The stories should be **estimated**. The product backlog is more than a list of work. It is also a planning tool. Again, place the highest priority on the top stories. Stories further down can get a rougher estimate.

Once the team understands the stories they can go through a few rounds of planning poker. This gives the product owner an estimate of how much effort it takes to deliver the story. The product owner can then use these estimates to reprioritize the work.

The product backlog should be **emergent**. A backlog is not static. It will change over time. As the team learns more about the product, new user stories will be added, removed, or changed.

The backlog should be **prioritized**. The backlog should be sorted with the highest-value items at the top. The least valuable should be at the bottom. This way, the development will always be working on the highest-value items.

Planning Your Sprints

The sprint-planning activity is where the team decides what to deliver for the sprint. The activity is usually timeboxed to four hours. In this activity, the team plans and forecasts the work for the next two weeks. The team will take the highest-value items from the product backlog and make sure that everybody understands what needs to be done.

It's essential that the product owner attends this activity. The product owner decides what's next and needs to be available for questions. The product owner will take the top value stories and present them to the developers. Then they'll *task out* the highest-value stories.

Pro Tip

Most agile teams use a task board for the sprint-planning activity. The task board is one of the most familiar artifacts in agile. You've probably seen the yellow sticky notes lined across a dry-erase whiteboard. The board is typically divided into four columns. Some of the columns have different names, but they're usually a variation of *stories, to do, doing*, and *done*. Some teams practicing extreme programming will add a fifth column called *done done.*

Your team could also decide to plan the sprint without a task board. Many agile software packages provide virtual task boards. This has the advantage of allowing the teams to see the tasks without visiting a real board. The downside is that it minimizes the importance of the shared workspace.

When starting out, it is usually best to plan your sprint without any software. You may have the ScrumMaster create a second software board with all the stories. That way, if you switch, you can still have the benefit of historical reporting. The reason it's usually best to start analog is that it encourages the team to sit in the shared workspace. Developers are usually technophiles and prefer to work with software. That might make this a tough sell for the team.

At the start of the sprint-planning activity, developers decide how they will contribute to the story. They'll write a yellow sticky note with their tasks for each story. The team usually starts tasking the highest-value items first.

A task should be no more than one day of work for each person. When a task represents more than one day of work, then the task board doesn't reflect the team's progress. You don't want one sticky to represent a task that is a day long and another sticky to represent a task that is a few hours long because then there would be no way to tell how much work is left after the sprint begins.

It is best if sprint planning is scheduled immediately following the demo (the activity to show the results of the last sprint). Since the demo just concluded, there shouldn't be any work left. It's a terrific time to plan without impacting the team's productivity.

The activity should begin with the product owner delivering the stories that they wish to complete in the upcoming sprint, but the product owner shouldn't drive the activity.

The product owner should think of themselves as being customers in a restaurant, except instead of ordering dinner, they're ordering what they want delivered in the sprint. You'd never have a customer going back and standing over the chef. The same is true with the product owner. They are there to answer questions and not drive the team to deliver. They can have their salad dressing on the side. What they can't do is force the team to deliver a full meal for less than a dollar.

Field Notes

I once worked for a company where a product owner was pushing the team to add stories to the sprint. The product owner would always say, "Let's just see what we can finish." The developers would accommodate the product owner, but they knew that they had little chance of delivering everything they put on the task board.

After the product owner did this a few times, the development team started overestimating the stories. It started to look like the classic project management practice of padding your work to meet an aggressive timeline.

Agile pushes for transparency when planning the work. When a product owner tries to drive the team, they will only damage the reliability of their estimates. In agile, the team's productivity is seen as a constant. The developer shouldn't have to be coaxed into being more productive.

The product owner is there to produce the highest-value stories. It's up to the team to decide how they're going to deliver.

After the product owner delivers the highest-value stories, the developers should start tasking. Hopefully, the team will have estimated the stories in an earlier product-backlog refinement, so this shouldn't be the first time that the team sees the stories in the product backlog. They would've also asked questions about the story as a way to create an estimate.

Sprint planning is usually when you find out how good you've been with refining the backlog. Converting a user story to daily work is not always a smooth process. It's not uncommon for the development team to say things like "That's what you meant by that? I thought you meant the other thing." Then they'll have to break down the story into smaller stories or quickly re-estimate.

Pro Tip

One of the biggest dangers in this activity is a story-breakout blizzard. That's when the team realizes that many of the stories are not ready to be tasked out. The team will try to task out one story and then realize they need to break it into two stories. One of the two stories becomes another two stories. Then the team has to estimate three stories and create tasks for each. The timebox is too short for all these activities.

The best way to avoid this is by putting a lot of time into backlog refining. When the team is just starting with agile they should spend more time backlog refining than on any other activity. It's not uncommon for a team to realize the importance of backlog refinement after a failed sprint planning.

As teams get better at backlog refining, they will spend less and less time talking about the stories during sprint planning. That way, they can spend less time focusing on what the story is and, instead, decide how they're going to deliver.

Demoing The Work

At the end of the sprint, the team schedules a review of the deliverable. This is sometimes called the sprint review. It's also commonly called the sprint demo. The team usually takes two hours to show the completed work to the project's stakeholders.

The product owner usually drives this activity since the product owner will have the closest relationship with the stakeholders and is probably best qualified to answer questions.

The sprint demo should actively engage the stakeholders. The theme of every demo is "here is what your money bought you over the last two weeks." A good demo will also get suggestions and feedback from the stakeholders.

It's a bit of a double-edged sword to call the activity a demo. On the one hand, you're much more likely to get everyone to attend. A demonstration activity sounds far more alluring than a review. On the other hand, you don't want to give the stakeholders the idea that they need to sit and watch.

In larger organizations, a demonstration is usually a slide deck with screenshots. For a sprint demonstration, the agile team walks through a working deliverable—most of the time, that's software.

Field Notes

I've seen many teams that are uncomfortable demonstrating working software to stakeholders. The team would prefer to develop software in a lab. Then they'll put screenshots on a slide to show the stakeholders. This is particularly true for organizations that have a strong affinity for slide presentations.

It's important that the team doesn't give into this temptation. This activity is just about walking through a working product. The stakeholders shouldn't be listening to the team talking about a product. Instead, the stakeholders need to be thinking about what they're buying.

The agile demonstration is about communication and accountability. This is the activity where the stakeholders justify what they've spent with what the team's delivered. They should be thinking to themselves, "Okay, I spent so much money and here's what I have to show for it."

The demonstration should be on the last day of the sprint, and it should be the first of the sequence of activities that end the sprint. The last day of the sprint will typically have a demo, then a planning activity, and then a reflection activity like a retrospective.

Pro Tip

Many teams choose to start their sprints on Thursday morning. This way, the big block of meetings happens on Wednesday. In larger organizations, it is difficult to have big meetings late Friday afternoon.

The agile demonstration is typically scheduled for two hours, but you may find that it is difficult to get project stakeholders to attend a two-hour activity late Wednesday afternoons. If your project has high-level stakeholders, then the team may be better off scheduling a one-hour meeting. But keep in mind that this arrangement puts more pressure on the product owner. They'll need to communicate more often with the stakeholders during the sprint.

As stated earlier, the product owner is the one who drives this activity. This is a common practice even though it's not explicitly stated in the Scrum framework. This is the only agile activity that has the development team sitting in the background. The talker in this activity is the product owner and the sitters are the rest of the team.

There are four reasons to have the product owner drive this activity. The first reason is that it helps the product owner feel like they have a stake in the outcome. The product owner should be keenly interested in the task board at the end of the sprint. They know that in a few days they'll be the one standing up in front of the stakeholders. Instead of some far-off deadline, the product owner has real-time skin in the game.

The second reason is that the product owner usually has the best relationship with the stakeholders, so you're more likely to get good back-and-forth feedback. The product owner should see the product from the view of the stakeholders and should describe the product the same way and have the same goal as the stakeholders.

The third reason is that you need to make sure that the stakeholders share the same vision with the product owner.

Field Notes

I was once on a project where the key stakeholder interrupted the product owner in the middle of the demo. They said they didn't think the team was working on the highest-value deliverables. Then they laid out their vision for how they thought the project should deliver.

It was awkward for the product owner, but it was a very good outcome for the team. Without that feedback, the team may have worked for weeks, or even months, disconnected from what the stakeholders wanted. This type of transparent exchange is what saves organizations money on lost efforts.

The fourth reason is that the development team is not usually very good at driving a demo. Often, the developers will talk about the product as a capability and not as a solution. They might talk about what software does and not necessarily why the software is valuable.

Sometimes the developers will do a NASCAR-style doughnut in front of the stakeholders. They may misinterpret this activity as a victory ceremony, and may view it as a good time for the team to get hard-earned recognition. Unfortunately, the demonstration is not nearly so satisfying.

If developers run the demo this way, it is likely that it will be lightly attended. The stakeholders might be patient in the beginning, but they will probably not want to sit through an activity every two weeks hearing about how great the team is doing developing great software.

Start running the demo correctly from the very beginning. The stakeholders are more likely to provide great feedback when they realize that this is their activity. Make sure that the product owner drives this activity. The rest of the team should be sitting in the background. Have them listen to how the product owner describes the product to stakeholders. If they have questions, they should save them for sprint planning.

Team Improvement

The self-improvement activity is limited to 2 hours and happens immediately after the product demo. This activity is often called a retrospective. Of the five activities, this one is arguably the most important because if the team can't improve, it will usually make the same mistakes each sprint.

In the beginning, the ScrumMaster may need to push the team to commit to specific improvements. Every organization has challenges and it will be the ScrumMaster's responsibility to keep the activity positive and productive.

If these five activities are done correctly, then the team will stay lightweight and productive.

Inviting The Right Groups

Agile activities are always timeboxed. Since the time is limited, there's always pressure to make the activities as efficient as possible, and it is the ScrumMaster who is responsible for setting up efficient activities. This means that the ScrumMaster is very careful about who contributes.

Often on an agile project, there are stakeholders outside the team that want to attend. Sometimes, agile is just starting in an organization, and these people want to attend out of curiosity. Other times, someone will have an interest in the deliverable and may want to have a connection to the project.

It's true that the agile team will almost always benefit from the added attention, but the challenge is to maintain the interest level without bogging down the team with overzealous participation.

The ScrumMaster should think about long-term efficiencies. It wouldn't be a good idea to tell an executive that they can't talk during a daily standup. If an important person passes through, it is best to let them contribute. What you do need to watch for are stakeholders who attend your activities on a regular basis. This is more about the senior manager who starts talking through your planning activities.

It's best to set a standard early in your agile project. If you let the activities turn into a group forum, then it will be very difficult to tie them down later. At the very beginning, the ScrumMaster should set the expectation that during an agile activity, not everyone is expected to contribute.

Pro Tip

To keep things from getting confusing, the ScrumMaster should try to think of attendees as either *sitters* or *talkers*. A sitter is someone who has an interest in the activity but shouldn't be contributing. A talker is someone who is expected to contribute as part of the team.

Trying to get everybody either sitting or talking will keep things moving. Sitting or talking is not a euphemism. A sitter should actually be sitting, and they should be sitting off to the side. This is a signal that they're not expected to contribute.

Sometimes it is a bit delicate to let someone know that he or she shouldn't be contributing. Some people interpret this to mean that they don't have anything valuable to contribute even if this isn't true.

The ScrumMaster needs to defend the agile activities and needs to stress to the participants that it's not about what they're saying, it's the forum. The timebox gives the activity very little wiggle room. This means the time is vulnerable to being hijacked.

Sometimes a sitter might hijack your activity and make an announcement or ask questions. The sitter may think there's no point in scheduling another meeting when everybody's already there. The ScrumMaster needs to ensure the sitter's concerns are addressed at another time and not during the focused agile activity.

The daily standup is the activity that's most likely to be hijacked. In the standup, the developers are the talkers. The activity is for them. The product owner, the ScrumMaster, and the project manager should always be sitters.

The activity will almost always break out of its timebox if the project manager hijacks the activity.

Field Notes

I've worked on a few projects where this has happened. The project managers would use the standup as their own daily status meeting. They would listen in on the developers and if they heard something interesting, they would interject with questions and concerns.

Field Notes (continued)

It was the ScrumMaster's responsibility to convince the project manager to sit and wait for the standup to finish. The ScrumMaster did this by scheduling another meeting immediately following the standup.

The product demo is another activity that is difficult to keep on track. The product owner usually drives this activity. They need to make sure that they agree with the sponsor on the vision for the project. What often happens is that the developers will want some visibility.

This makes sense. The development team has been working on this project and they have some pride in the deliverable. They'll want to show the sponsor all the bells and whistles. There is also an urge to spike the football. If the sponsor mentions something that was well done, then the developers might want to accept their share of the credit.

The product demo is also timeboxed. To run efficiently, the development team needs to sit and not contribute. The only time the developers should contribute is when the product owner asks them a question. Otherwise, the team should do its best to communicate that this is the product owner's activity. The rest of the team is there to sit and watch.

Often sitting and listening will give the team a much better sense of the activity. I've seen many demos were the development team picked up on cues that the product owner missed.

Pro Tip

Keeping the sitters from talking is a necessary part of well-run agile activities. But it is easier said than done. It requires some tact from a savvy ScrumMaster.

The ScrumMaster needs to differentiate between the people who are involved in the activities long-term and the people who are just stopping by with a few concerns. Once you identify your sitters and talkers, work hard right at the start to communicate to them your expectations for the activity. A little work at the beginning usually saves a lot of headaches later on.

Gathering The Roadblocks

An organization is always looking for leaders. Managers complain that they need more leaders. Executives look for leadership qualities to promote or hire. They'll send senior managers to leadership seminars. They'll recommend the best leadership books.

Leadership is associated with someone who takes responsibility for outcomes and who drives the team forward.

There's no doubt that leadership plays a role in organizations. A great leader can do great things. But a lot gets done by people who aren't leaders. Not every great change requires great leadership. It's not always the person pushing forward. You also need people to keep the team from sliding backward.

That's where the ScrumMaster comes in. The ScrumMaster needs to remove the obstacles, so the team can focus on delivery. These obstacles can mean many different things. Sometimes it's hard for ScrumMasters to sort out the difference between removing obstacles and managing the team.

There is no clear list of every obstacle. The list will change depending on your organization. Even within the same organization, you're bound to run into many new obstacles. Instead of thinking of obstacles individually, try to think of them in terms of groups. In general, there are five groups of obstacles that you'll run into on your project. If your obstacle is not in one of these groups, then you might be in danger of managing the team.

You can remember the five groups by thinking of the word SMITH, which stands for setup, mentoring, input, training, and hiring. These are the five groups where you'll find most of your obstacles.

Setup: In some organizations, setting up a shared workspace is an enormous obstacle. If your agile team works on a floor with rows of cubicles, then it may be difficult to create a shared workspace. The organization may think these cubicles are the best way to work.

Setup is not just limited to a shared workspace. It also includes team roles. Sometimes an organization won't dedicate a product owner to the team. It will be the ScrumMaster's responsibility to convince the organization that the team won't succeed without a product owner.

Mentoring: This is the coaching part of the role. The ScrumMaster should be very knowledgeable about agile, particularly since the rest of the team may not know that much about the process.

This is particularly true with product owners. In many ways, product owners have the most to learn. They'll know the product, but they may not know agile. The ScrumMaster should work with them from the beginning to help them define their role and create a product backlog.

Another obstacle ScrumMasters could face is that the developers might not embrace self-organization. The ScrumMaster may have to coach them as well. The ScrumMaster should sit with the team and offer guidance. If an individual developer is having trouble with self-organizing, the ScrumMaster should pull the developer aside and set up time to help.

Input: The ScrumMaster will often come from a technical background. They're not developers in the project, but they might still offer best practices to the group.

It is very important for ScrumMasters to distinguish between input and direction. As a general rule, input is asked for and direction is given. Input is when the developer approaches the ScrumMaster and asks for an opinion on a JavaScript library. Direction is the ScrumMaster having a meeting with the developer, then encouraging the use of a JavaScript library the ScrumMaster has used in the past.

Training: It's the ScrumMaster's responsibility to assess the team's knowledge of agile. Many developers have worked on *agile-like* projects, but some of their practices might be wrong. Depending on the experience of the team, they might be spreading these incorrect practices. Other times, the team starts agile without any training.

In either case, the ScrumMaster needs to identify this as an obstacle. Agile training is a good way to get everyone to understand the framework, and it is also a good way to get everybody doing the same thing.

Hiring: The ScrumMaster's role in hiring is an advanced topic. A self-organized team should have control over their own developers. If not, you're giving the team responsibility for delivery but no authority to make any changes. Also, the team should know the most about what makes a successful developer.

But you don't want the team interviewing developers and posting jobs. It will take too much time away from development. Also, many organizations don't like other team members knowing one another's salaries.

Pro Tip

The best way to think of the ScrumMaster's role in hiring is to think of them as an administrator. They post the job and arrange the interviews.

When they find a candidate, they schedule an interview with the rest of the team. If the team approves of the hire, then the ScrumMaster will negotiate the new person's salary.

It's not about controlling who's on the team. It's about keeping the team focused on delivery.

Keeping The Activity Moving

To become fully agile, the team needs to abandon much of the traditional project management mindset. Traditional project management can be high stakes. If you're wrong about an estimate, then the project will need more money. That's usually not a happy result for the project manager.

Agile activities are different. An agile team needs to accept these differences. One of the big differences is that agile doesn't assume immediate expertise. It's pretty much accepted that a new agile team will be terrible at estimates and slowly get better. The same is true with sprint planning. The team will be bad with tasking, and the stories will usually be worse.

To be productive, an agile team has to have the courage to be wrong. Fear of the unknown cannot be an excuse for inaction. Projects, by definition, are almost always something new. Even longtime professionals will have a learning curve.

That's why in Scrum and extreme programming, there are several references to courage. It takes courage to accept that you might be wrong. The team still needs to move forward. Many organizations put a high penalty on being wrong. Accepting that they might be wrong may not be easy for developers who've worked on traditional projects for large organizations.

Pro Tip

In traditional project management, a slow meeting is usually the result of a lack of direction. In agile activities, the agenda is set. What usually slows down an agile activity is a lack of commitment and courage. Each of the agile activities will have its own telltale signs that the team is being too timid.

Moving The Daily Standup

Watch for developers who don't mention obstacles in the daily standup. This doesn't mean that they don't have obstacles. On the contrary, it sometimes means that they've stopped working.

Field Notes

I once worked on a project in which the developer was tasked with creating a script that would move data into a new database. Every standup, they would mention the same task, "worked on the script yesterday, going to work on the script today, no blocks."

After about a week, the ScrumMaster noticed that the task hadn't been moving across the board and asked the developer if he were sure he had no obstacles. The developer had discovered that the authentication method needed to run the script was not supported by the database, but hadn't told anyone. Instead, he had been trying to find a workaround. It turned out that the assumption that the developer made about the database was wrong, and, instead of communicating the trouble at the standup, he decided to try and create a fix.

It takes courage to stand up in a meeting and say you were wrong. Many developers strongly prefer to quietly engineer a fix before anyone notices. The challenge is when these fixes take time away from the sprint. Instead of being transparent, they start to work on fixes that the other developers don't even know about.

Moving The Backlog Refinement

Relative estimating is another area where the team needs to be comfortable with uncertainty. When many developers hear the word *estimate*, they think, "What is the longest I think this will take?" A relative estimate is not the worst-case scenario. It's not even really an estimate. It's a best guess.

One warning sign that the team is having trouble in this area is when the team complains that they don't have enough information. When the developers complain about this, what they're actually saying is, "I don't know what it takes to finish what you're asking for."

When that happens, you need to remind the team that it takes courage to guess. Not knowing how you can finish doesn't mean that you can't get started.

Pro Tip

Relative estimates are a fiction. They're like style points. They're not designed to convey a lot of information on their own. If you think about it, you can create a relative estimate for almost anything.

I would guess that it takes roughly six times as long to make a wedding cake as it does to make brownies. I've never baked a wedding cake, and I've only made brownies a few times.[26] But I can still make a pretty good relative estimate. I can plant my flag in the ground.

The estimating activity will quickly exhaust its timebox if everyone debates what they don't know. Is it a chocolate cake? Is anyone a vegan? Do you know if the groom is gluten-free? All of these are signs that your team is scared to commit. These estimation sessions seem to go on forever.

Moving The Sprint Planning

You may also see this lack of commitment when tasking. The sticky notes need to represent one day of work. Many developers don't like to break down the stories into tasks. They're concerned that they might run into something that will take much longer than expected. So they'll create one large task that spans several days in the sprint.

[26] Unfortunately, they were awful.

Listening To Feedback

Agile doesn't have much up-front planning. The team instead relies on real-time feedback to keep their project on track.[27] These feedback loops are the best way to respond to changes.[28] That's why agile gets real value from project changes. It's the engine that drives the team to produce and improve.

The agile activities are designed to help create these loops. If there's no feedback, then it's probably because the team is not following these activities. It could also mean that the team is following activities, but not everyone is participating. If feedback is stalled, the project will most likely grind to a halt. It's very important to keep these feedback loops working so that the team can deliver something of value.

There are a few warning signs to look for when the team is not creating feedback loops.

Feedback During The Daily Standup

Feedback in a standup is a little tricky. It's a pre-feedback activity that gives you the information that you need before you can offer any feedback. In general, you want to announce challenges in large meetings and solve them in small meetings.

The standup activity is the large activity where everyone gets updated. It's a one-way conversation. The team members individually relate their tasks and obstacles. They don't try to solve anything.

What you want is feedback *after* the activity. The team needs to coordinate after the meeting. Developers should be reacting to what they heard. They should be sewing their work together. The ScrumMaster should be getting the information they need to remove obstacles.

The team is not having those conversations if after the activity, they scatter like a box of spilled cereal. If you're the ScrumMaster for the team, then you need to fix this loop. Is the team breaking the project into areas of responsibility? Is everyone waiting on someone? These are the types of obstacles you'll need to sort out.

Feedback During Product Backlog Refinement

The product owner should be scheduling as many refining activities as necessary to prioritize the backlog. The product backlog should be an ever-changing list. The team should take a

[27] *The Agile Manifesto* Principle 2 is: "Welcome changing requirements, even late in development. Agile processes harness change for the customer's competitive advantage."
[28] The fourth value in *The Agile Manifesto* is responding to change over following a plan.

look at the new ideas in the backlog. The product owner may have to reprioritize some of the user stories. They should discuss the impact of the change with the team.

If the product owner doesn't have these activities, this feedback loop will be broken and the product backlog will freeze. Then the team may not be working on the highest-value stories. This usually happens when the product owner doesn't dedicate the time needed to successfully fill the role. What you end up with is a concrete requirements document that seldom changes.

This is another time when the ScrumMaster should see the problem and talk with the product owner about a possible solution. Sometimes the product owner just doesn't have the time to maintain the product backlog. When that happens, it might be a good idea to ask the product owner to dedicate an assistant to fill the role full time. It's better to have a product owner with more time and less clout than a product owner with no time. A product owner without sufficient time will end up slowing down the team.

Feedback During The Sprint Demo

One of the most important feedback loops is the sprint demo. This activity needs to ensure that the customer is giving feedback to the product owner and that they share the same vision for the deliverable. There are a few things to look for if this feedback loop isn't working well.

The first is when you hear the customer asking the same questions over and over again. If that happens, the product owner might want to create a *heard it/did it* board. This is a simple way to record what the customer is saying during the demo. It might mean that the customer is not being heard or it might mean that the customer isn't recognizing the request in the product backlog.

The product owner creates a whiteboard with two columns. As the deliverable is being demoed, the product owner should put all the feedback under the *heard it* column. For the next demo, the product owner should move everything they completed from that sprint to the *did it* column.

This whiteboard shouldn't be a replacement for the product backlog. What it can do is give a high-level view of the feedback that goes into creating the backlog. It can help the product owner start a conversation about the priority of the work. If the same feedback is in the *heard it* column after each demo, it might mean that the product owner is not doing a good job prioritizing the work.

Feedback During The Retrospective

A lot of teams think that the retrospective is the most important of all the activities. This is when the team gives feedback to one another about the work. Again, it's much easier said than done.

When the team is starting out, they don't really know how to give one another good feedback. On traditional projects, there isn't a standard way for everyone to give each other feedback. Sometimes, there might be a meeting after the project is complete, but usually there is only a meeting while the work is ongoing.

The facilitator for the team needs to make sure that everybody in the retrospective is talking. Often the quietest people on the team have the most to say. They just need to be coaxed to share their feedback. The facilitator needs to be careful not to be too active, though, because it might stifle the rest of the team. The facilitator should organize this activity, not drive it.

If the retrospective is too quiet, then the facilitator may want to ask some very open-ended questions. They can use themselves as a way to get people talking. Something like, "What could I have done better this last sprint?" and "What did I do really well this last sprint?" If that works well, then just ask the team to pose those questions to one another.

Agenda Setting

You need to be careful that your activities are not taken over by people who do not have "skin in the game." Not everyone needs to participate in your meetings or is committed to the process.

Bonus Fact

There's an old joke about agile activities. It starts out with a pig and a chicken. The pig and chicken are both entrepreneurial so they decide to open a restaurant. They sit together in their empty restaurant and decide what to put on the menu. The pig asks the chicken, "What do you think we should serve for breakfast?" The chicken responds, "What about bacon and eggs?" Then the pig says, "Wow, if we served that you'd be involved, but I'd be fully committed."

You should think about this joke when you start your agile activities. Who's really got skin in the game? In agile, you routinely hear about chickens and pigs. The chickens don't have any skin in the game. They are free to listen. But the activity is not for them. It is always for the pigs. They are the people who are truly committed to delivering the project.

Even though the pigs are fully committed, it doesn't mean that they drive all the activities. Pigs are sometimes sitters and at other times talkers.

Pro Tip

A product owner is a sitter for the daily standup. They're not expected to talk. They're listening to make sure the team's working on the highest-value stories. That doesn't mean they don't have skin in the game.

The same is true for the product demo. The development team certainly has skin in the game, and even though they're pigs, they are still sitters for this activity.

In some organizations, the senior managers will stop in to watch the daily standup. It's a good way to see the team's progress. The ScrumMaster needs to communicate the fact that they shouldn't participate in the standup. They might be senior managers in the organization, but on a Scrum team they're chickens.

Depending on the organization, your activities might be overwhelmed by chickens. It's the ScrumMaster's role to make sure that the chickens don't take over your pig team. Sometimes getting chickens to accept their status is not an easy assignment. Chickens are always sitters and never talkers. It's difficult to keep salespeople and managers from talking to the team during the standup. They almost always want to offer guidance and advice.

One way that the ScrumMaster can help is by sitting down in between the chickens and the developers. The ScrumMaster can physically block access to the team. Managers who don't know agile very well will often misinterpret this activity. They assume that the team is giving a status update to the ScrumMaster. They think the ScrumMaster is a manager and the team is giving a progress update. The ScrumMaster can sometimes quash interruptions by just asking that the chickens save any questions until the end of the standup.

This is one of the challenges associated with being a ScrumMaster. Sometimes you'll have to "speak truth to power" to protect the team. In some organizations, the agile team will have different organizational managers. It will take some finesse to tell a manager that they can't question someone who works for them.

The key is to focus on the agile process and how things are run. If you're the ScrumMaster, try to emphasize that you're not saying they can't talk to someone who works for them. You're only asking if they could refrain from asking questions during this 15-minute activity.

Reporting Status At Standups

There are a lot of challenges around having a good daily standup. Overzealous managers could hijack the activity—the people who should be sitting decide to talk. The agile *chickens* may see this as a town-hall sharing session and may begin taking up valuable time with questions or visioning.

All these obstacles are there and you should be aware of them. But the team has its own challenges. Even without all these distractions it's difficult for the development team to get into a 15-minute rhythm.

There are usually many different personalities on a development team. But there are some common personalities that may cause problems during a standup. The ones you'll most likely see are the **late risers**, the **Oscar winners**, and the **educators**.

The one I'm most sympathetic with are the late risers. These are the developers that have trouble focusing first thing in the morning. You can usually identify them by the telltale giant coffee mug.

A good agile team should have about five to nine developers. Each one should talk for about three minutes. That's their three questions, one minute each. That gives 15 to 30 little bits of information. That's a lot of information. It is especially a lot for someone who doesn't spring out of bed. It's very easy to start zoning out.

Typically a late riser will zone out for everyone except for the person immediately to the left and right of them. The standup almost always takes the form of a circle. It's easier for a late riser to listen to the person who's next to them than it is to listen to anyone across the room.

The ScrumMaster can usually tell the late riser because they won't talk with anyone immediately after the standup. They'll want to plug into their computer and just start working until they wake up. Unfortunately, the conversations after the standup are key for communication. When a late riser skips these activities, they are missing out on a crucial self-organization exercise.

The second personality that might give you trouble is the daily standup Oscar winner. Have you ever watched the Oscars when someone wins and stands up in front of a crowd holding

Pro Tip

Even the best ScrumMasters can't turn late risers into morning people. What they can do is force them to focus during these activities. The best way to do this is to get a daily standup koosh ball. Those are the balls made up of thousands of rubber strings. They're strangely satisfying to flip and spin.

Use the koosh to randomize who goes next during the standup. The ScrumMaster can toss the ball to one random person. They'll go through their standup and then that person tosses it to the next person. Try to encourage the developers to not just hand it to the person next to them.

It might seem trivial, but it does work to help the team focus for 15 minutes. The team will retain more of the activity's information if there's something stimulating and interactive.

their new gold statue? They thank their friends and relatives. Then the music starts. They start trying to shout over the music. Finally someone shows them back to their seat.

There are times during the standup where you might wish you could summon your own orchestra to encourage a team member to finish up. There are some developers who cannot answer the three questions succinctly. Sometimes, it's because they talk very slowly. Other times, it's because they thank other team members for their help. Maybe they'll remind the ScrumMaster that there is still an outstanding obstacle. Whatever the case, the additional chatter will quickly eat up time for the rest of the team.

It's the role of the ScrumMaster to keep this activity moving. They may want to talk to this person after the activity and remind them of the timebox. Sometimes that's not effective. For those tougher cases, you may want to bring back your koosh ball. No one wants to tell someone they need to stop talking, it just feels rude. It's much easier to tell a long-winded developer that it's time to "throw the ball." If you remind the developer enough times, then after a while it usually becomes a natural habit.

The final personality that might get you into trouble in the standup is the educator. You definitely want a lot of knowledge sharing on an agile team. Ideally, each team member should be able to work on everybody else's tasks. What you don't want is for that knowledge sharing to happen during the standup. The activity just doesn't have a timebox to accommodate that extra information.

It's very typical that developers will want to share some of their solution when talking about their work. That's just how many good developers think. It's difficult to separate the work from the solution.

The team can run into trouble when the daily standup turns into an ad hoc brainstorming session.

You want developers to talk about what they did, but not why they did it.

Breaking The Sprint

Breaking the sprint is when the team cannot create a high-value deliverable at the end of two weeks. This is also called *abnormally terminating*. If your team has old-school developers, they might use the dorkier *abnormal ending* or *ABENDing* the sprint. This is borrowed from the language of software crashes. Some teams even call it "blowing up" the sprint.

There are good and bad reasons for blowing up a sprint. A few of the bad reasons to blow up the sprint have to do with challenges the agile team had to face. Maybe the team was terrible at estimating, or sometimes people get peeled off the team for emergency projects. Other times the team runs into an obstacle they can't overcome.

Some of the better reasons for blowing up a sprint have to do with the product owner and the backlog. Maybe the highest-value work suddenly changed. When that happens, the product owner doesn't want the team delivering something that the customer no longer wants.

Field Notes

I once worked on a project in which the product owner had misunderstood the customer. They thought they were asking for a major redesign. The product owner scheduled a meeting to understand the new look.

In the middle of the meeting, the customer corrected the misunderstanding. They said that they liked the way the product looked and all they wanted to do was make a few changes.

The product owner knew immediately that this was much different from the sprint plan. The product owner had already created high-priority user stories for the new design. The team had started working on the new design at the beginning of the last sprint. Right after the meeting, the product owner asked the developers to meet in the shared workspace.

The product owner told the team they were mistaken about the highest-value stories for that sprint and they needed to take these stories off the board and replace them with new ones.

At that point, the ScrumMaster intervened to let the product owner know that the framework doesn't support reprioritizing the work in the middle of the sprint. If the product owner changes the goalposts, then the team is in danger of not delivering.

The team agreed that there was really only one option. The product owner didn't want the team to work on a mistake. Instead, they had to stop work and blow up the sprint.

The team cleared the task board and scheduled a new planning meeting for the next day. This also pushed back the final delivery of the product. The days of the broken sprint were lost work.

Breaking the sprint takes away some of the predictability from the project. The lost time causes a chain reaction that pushes all the future work forward.

On this project, the team committed to delivering in 20 sprints. That means the stakeholders were expecting a product in 40 weeks. When the team broke a sprint, there was a new chunk of missing time. The team will either have to scale back on the deliverable or add time to the delivery date.

On this sprint, the product owner was responsible for the mistake. The product owner recognized the gap and quickly moved to make changes.

Other times, the development team pushes to end the sprint. It's a lot more treacherous when developers want to blow up the sprint. It is the ScrumMaster's responsibility to determine if they're working within the framework.

There are a few common reasons why the development team would want to blow up the sprint.

When the team is just starting out, they will most likely be very bad at estimates. They may have underestimated some of the highest-value stories. There may have also been some unforeseen event. Maybe the entire development team ate at the same restaurant and all got food poisoning.

In general, bad estimates and unforeseen events are not good reasons to blow up the sprint. Often the development team is really trying to avoid an embarrassing demo. The team can only show their finished deliverables at the end of the sprint. It would be awkward if the team can't show any deliverable. Even worse, they may try to create a smoke-and-mirrors demo with slides and screenshots.

When that happens, the ScrumMaster should try to keep the developers from blowing up the sprint. That would be cheating the framework. The development team is trying to put their

Pro Tip

The product owner is always the final word. It is very unlikely that the ScrumMaster and the product owner would disagree, but if they did, the product owner would prevail.

thumb on the scale. They're giving themselves bonus time for bad estimates. As the protector of the framework, this is the only time the ScrumMaster should weigh in on this decision.

All other times, it's solely the product owner's decision whether to blow up the sprint. The development team is delivering the highest-value stories for the product owner. It's ultimately the product owner's call whether there is enough to demonstrate.

It's the ScrumMaster's roll to guard the framework, but the team still works to deliver value for the customer. It's not realistic to try and force the product owner to demo something that isn't ready. The ScrumMaster can make the case, but ultimately it's the product owner's decision.

Chapter 8

Reporting With Agile Charts And Boards

Agile uses a number of different methods to keep track of the work being done and the work that needs to be done. These charts and boards are an easy way to quickly determine how well the work is progressing.

Keeping Agile Transparent

As a project manager, I would sometimes manage successful projects that ran slightly over budget. Sometimes, it was because the team was completing work too quickly. Other times, it was because one of the developers put in much more time at the beginning.

I would also sometimes run projects that were in danger of not delivering. The budget would look fine because developers weren't putting in the hours.

Often, there are many different types of reports. These reports can say the same thing in different ways. Some of them will be out of date. Some of them will have incomplete information. The closer you look, the more confused you get about the overall health of the project.

Free Analogy

When I was younger I used to hate going to art museums. I was always hungry or tired. I could only digest the artwork in batches. It was like trying to read billboards while driving on the expressway. I could never stop too long in any one place. If I spent too much time looking at the mummy's tomb, then I would miss whole periods of artwork.

I remember I liked one art form in particular. It was a painting style called pointillism. It was a form of Impressionism that used small colored dots to create a larger work. It was an early form of dot-matrix printing. If you stood a few inches away from the painting, then it would just seem like scattered dots of color. If you took a few steps back, you would see a wonderful image.

What I liked about these paintings is that they were tricky. If you came too close they would hide. They would only reveal themselves when you stood farther away.

Agile takes a different approach to reporting. Instead of numbers and variances, agile communicates larger truths with simple images. The team should have these reports prominently displayed in their shared workspace.

These images should be clear and simple to read. It will show the team's momentum. Are they going fast or slow? Will they meet the deadline? How much work is left until the end of sprint?

These are simple questions. Agile reports try to give a simple answer.

This is commonly called the team's **transparency**. The truth might be good or bad but it should be available to everyone. The team will have the project's status displayed and easy to understand. Anyone with some knowledge of agile should be able to walk into the shared workspace and see how the team is performing.

Transparency is easy to talk about but much harder to actually do. Teams usually want to celebrate their successes. They'll post completed milestones and other accomplishments. It's much more difficult to be transparent when the team's behind schedule.

It's also common for teams to be optimistic. They think they might be behind schedule today, but next week they'll be able to catch up. The charts help people outside the team figure out if they're being too optimistic. The product owner can step in and change the priority or eliminate some work.

The reports and transparency are the foundation of trust between the team and the product owner.

All the reports in agile should share two common traits. They should be **simple** and highly **visible.** That way the project is open to many more participants. The team's work is transparent and open to feedback.

One of the most common charts is the team's burndown chart. This is a simple line graph that shows how much of the team's work is complete. The team can have a burndown chart for each sprint or for the entire release.

The burndown charts are usually displayed in the shared workspace. These charts are typically called **communication radiators.** Instead of giving off heat, they give off information. They should be ever-present artifacts radiating information about the team.

Another report that you commonly see is the team's task board. The task board is another simple information radiator. It will have the user stories and tasks on 3 × 5 cards and sticky notes. Even someone who doesn't know about agile should be able to see how the work is moving across the board. That way when the manager peeks in on the shared workspace they can see the team's progress. Too many sticky notes stuck in the *to do* column might be a red flag. This is especially true on the last days of the sprint.

One of the most important reports in agile is the product backlog. The product backlog is a simple list of user stories ranked by value. The top of the list has the highest-value stories. The product owner should be able to use the product backlog in most of their meetings. Not everyone will know about agile. But they should know what the product owner sees as the highest priority. It will be a simple display from top to bottom.

Communicating Progress

Traditional projects are like a submarine. Most of the work happens below the waterline. Then every so often, the project will surface and send a signal to waiting stakeholders. These signals usually come in the form of executive summaries and high-level status reports.

The signals take a lot of time to create. They are also not needed by the rest of the team. The team is hard at work within the submarine. They don't need to be updated on their own progress.

Alternate Universe

When I worked as a traditional project manager, I used to create two sets of reports. One I would create for myself. The other I would create for executives and managers. The status reports were a high-level view of milestones and accomplishments. Sometimes they were simple reports that looked like traffic lights. Green was clear and red signaled unresolved issues.

These status reports were the trade-off for traditional project management. The project would have a lot of up-front planning. After it began, the stakeholders would quickly lose sight of the project's inner workings. The status report was a mechanism to keep the stakeholders connected to the project.

I would work on each set independently. I updated the internal reports daily. Then I would translate that same information into an executive overview. Executive reports almost always coincide with an upcoming status meeting. I would create the report and then explain the information in that meeting.

I was spending a good deal of my day communicating the team's progress in both directions. I would ask questions of the team. Then I would report the answer up to executives and managers.

In agile, the team focuses on working software. There is much less of an emphasis on creating documentation. The time the team spends on reports is time they're not spending developing software. But that doesn't mean reporting isn't important. What it does mean is that an agile team should be more disciplined in how they spend time with their reports.

An agile team uses three techniques to try and make reports more efficient. The team should avoid **duplication.** One set of reports should work for both the team and the stakeholders.

There's a lot of potential for miscommunication on a project. One way to keep that from happening is to make sure that everybody's looking at the same information. There should be one chart that everyone can stand over. The same report should be circulated between the team and the executives.

Most product owners see documentation as a low-value item. Product owners usually drive the team to produce working software. Remember that all of the team's work is timeboxed. There is no free work. That means that when the team is working on documentation, they are not working on creating functioning software.

Pro Tip

The product owner is often one of the team's strongest allies in the struggle against too much documentation. If there is a strong drive to produce a duplicate set of documentation, then the ScrumMaster might want to enlist the help of the product owner to highlight the team's lost productivity as a result of having to create these duplicate reports.

The team should also use reports designed for **improvement.** Stoplight reports are not useful in helping the team improve. They're designed to communicate when things have gone wrong. An agile team should use the reports as a way to continuously improve.

In lean software development, this is often called "kaizen." It is a reasoned and attainable path aimed at helping the team improve. A report should be a steep hill instead of a red flag. When the team looks at the report, they should think to themselves, "If we fix this, we can still reach our goal."

An agile report is not just about showing progress. It's a way to show trends and areas to optimize or improve. A burndown chart shows long-term work patterns. The task board helps the team create a sustainable pace. If the only goal for a task board was to show progress, then there would be just two columns: one for "to do" and one for "done."

Finally all reports should communicate **movement.** This should be the case whether it's up and down or left to right. The development team should always communicate forward progress. If the boards are not changing, then it means that the team is probably blocked.

It's also very motivating to have the board showing movement. The team is always pushing to burn down, or move toward completing the work. They also get a degree of satisfaction from moving tasks from left to right. They're doing work and that work is reflected in the reports.

Traditional project milestones are often spaced months apart. It's almost as if the team is walking up the side of the mountain. Each day, there is a little bit less up top and a little bit more below.

An agile report gives that satisfaction every day. You don't have to guess how much further there is to go. Each day, you can visualize the team's progress. For example, picture having to drive to the airport. You know you have three bags of luggage that you need to put into the trunk. Each trip downstairs, you put another bag in the trunk of your car. You might start with three, then two, and then one. You're not walking up the side of a mountain. Instead, you're moving things a little bit at a time from one place to another.

Pro Tip

All of your agile reports will reflect this type of movement. They'll burn down one sprint at a time. Each story will move from left to right and into the *done* column. Even the product backlog moves from top to bottom. As each story completes another one springs up to take its place. This movement is a big part of communicating progress.

Creating A Task Board

The task board is one of the most recognizable agile artifacts. It's a visible agile signpost. It's like a billboard that reads, "Quiet please. Agile team working." Often managers will use the task board as a signal of progress. They'll gesture toward it and say, "This is our agile team."

Something about the board attracts *oohs* and *aahs* from people who enter the shared workspace. It shows that the team is doing something different. It takes your team from theoretical to practical.

There are many different ways to create a task board. It's usually displayed on a large whiteboard with marker columns. The columns are labeled something along the lines of *stories, to do, doing*, and *done*. Sometimes it will be created with simple blue tape on a white wall.

Pro Tip

If a team is short on space they might use markers to scribble their board on a glass window. The boards can range in size. Some large teams will have a board that takes up the entire wall. Other teams fit it on something as small as a corkboard.

The task board is a simple swim lane diagram. Swim lane diagrams were commonly used in software development projects starting in the early 1990s. They got their name because they look like the swim lanes that divide Olympic swimming pools. They have long vertical columns with starting blocks on the top of each lane.

The column names are on the swim lane's starting blocks. The first lane will have the user stories. The other lanes will have the other column names. Each of the tasks is placed in the swim lanes starting from top to bottom. The tasks will lane hop from left to right and move across the board. When the developer starts working on a story, it is moved from the *to do* swim lane into the *doing* lane.

The task board should show a flurry of activity. Each day the board should be different. There'll be a rhythm of tasks moving from left to right. The highest placed tasks should go from *to do*, to *doing*, and then to *done*.

The stories should also finish from top to bottom. The top story should finish first. The second story should finish second and so on until the end of the sprint. There is some room for flexibility, but this should be the general pattern of work on the board.

Most teams place their task board prominently behind their desks. Other teams will just place it where they have their daily standup. The board needs to be where everyone can quickly step up and see the work. Anyone from the team should be able to walk up to the board and see all the work in the sprint.

You can tell a lot about the team by looking at how they organize the board. Some boards are simple. They communicate the bare minimum amount of information. Other boards look like engineering projects in themselves. Each story and task is connected with arrows and notes. The board itself looks like it might need a smaller board to explain how it's read.

Pro Tip

You can sometimes predict the team's blind spots by how they've decided to create their board. A board without much detail would suggest that the team might miss some crucial bits of information. A board that is immersed in detail might suggest the team will over-engineer parts of the project.

If you're the ScrumMaster for the team, you may want to keep an eye on the board for signs of future obstacles. If the board is too broad of a picture, then you might want to encourage the team to add greater details. If the board is too complicated, you may want to remind the team that the board is designed to be lightweight and easily read.

Field Notes

You should also be ready for how a task board can spur interest from the rest of the organization. I once worked for a team that spent months planning their agile initiative. The rest of the organization was heavily invested in traditional project management. All the meetings were quiet and passive. The project managers watched the agile slide presentations with a casual collective yawn.

No one said anything when the agile team moved into a shared workspace. It was also quiet when everyone went through the agile training. All the agile checklist items were finished and ready to go.

Then the team created their first task board. The new board set off a flurry of activity. Suddenly, they were doing something real. It went from an idea to actual change. The project managers wanted to know why the board wasn't using milestones. The team had to push back their start date so that everyone could get reoriented.

If your organization is just starting with agile, then you should immediately put up the task board. You should create the columns and swim lanes weeks before the team starts working. It will send out the message that something new is happening. If the organization is uncomfortable with change, the task board is a great way to show you're serious about going agile. The board is like a flag firmly planted in the ground. It says, "There will be agile here."

That's also why it's usually best to start out with an actual physical board. There are many task-board software applications available which will allow you to update a virtual board from your smartphone or computer. These are especially useful if part of your team is remote. But it's not always a good idea to start with software. The board provides a tangible symbol that the team is starting their work. With the software, the whole team could start using it and no one would notice. When the board is up, everyone sees it. It advertises that work has begun.

Reading The Task Board

A task board radiates information about the team. Even if you don't know much about the project's inner workings, you can still get a sense of the big picture. The team needs to make sure that the board is complete enough to be useful, but it also needs to be simple enough that anyone outside of the team can understand the value of the work.

The board is the team's most widely used information radiator. It radiates information without anyone having to look too closely. A simple glance should be enough to take in all the information you need.

It doesn't just radiate the team's work, it also radiates the team's passion and commitment. When you walk into a shared workspace and the task board is proudly displayed, then you know that the team is excited about their work.

Just looking at the task board will provide you with a lot of information. Is the board up to date and filled with tasks? Then you probably have a motivated team with a good deal of agile experience.

Pro Tip

Sometimes, you'll see a board filled with stories but only a few tasks. They're all gathered in the *doing* column. That probably means that the team is not working on the project. They may be blocked or not dedicated full time. It also might mean that the teams are not reporting to one another. They may not be working together to deliver the project.

If you're the ScrumMaster, make sure you make frequent visits to the task board. If the board's neglected, it can be an obstacle for the team. Be sure to ask a few questions when evaluating the board. Is the board placed prominently? Are there a lot of tasks stuck in the *to do* column? Are there any tasks in the *doing* or *done* column? Is the board well kept or have the yellow sticky notes fallen and gathered underneath like little autumn leaves?

Pro Tip

The team is responsible for maintaining the task board. They should feel a sense of ownership. A board that looks abandoned or neglected usually means that they're not sharing responsibility for the work. They might come from a traditional project management background, so they might expect project managers to report their status to everyone else on the team.

In agile, that's not the project manager's role. Team members are responsible for reporting the status of their own work. No one manages the developers. The team should understand that. The board is usually a pretty good indicator of whether that idea has taken hold.

The team should update the board every day. It should be the most active of all the reports. It's a vital part of the rhythm of the project. It's almost like a large flight monitor. It shows where the team is going and how far they've got until they get there.

After the task board is up, the ScrumMaster should be very clear about why the team uses the board. Some teams have trouble accepting that it is by-the-team and for-the-team. They'll mistakenly see it as a status report designed to give managers insight into the project.

When the team doesn't see the value in the task board, then it isn't useful to anyone. The ScrumMaster should make sure that everyone recognizes why the board is valuable.

The board is designed to show everyone on the team what everyone else is doing. In software development, the team will often have to closely coordinate their work. That's why the team usually sits in a shared workspace. The board will give each of the developers a daily report of how their work impacts the rest of the project.

Let's say one person on the team is working on updating a database and other team members need to know when the database will be updated so that they can start on the next task. With the board, they can easily see who is working on this task and when it will be completed. This kind of real-time, whole-team communication is essential for self-organization.

The board is also a good way for the ScrumMaster to see if there are any unreported obstacles. As a ScrumMaster, you'll need to recognize when the team is having trouble moving tasks across the board. You'll be able to tell there's a problem when there are 20 tasks left on the board and there are only two days left in the sprint. It could be one big obstacle, or it could be several smaller obstacles. The board will alert you to the need to start determining whatever it is that's stopping the team from finishing the work.

If you're the product owner for the team, you might also want to make sure the team is working on the highest-priority work. Remember that, in general, the team should be working on the user stories from the top down. The highest-value stories will be on the top of the far left column.

If the team is working on all the stories at once, you'll see tasks spread out all over the board. When this happens, there is some danger that the team is not focusing their efforts.

This is sometimes called plateauing. It's when the team works on all of the stories simultaneously and delivers everything all at once at the end of the sprint. It's called plateauing because the number of *done* stories is zero until the end of the sprint. Then the *done* column fills up with all the completed stories.

As a product owner, you need to make sure that the team is working on the highest-value items. The team should try to finish the highest-value story before moving on to the other work. When you see the tasks evenly spread out, you should bring this up as an obstacle for the ScrumMaster.

Sizing The Task Board

The task board shows all the work that is delivered in the sprint, and every two weeks, the team will clear the board and start over. They'll add another two weeks of stories during their sprint-planning activity.

The board acts as a constraint on the team. The team should never be working on stories outside of the sprint. The board represents what the team can deliver in two weeks. So if something is added to the board, something will have to fall off. That's why the task board is fixed after each sprint-planning activity. It would be near impossible to prioritize the work if new items were coming in and out of the sprint.

In many ways, this is the same problem as multitasking. Remember that multitasking usually creates more problems than it solves. Each person is constrained by the number of hours they can work in a day. When you add too many tasks, the person becomes overwhelmed with inefficient bottlenecks. In general, people get a lot more accomplished when they can finish one thing at a time.

The same can be said of teams. The team is constrained by the number of hours they can work each day. They're also constrained by the number of people on the team. There are a certain number of people that will be able to produce work for a certain number of hours. If you overload the team, it will also create bottlenecks. The bottleneck may slow or even stop all the team's work. They're much better off setting a pace and staying within their constraints.

Free Analogy

You've probably seen the same thing when you're driving in heavy traffic. If everyone tries to cram into the same lane, it slows traffic to a stop. If everyone slows down, they can create a more consistent pace. The cars create a rhythm. First you go, then I go, then the next person goes, and so on. The drivers stay within their constraints of only one car at a time. When one or two cars try to break the pace, they create bottlenecks and the whole system slows down.

The task board is a key tool to helping the team stay in rhythm and within their constraints. Each of the agile frameworks deals with this in a different way. The Scrum framework uses sprints. Extreme programming uses equivalent sizes for features. Kanban uses work in progress. That means that the task board can be used in different ways and have different names based on the agile framework you use.

If your team is starting out with agile, then Kanban is a terrific way to get the team thinking about lightweight delivery. In Kanban, the board is the only thing the team needs to start working. There are no roles, activities, or other reports. That means there's no ScrumMaster, product owner, daily standups, demos, or retrospectives. Just put up your Kanban board, and you're ready to go.

Kanban comes from the Japanese word for "billboard." A Kanban board is almost identical to a task board and some teams will use the term interchangeably. For example, Scrum teams will sometimes refer to their task board as a Kanban board.

The key difference between a Kanban board and a typical task board is how the team uses the *doing* column. In Kanban, this column will often have a number. The number will represent the maximum number of tasks that the team can be doing at any one time. In Kanban, there are no two-week sprints or velocity. Instead the work is always ongoing. The key constraint is the maximum number that you put in the *doing* column.

The key difference between a task board and a Kanban board is how you think of constraint. In Scrum, you constrain the work with two-week sprints. In Kanban, you regulate the flow with the work in progress.

Even though the boards are used differently, they are still agile. They're all lightweight and incremental with a focus on delivering value early and often.

Bonus Fact

When I was in college I took a few courses in philosophy. During one of the lectures, the professor told the story of Zeno's paradox. The story was about a race between the famous Greek warrior Achilles and a tortoise. The tortoise told Achilles that it could beat him in a foot race. The great warrior laughed and said it was impossible. The tortoise said it was certainly possible as long as he got a small 10-meter head start.

The tortoise asked Achilles how long it would take him to run the 10 meters. The warrior responded it would take him no time at all.

The tortoise then asked how far Achilles thought the tortoise *would have travelled* when Achilles reached 10 meters. Achilles said maybe a meter at the most.

The tortoise then asked how far he would have travelled before Achilles covered that meter. The great warrior thought about it and stated the tortoise would have covered a few centimeters.

The tortoise responded that every time Achilles caught up with him, the tortoise would have run a little bit further. Achilles could never truly catch him, so the tortoise would always win the race. With that, the mighty Achilles conceded the race.

Burndown Charts

An agile project needs a way to ensure that things are on track and that the team is following the agile method. Burndown charts are an easy and important way to do this.

Free Analogy

When I was younger, I would go away for the summer to camp. After several days of camping, we all had to face the dreaded prospect of showering. At camp, the showers were lined up against the wall of a large room with four showerheads on each side. Each shower had its own tiny electric water tank. After you turned on the water, you had about two minutes of warm showering. After that, your experience changed dramatically as the warm water would stop and your shower water turned frigid.

Free Analogy (continued)

One year, on the opposite side of the wall, the camp installed high-efficiency showerheads. These new showers constrained the amount of warm water that could come out, causing the warm water to come out in a slow and steady trickle.

So each day, we all had a choice. We could have a five-minute warm shower with a slow and steady trickle of water, or we could have a two-minute shower with a short burst of warm water that would end abruptly.

This resembles the two ways you can use your board with agile. If you use Scrum, then the constraint will be the days in the sprint. Every two weeks, you fill the board with a number of tasks the team will deliver. The work will end abruptly at the end of the sprint. With Kanban, you can fit as many tasks as you want on the board, but the workload will be slow and steady. It'll be limited by whatever constraint you put in the *doing* column. You'll be regulating the flow of work that comes through the team.

The paradox is that every time you travel halfway to your destination, you're still a distance away from finishing the race. One day you'll be half the distance, the next day you'll be one-quarter the distance, the next day you'll be one-eighth the distance and so on. But you'll always be one step short of completion.

As a project manager, I was always running into this paradox. We may not have called it an endless race, but it certainly felt like it. I would ask the developers how close they were to finishing the next milestone and they would invariably say they were about 80% complete. The next time I asked, they would say 87% complete. The next time, they said maybe 87% complete. Things never seemed to end.

This is the problem when you use a measurement that can always expand. The team will always split the difference and have trouble completing the work. If this happens with too many tasks, then you might have an unpleasant surprise when you reach the completion date. You could have a lot of tasks that are only 80% complete.

In traditional project management, you'll typically use Gantt charts or timelines. These are horizontal bars that stretch out over time. The bars end when there is a release date. There are also diamonds that represent milestones. The bars will travel the horizon of the project. They'll reach across time chasing those distant milestones.

With these charts it is very easy to add a little bit more over time. You just expand the bar a little bit further. Sometimes people don't even notice. Without knowing it, your project will run like the mighty Achilles—closing in on the milestone but not quite completing the distance.

Agile tries to combat this tendency by breaking everything down into discrete chunks of work. Each of these chunks has to be delivered within a timebox.

The challenge is to show this workflow in an easy-to-read chart. The project stakeholders need to be able to see that these chunks are finishing at a predictable rate.

The most widely used of these high-level charts are agile burndowns. These charts are easy-to-read graphic representations of how much work the team has completed. It also shows how much work the team is expected to complete. The chart follows a predictable linear pattern.

The purpose of these charts is to show how much work the team has completed over time. On the far right of the chart, there's the finish date. The team should complete the work and zero in on the final date. The chart should *burn down* to the due date.

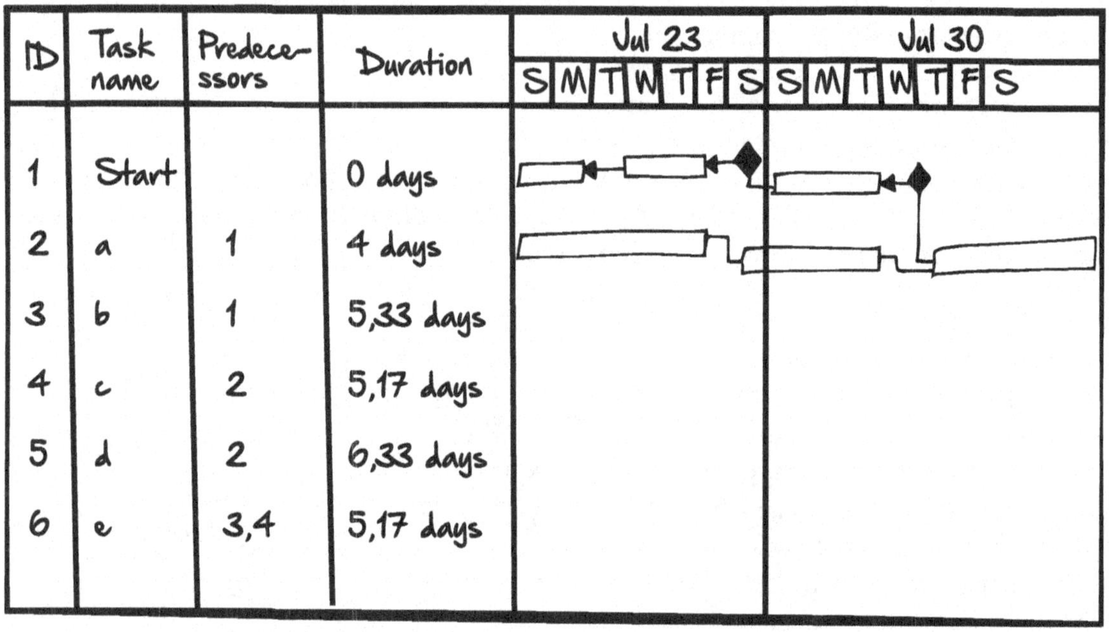

ID	Task name	Predecessors	Duration	Jul 23							Jul 30						
				S	M	T	W	T	F	S	S	M	T	W	T	F	S
1	Start		0 days														
2	a	1	4 days														
3	b	1	5,33 days														
4	c	2	5,17 days														
5	d	2	6,33 days														
6	e	3,4	5,17 days														

Free Analogy

The lines on the burndown look a little like a subway map. If you ride the subway, you might see the dark line representing the current train. Sometimes there's a dashed line to show future train lines. You can see all the stops in a linear pattern. Where the train line ends, the future dashed line continues in the same direction. Then there's a label that says *future stop* with the completion date. You can see the linear expansion of the subway. One day, the line will go one stop further.

The burndown chart works the same way. The work burns down in a predictable direction. The line goes all the way to the current day. The future work is a dashed line that shows how much of the work is left to complete.

Burndown charts are very popular for a few reasons. The main reason is that everything in agile is timeboxed. That means that the team will always be working in predictable chunks of time. There's also a strong motivational factor in using the chart. There's something very satisfying about the team zeroing in on the due date. It's much more emotionally satisfying to move toward completing the work. Each day or each sprint, your team is a little closer to the fixed goal.

One of the most powerful aspects of the burndown chart is that it cannot expand beyond the due date. The cost and time are fixed. The chart is designed to burn down to zero. The team will not be able to split the difference. There's no danger that the chart will increase incrementally over time. It can't, like Achilles, be inching forward but never closing the distance.

The only way the chart makes sense is to eliminate work. You can only add or remove scope. You can't break the timebox, but you could remove user stories.

There are two common types of burndown charts. There's the sprint burn down and the release burn down. Each of these charts follows the same pattern. On the bottom of the chart, along the x-axis, there is a fixed measurement of time. Up the y-axis, there is a fixed amount of work to be done.

Pro Tip

When you create these charts, make sure that you label them appropriately. You won't want to put your sprint and your release burndown charts next to each other. This might cause some confusion. It's usually best to put your sprint burndown chart next to your task board.

The Sprint Burndown Chart

With the sprint burndown chart, the x-axis will cover the days that make up the sprint (two weeks) and the y-axis will cover the number of story points for that sprint.

There is also one vertical dashed line that represents the team's projected productivity. It's like the dashed line on the subway map. It's showing where the team should be going. This is the team's velocity and is based on their historical productivity. If the team has a velocity of 50, then the dashed line will start at 50 on the y-axis and work its way down to zero at the end of the sprint. This is the amount they're expected to deliver during the sprint based on past performance. The actual team performance is plotted on the chart and compared to the estimated performance.

The lines on the sprint burndown chart help you to visually extrapolate the team's progress. Even for someone who doesn't know very much about the project, they can tell the trajectory of two lines. Both lines, the team's velocity and actual work, should be close together. When these two lines are not closely weaved together, then you probably have an obstacle.

The Release Burndown Chart

The second burndown chart the team will work with is the release burndown, which is very similar to the sprint burndown. This chart is usually more for the benefit of the stakeholders. It gives a much broader view of the team's progress. This chart should be less of a surprise for the team, but it could be useful for managers who are focused on the big picture.

The release burndown chart will have the familiar story points along the y-axis and the time along the x-axis. The main difference is the duration and the number of story points. In a release burndown, the velocity is estimated across several sprints. If the team's velocity is 50 then the release burndown will use 50 multiplied by the number of sprints in the release to chart the work. For example, if there are 10 sprints then the number at the top of the y-axis will be 500.

This chart will also have the dashed vertical line starting from the top of the y-axis and making its way to the end of the x-axis. This line still represents the estimated amount of work to be done but it will cover the whole 10 sprints instead of just one sprint.

Pro Tip

You can put the release burndown chart in a less prominent position in the shared workspace. You don't necessarily want to take up valuable wall space with your release burndown chart. Since this chart represents the big picture of the entire project, the team won't need to use it every day. Your best wall space should go to reports that are more frequently updated. These will usually be the team's task board, the backlogs, and the sprint burndown.

Updating The Burndown

It's inevitable that at some point a stakeholder is going to ask, "How's it going with your project?" When that happens, you won't want to give them a rundown of the team's velocity or estimates. Instead, they'll want something like "we're on track," or "things are looking good." Then you can point to a high-level report. For most agile teams, this high-level report is a burndown chart.

Like all reports, the burndown chart is only as good as the information that goes into it. To get the most from your burndown, you'll want to make sure that the team updates the chart in a regular pattern. Typically, in an agile team, the ScrumMaster is the person responsible for keeping the charts up to date.

Also note that the burndown chart will always be a few steps behind the team's velocity.[30] That's okay. Each of these charts is time lagged to make sure they're accurate. The sprint burndown is yesterday's progress. The release burndown is accurate to the last sprint.

The two different types of burndown charts are updated at different times.

Updating The Sprint Burndown Chart

Typically, the ScrumMaster will update the sprint burndown chart before the daily standup. The sprint burndown will reflect yesterday's work. The ScrumMaster looks at the *done* column on the task board. When all the tasks for the story are complete, they add that user story's points to the burndown chart.

Let's say a team has a velocity of 50. That means that the team is expected to complete 50 points worth of user stories within the sprint. Each day before the standup, the ScrumMaster will create a point on the burndown. That point will be the number of story points that the team has burned down from the velocity.

30 *The Agile Manifesto* Principle 7: "Working software is the primary measure of progress."

If the team has completed one user story worth five points, then the point on the burndown will decrease by five. If they did that on the first day, the ScrumMaster would create a point on the chart near the number 45 on the y-axis. This point will line up with the day of the sprint on the x-axis. In this case, they'd do this on the first day of the sprint.

Each day the team should burn down a certain number of user stories. If the two lines are not closely matched, the ScrumMaster might ask about any unreported obstacles. Sometimes, this means that the team is having trouble finishing the work.

Updating The Release Burndown Chart

The ScrumMaster should update the release backlog just before the product demonstration. Remember that these activities are at the very end of your sprint. They will happen just before you demonstrate that sprint's deliverable to the project stakeholders.

Typically, the ScrumMaster will take a final tally of the story points completed. Any stories that were not completed will be moved back to the product backlog. Sometimes, you'll have stories that are partially completed. For those, it's best to take the task's yellow sticky notes and stick them onto the back of the story card. Then put the stories and tasks back into the backlog.

The ScrumMaster will then take this final tally and put a point on the burndown chart to represent the number of stories completed. This can then be compared to the estimated work.

Seeing Trouble

The burndown charts can be a powerful information radiator. Senior managers, ScrumMasters, and product owners will have a keen interest in these reports.

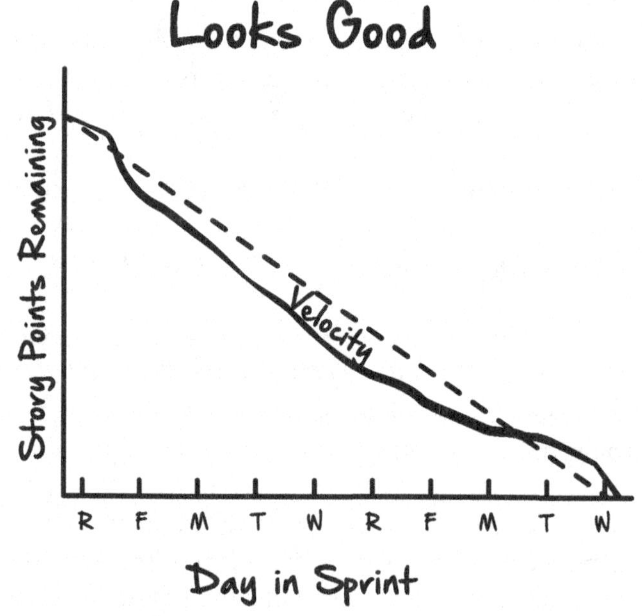

They just need to be updated regularly and filled out correctly. If you're the ScrumMaster for the team, try to make sure that you stay on top of these reports. They'll help you keep track of obstacles and recognize problems that are being reported by the team.[31]

Although each chart is different, there are a few common problems

[31] "If you can't measure it, you can't manage it." – Peter Drucker

that you can identify by looking at the burndown charts. These trouble spots will mostly be visible in the sprint burndown chart. The release burndown is usually too high-level to isolate problems for the team.

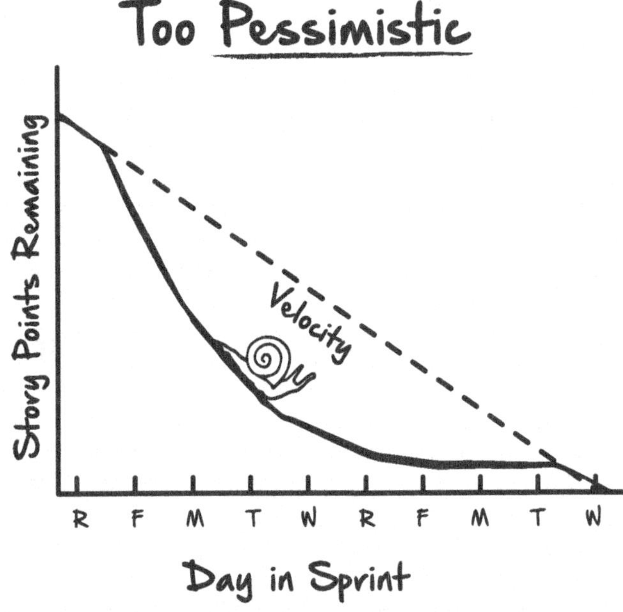

An easy way to remember these problems is to think of the acronym PEACH, which stands for pessimistic, epics, adding, creative storytelling, and hang gliding. These are the five most common challenges identified by the burndown charts.

Pessimistic: Trouble can arise when the team is too pessimistic about what it can accomplish in the sprint. Often the teams will just not add enough work. This is very common when the team is just starting out with agile. What this will usually look like on the sprint burndown is a steep and steady decline with a long horizontal line at the end.

Sometimes what happens is that the team will realize that they didn't add enough work and then they'll slow their pace to fill the sprint. This will give the chart its steep and steady decline that leads to a long tailing off at the end. If you're the product owner for the team, you want to bring this up during sprint planning. It usually means the team is not pushing itself hard enough to deliver with an aggressive but predictable pace.

If you're the ScrumMaster for the team, you probably see this in organizations that are heavily invested in the waterfall approach. Often in these organizations, the developers are used to padding their estimates. They see them more as commitments. They under-commit to the sprint as a way to protect themselves from unknown risks. You'll want to bring this up at the standup. Use the burndown chart as a way to start the conversation.

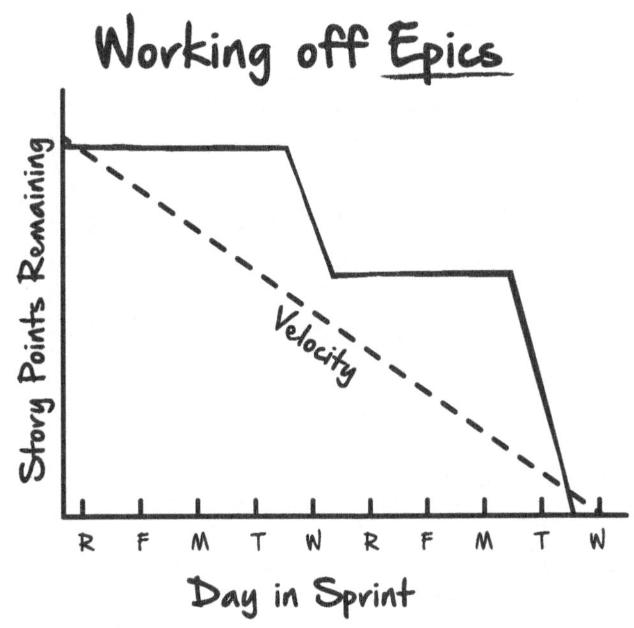

Epics: Sometimes the team won't break their epics down into the stories they need to deliver the sprint. Instead of a smooth predictable delivery, the burndown chart will look like a stepped plateau. There'll be a big delivery and a long wait.

This could mean that the team is having a couple of problems. The first is that the product owner might have trouble breaking the epics into user stories. The product owner just might need more experience with creating good stories. The second is that the development team might not recognize that these are bad user stories. Estimating the epics at 21 points or higher means that they might only have one or two user stories for each sprint.

When this happens, the ScrumMaster might want to coach the team on how to effectively write and estimate user stories.

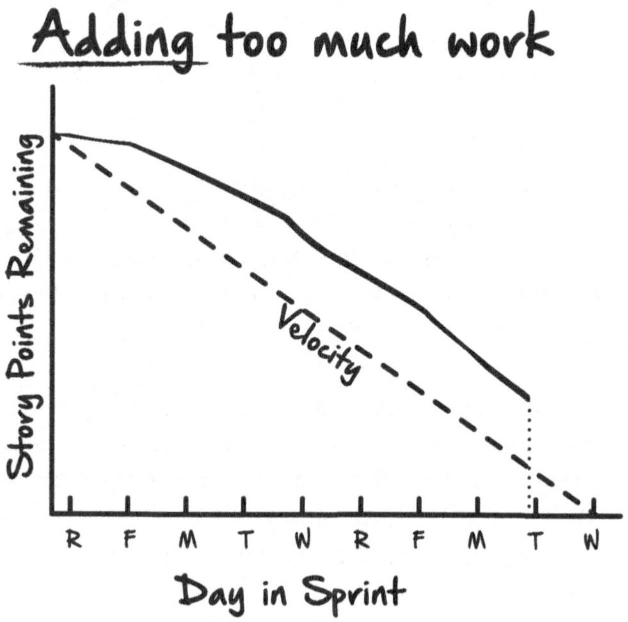

Adding: Another problem is adding too much work. When this happens, the burndown chart will have a slow decline. It will be clearly visible after the first few days that the work line has a trajectory well beyond the end date.

Remember that the y-axis is the team's velocity. Velocity is the historical average of how much the team can accomplish in a sprint. How can the team be wrong about their own estimate on what they can accomplish? The answer is they usually aren't.

This is almost always due to an outside influence on the team. Typically what will happen is a senior manager will encourage the team to "increase their velocity." Then the team will add a bunch of user stories to the board. This can also happen when the product owner is overloading the team.

The ScrumMaster should try to protect the team from being overloaded. The ScrumMaster usually creates the board, so it should be very apparent that the team is burdened with too much work.

The team might want to invite the product owner to the sprint retrospective and then have a frank discussion on how to avoid this from happening in the future. The team needs to produce at a predictable pace.

Creative Storytelling: Sometimes the team won't see very much value in the sprint burndown chart. Maybe they'll see it as too much documentation. Or they'll think it's just a different way of looking at the task board, so they'll create a fiction to appease any managers who might look in on the team.

A fictitious burndown chart is one of the easiest problems to spot—it will be too perfect. There'll be the dashed vertical line to show the team's velocity. The solid line will be right on top of it. It will be perfectly aligned. This could mean that the team is not reporting their progress, or it could mean that the ScrumMaster is not recording their progress. Either way, it's a sign that the team thinks that lightweight documentation means no documentation.

Hang Gliding: This is when the burndown has a long, smooth work line up until the last few days of the sprint. Then just before the sprint ends, the work takes a deep vertical dive on the day before delivery. On the task chart, the tasks will all be stuck in *doing*. Then on the last day, everyone will move their tasks to done.

This usually means that the development team is not working on the highest-value stories. Instead, they're working on all the stories at once, then finishing them on the last few days of the sprint.

If you're the product owner, you are going to want to push the team toward value-driven delivery. If you see hang gliding on the sprint burndown, you want to talk to the team. Work with the ScrumMaster to ensure that the team understands that they should deliver the stories from top to bottom, ideally finishing the top stories before moving on to the next ones.

Much like its real-life counterpart, hang gliding can be a dangerous business for the team. If they don't finish the highest-value stories first, then they're in danger of not delivering at all. Remember that only the finished work is delivered in the sprint demo.

Dealing With Challenges

There are a number of challenges you will have to deal with in your quest to turn your company into an agile company. Even though there are a number of challenges, you can alleviate their impact.

How To Avoid Expanding The Burndown

In many ways, the burndown charts are bookended. The charts depend on the idea that you can't increase capacity or add time. So each side of the chart will have a start and a finish. For the y-axis, the team will have a finite amount of work they can deliver. For the x-axis, they will have a finite amount of time. Both points are fixed on the burndown from beginning to end.

This is not usually much of a problem with the sprint burndown. The sprints are also locked from start to finish. There isn't much of a need to add work to the sprint. Even if the team is pessimistic, they usually ride out the rest of the sprint and just add more stories the next time around.

It's far more common to try and add more stories to a release. Sometimes, the development team can work with the product owner to swap out equally sized stories, but other times, it's just not going to happen. The product owner wants more than the team can provide.

The trick is to allow for this, but at the same time, record the new stories in the burndown chart. In a sense, you're going through a controlled destruction of your burn down.

With traditional project management, this wasn't much of a problem. In a Gantt chart, all you have to do is extend the lines a little bit further in time. Your sponsor wanted a little bit more scope, so you added a little bit to the bar and pushed out your milestones.

Pro Tip

With burndown charts, you have finite time. In order for this chart to work, you need a non-expanding unit of time. There is no easy way to edit the chart for a later deadline. The whole project burns down to zero. In a regular burndown, there is no way to express negative time.

So you have a problem. On the one hand, the chart is designed to enforce restrictions on time and story points. On the other hand, you have a product owner who's excited about the project and is adding work for the team. Sometimes, it just isn't realistic to deny additional work. Typically, there are two ways you can deal with this problem. The first way is to scrap the idea of the burndown chart. Your team can use much more sophisticated charts. These charts are usually a sequence of stacked bar charts that show the added work.

The stacked bar charts work a bit differently from a standard burndown. These charts use a bar instead of a point that intersects the x- and y-axis. That means that each sprint will have its own progress bar. The bars will line up along the baseline of the x-axis.

The key difference is that this chart allows negative progression along the y-axis. Remember that your y-axis is the number of story points. This gives your product owner the freedom to commit more work to the development team.

The second way to deal with this problem is to create a *wormhole* burndown chart. Much like its science fiction counterpart, this chart will wormhole forward through time. It will burrow past the original finish date.

Both of these solutions are ugly in their own way. The bar charts give up a lot of the simplicity and readability that you get from a regular burndown. Instead of a simple information radiator, you get a much more sophisticated report.

The wormhole burndown is a bit ridiculous. Why create a burndown chart if the product owner wants to go on forever? It's inherently un-agile. You're breaking timeboxes and adding complexity.

Nevertheless, these alternatives might be necessary. The thing to keep in mind is that with both these scenarios, you're upending the intended purpose of the burndown. You want to communicate to your stakeholders and your team that time is limited.

In many ways, this is the same challenge you have with breaking a timebox. Remember, the timebox is the amount of time that is set aside for most agile activities. When you break the box, it adds uncertainty to the project. The team has to figure out a way to make up for lost time. That may mean the need to scale back on their commitments.

You run into the same problem when you continue burning down past the release in the release burndown chart. It adds uncertainty. It makes it seem like the project could go on forever. This will make it more difficult for the team to stand by their commitments. They'll be less sure of how much time they have to deliver on their promises.

Retrofitting

I once worked for an organization that was heavily invested in traditional project management. They maintained a shared document library with templates for almost every report imaginable. It represented decades of work. It was a treasure trove of effort from previous project managers. The project charter template was so old that it included a brief explanation of email. I remember it saying, "This charter can be redistributed using an electronic messaging format."

It was a great resource for the organization. If you were a new project manager you could easily plug the templates into any new project. Everybody knew what to use and everybody knew what to expect.

But this resource for traditional project managers ended up being a serious obstacle for the agile project. After years of standardizing, the organization relied on these reports. The executive assistants had created macros to copy and paste fields from the spreadsheets. Everyone in the project management office (PMO) knew exactly what to look for in each of the documents.

The agile project didn't fit into this established library. The new agile team was even having trouble establishing itself as a project. The PMO would only create a new project if there was a project schedule with a list of milestones.

This was a bit of a challenge for the team. No one wanted to reinvent decades of work. This was especially true because the agile project was just starting. At the same time, the team didn't want to submit documentation to the organization that was a complete fiction.

There were several templates for Gantt chart and milestones. The team could create them, but they would be updated as soon as they came off the printer. The product owner would likely change them after a few sprints.

It also seemed that if the team created these documents, they would be working against their own long-term interests. Everyone had been through training. Many of the stakeholders understood that this was something new and different.

The team was worried that the project would no longer be seen as new and interesting. Instead, it would look like a mismanaged and poorly documented traditional waterfall project. Each week, the executive sponsors would get a report with a red traffic light next to the project saying it wasn't on schedule or milestones were missed.

Before we started the project, the team decided to meet and discuss whether to retrofit the organization's documentation to fit agile. We had to decide whether we wanted to try and change the organization, or did we want to create reports that didn't really reflect our actual work. If it helped us to get started, then in the future, we could go back and work more closely with the PMO.

The team had executive-level sponsorship. They could've attempted to persuade the PMO to let the team run outside their normal process. The project could be a rowboat, trailing alongside the larger and more established PMO. The team wouldn't benefit from the PMO's resources, but it wouldn't have to play by their rules.

The team decided that this made the project more vulnerable. It was independent, but it wasn't setting the stage for any organizational change.

In the end, they decided to retrofit only three templates out of the library. The team worked with the project manager to create an agile counterpart to the project charter, the project management plan, and the schedule.

The project charter was a relatively easy transformation. Instead of milestones, the charter established a half-dozen high-level epics that the product owner committed to delivering. It was likewise fairly simple to convert the vision, mission, and success criteria of an agile project charter.

The project management plan was a bit more challenging. In traditional project management, the project manager *manages* the plan. In agile, the team was self-organized. There's no one person who knows everything you need to know about the project.

The team decided that they would invite a project manager to the sprint planning. The project manager could update the project plan with new deliverables. The project manager warned the PMO that this plan would be designed to be flexible and would frequently change. It couldn't go through a traditional project's change-management process.

The project schedule was the most difficult to retrofit. An agile project, by design, does not have a lot of planning up front. It gives the product owner the flexibility to prioritize the project. The schedule is a byproduct of the thoroughly planned project. The team didn't want to feel like they were taking something away from the product owner.

Nevertheless, the team found that by working with the project manager, the product owner could create some high-level milestones. When the project manager attended the sprint-planning activity, they would backfill the milestones with project deliverables.

The team found that when they were retrofitting the reports, the most important relationship was between the product owner and the project manager. They could work together closely without taking up too much of the developers' time working on low-value documentation. The ScrumMaster worked to make sure that the team wasn't spending too much time in sprint planning producing traditional documentation.

The triangle of responsibility worked well. The project manager was able to create some useful retrofitted reports. The product owner lost some flexibility, but was able to work more smoothly in the organization. The ScrumMaster guarded the framework and made sure that the team wasn't traveling too far down the path to waterfall.

Working In A Distributed Workspace

There are a lot of challenges with distributed agile teams. One challenge is how the team coordinates the reports. In agile, there's a lot of emphasis on working in a shared space. The team should be working together closely to deliver high-value user stories.

The team will be layered. They'll need to blend their expertise to produce a complete deliverable. There's no way to add vertical slices to the team's layers without a disconnect occurring.

That being said, it's often unrealistic to have everybody in the same room. Many large organizations outsource parts of development to large shops that specialize in a niche technology. Often the teams are more local but some members have the opportunity to work from home.

Pro Tip

The agile team depends on their information radiators. The task board, product backlog, and burndown charts are all reports that need constant feedback from the team. These reports are only as good as the effort that goes into making and maintaining them. The reports are much more challenging to maintain when part of the development team is at home or in a different country.

Some agile teams strongly feel that the developers are the ones who should maintain these reports. That might work well if the team is small and consistently in their shared workspace, but when you're working with distributed teams, it's usually much easier to make the ScrumMaster responsible for keeping reports up to date.

The ScrumMaster can act like a switchboard operator by coordinating with individual members and being their remote hands to update the board.

There are also several software packages available that allow the team to update their work remotely. These software packages have virtual task boards that will create automated burndown charts based on the stories' swim lane column.

Both of these solutions have their downsides. When the ScrumMaster updates the reports, it might be okay for the local team, but it doesn't do much for the person who's working remotely. It also makes the ScrumMaster an impediment to self-organization.

It will start to feel like a ScrumMaster is working like a traditional project manager. It's hard to distinguish between someone asking for an update for the project versus someone asking for an update for a report.

The software also has its own downside. Developers are all too happy to rely completely on software. Most of the time that's what they're producing. It makes sense that they would see it as a great tool. But that's not always the best thing for an agile team.

Many agile reports force the team to interact. If the task board is a real board, the team has to sit together when they plan their sprints. When the task board is software, then the team can be at home, on another floor, or in another country. The benefit of the software can also be the flipside of the problem. This freedom allows developers to work on their own. They have greater flexibility to isolate themselves from the rest the team. This could be a slippery slope to less interaction and more miscommunication.

Field Notes

I once worked for an organization that went through a serious reorganization in the middle of an agile project. Many of the team members were pulled into different groups. Some of these different groups were in different buildings. Everyone agreed that this change should not impact the project's deliverable, but it made it much more difficult for the team to be in the shared workspace. Everyone was always being called over to different buildings for different meetings.

The team decided to supplement the shared workspace with a very popular software package. The software allowed for a shared task board and automatically created the burndown charts.

Before the reorganization, everyone would come together for the morning standup. After the software was installed, only about a third of the team attended the morning standup. The other two-thirds of the team listened in on a conference line. The team projected the virtual task board on the wall and virtually moved their stories across the board. What started out as a very nice morning ritual quickly turned into a tedious exercise in a dimly lit room.

The software gave everybody the freedom to stay in their building, but this came at a cost. It limited the spontaneous conversations that the team had after the standup. It also made the team feel less cohesive. There was always part of the team that was no more than a distant voice on a conference line.

It's important to remember that agile reports are an artifact created by the team, but they're also a vehicle for bringing the team together. The ScrumMaster and the software can be stopgaps to help create the reports, but this convenience can come with a cost. If you're the ScrumMaster for the team, you should work to keep the team in the shared workspace.

If it's not possible to keep the team together, then try one of these two alternatives. Just keep in mind that the team should make an extra effort to make sure they spend the maximum time collaborating.

Sometimes it's better to have smaller teams that are working together. If the team is depending too much on the ScrumMaster to run the software, then it may be worth a discussion with the product owner to break the team into smaller groups.

Chapter 9

Getting Better With Agile Retrospectives

A retrospective activity is not an informal gathering. It should be well run and very structured. That's why many teams choose to have a dedicated facilitator. The point behind a retrospective is to look at how the team performed and how the team can improve.

Successful retrospectives depend on many of the setup details. This is true more than with any other agile activity. There are a lot of details that really matter. It matters who attends. Equally important is who's not attending. Who facilitates your retrospective is important. Where you have your retrospective is also extremely important.

Team Reflection

Every so often something will happen that captures everyone's attention. Maybe it's a famous court case. It could be a natural disaster. There may be a rally in the stock market. A famous company might have gone bankrupt. Afterwards you'll see experts talking on television. People will write articles. People at work will tell their own version of the story.

When this happens you might notice that it seems as if no one person has the whole picture. People usually have their own little piece of the story. They have their own perspective on what happened. Only after months or even years do you start to get the books and articles that put together the whole story from beginning to end. In many ways, people seem hardwired to only understand events after they become history.

In retrospectives, this is called the team's reflection. It's the time when everybody combines their little piece of the story and tries to come up with the end-to-end history of the sprint.

This reflection is an important part of team improvement. It gets people out of day-to-day firefighting and into looking at a long-term strategy on how to improve. Agile does this reflection at the end of every sprint. That usually means you don't have to wait for the project to end to see a real improvement.

Starting Simple

One popular book used by many teams is *Agile Retrospectives: Making Good Teams Great.*[32] In the book, the authors outline a simple framework for running your retrospectives. They break the retrospective down into five phases. There is the **start**, **data gathering**, **insights**, **decisions,** and **closing**.

[32] *Agile Retrospectives: Making Good Teams Great*, by Esther Derby and Diana Larsen (2006)

The **start** is all about creating structure and safety. You'll want the team to feel comfortable. At the same time you want the team to feel that they're doing something different and new. Some facilitators start this activity by asking everybody to write down what they hope to get from the retrospective. Each person will write this on a Post-it® note. Then they'll gather up the notes before anyone goes any further. After the retrospective, they'll read some of the notes out loud and ask if the retrospective met their expectations.

The second phase is **data gathering**. Here, the facilitator would usually use a chart to establish the agenda. Some of the most commonly used charts are the starfish diagram or the PANCAKE list of agenda items (more about these later). This phase is all about extracting information from the team. It's very common for each person to have a stack of Post-it notes. They'll come up with events and action items to put on the chart in the front of the room.

The facilitator will often use different practices to inspire the team to create this information. They can try to ask the team good questions. They can also use common lean techniques such as "the five whys." We'll see more about this technique later in this chapter.

Once they have identified these issues, the facilitator will push them to come up with SMART goals to improve the team. SMART goals are simply goals that are clearly defined and follow a specific format. We will discuss SMART goals later on in the chapter so you know how to develop them.

One of the key challenges with data gathering is making sure that everyone has a shared understanding of what happened. When something happens to a team, there are usually different versions of the same event. Everyone has their own memory of what happened. The facilitator will want to take each one of these memories and create a shared understanding. Only with this shared understanding can the team move onto the next phase.

The third phase is about generating **insights**. This is one of the most important parts of the retrospective. The team isn't there to celebrate or complain. It's about making the team better. The best way to make the team better is through real learning. The charts really help with this phase. A good facilitator should ask the team, "What are the patterns that you see?"

The key is to push the team to understand their challenges as a whole. Some teams think that if they only fixed a few problems they would be hyper-productive. Most teams struggle for a variety of reasons. It's like a machine that has many rusty parts and you have to decide which ones are the easiest to replace.

It's important for the team to focus on the process. They shouldn't blame any one individual. If you want to fix the machine, you don't blame a part for being rusty. Instead, you need to focus on why that one part *became* rusty. The same is true with a retrospective. The retrospective focuses on the process and not individual people. Most challenges are not the result of one bad actor. They're usually a few people struggling with a flawed process.

The fourth phase is about having the team make **decisions**. Many teams run out of time before this crucial step. It's great to have the team gather insights. That itself is a good way to build team safety and trust. Still, at the end of the day, the team needs to improve. The best way to do that is by creating very clear action items.

In many ways the action item should be the flipside of the SMART goals that get created earlier in the process. The facilitator should push hard against these insights. The team should be able to break them down into action items and spell out how to apply some fixes. They should think about the what, how, who, and where of each item. Each of these action items needs to be delivered in a two-week sprint. They should be ambitious enough to make an impact, but still small enough to fit in that time frame.

The team should be empowered to improve their own process. That's a core part of agile. They should be motivated and self-organized. Each team member volunteers to accept at least one action item. The facilitator should point out any action items that are not addressed. The facilitator needs to make sure that the effort is distributed equally among the team.

Finally, the team should **close** out the retrospective. The facilitator should ask whether the retrospective met everyone's expectations. If there were problems with the activity, then it's the facilitator's responsibility to write notes and apply the changes to the next retrospective. Think of this as the retrospective's retrospective.

The team should then decide what they want to do with the reports. Some teams keep up the starfish diagram or the PANCAKE agenda throughout the sprint. Other teams clear the board and focus on the action items. They might create a chart that just lists the action items along with their action "owners."

If you're the facilitator, try to make sure that everyone feels positive and feels that the retrospective was productive. How you close out the retrospective will have a big impact on how the next one starts.

Understanding Retrospectives

Retrospectives have been around since the beginning of agile. Soon after the manifesto, the agile alliance listed out several core principles. These principles were supposed to help clarify the short list of agile values. The twelfth principle says that, "At regular intervals, the team reflects on how to become more effective, then tunes and adjusts its behavior accordingly."

The team should reflect, tune, and adjust. This is the same way they should approach the project. The retrospective is about the team being agile about their own improvement. They use the same tools and techniques and turn their efforts inward to reflect on how they can better run as an agile team.

With an agile project, you use iterations to adapt to customer changes. Retrospectives iterate over the team's work. They adapt how they work at the end of every sprint. Typically, the team will meet for two hours on the last day of the sprint. Then they reflect on things that went well and what could be improved.

Retrospectives are a very lively area in agile. Norm Kerth applied the term to software right around the same time as *The Agile Manifesto*. Since then, there have been numerous books written on how to run retrospectives. There are even special facilitators who can help the team get the most out of their time.

Some organizations see retrospectives as being self-indulgent. They feel they're hiring developers to focus on software. They shouldn't spend time reflecting on their behavior. They see any time spent on retrospectives as lost development time.

Many of these organizations say this explicitly, while others may just give the team lukewarm support. Even more, open organizations simply don't give the team any time. They're welcome to reflect—they just have to do it when all the work is done, which in many projects is just another way of saying "never."

All of these challenges make it very difficult to have a scheduled retrospective. The ScrumMaster has to work closely with the product owner to make sure that the team has this crucial reflection time. Without a retrospective the team will continue to make the same mistakes. They won't have time to improve or adapt.

Field Notes

I once worked for an organization where it was a real challenge to hold the team's retrospective. It wasn't the product owner who was having trouble accepting the practice. It was the senior manager.

The software department had a reputation for spending too much time updating their own tools. The managers thought they did this at the expense of delivering business value.

There was some truth to the criticism. That's one of the main reasons the team was transitioning to agile. In previous projects, former software developers had managed the team. These project managers were very open to spending time exploring the newest software.

Field Notes (continued)

For the senior manager, this looked a lot like history repeating itself. When they heard the term *reflection* they imagined the team spending hours researching new trends. The manager's view was that they could reflect as much as they wanted after the project was complete.

Yet the product owner understood the value of the retrospective. They've been through the training. They also saw the team getting better. They were improving over time and the product owner knew that this was part of the process.

The product owner knew agile well and had seen other teams benefit from the practice. The ScrumMaster and the product owner convinced the senior manager to sit in on a retrospective. The ScrumMaster facilitated this first retrospective so that they could explain the process.

All of the developers convened in the room and immediately started talking about the project. The ScrumMaster asked the team to list out what went well in the last two weeks. They listed these out on the whiteboard. Then he asked what could be improved. The developers sprung to life and came up with twice as many areas of improvement. Most of them were about communication and outdated processes.

After the retrospective, the senior manager felt much different. They liked how the activity was structured. They also saw that without this refection the team would make the same mistakes over and over.

Scrum teams don't usually allow product owners to sit in on their retrospectives. They feel it's not a good idea to let the customer see the team's challenges with a transparent discussion, but in this case it was necessary in order to get the senior manager to agree to the retrospective.

If you're the ScrumMaster for the team, try to keep these points in mind. The retrospective is a time for improvement. Keep this activity structured and productive. It isn't an informal gathering. The team should use charts to record everyone's ideas. Then they should create action items and even use some communication games.

All the time in the retrospective should be planned and organized. That's why some teams even use outside retrospective facilitators.

Pro Tip

Keep in mind that retrospectives are one of the most misunderstood agile ceremonies. Some development teams see this as a biweekly brainstorming session. They focus on the software and the project. This isn't the purpose of a retrospective. It's about improving the team. It's about making the team better at working together.

Following The Prime Directive

Like many agile practices, a good retrospective depends on a highly motivated and self-organized team. The team needs to accept responsibility for their self-improvement. That's why Norm Kerth created a short retrospective statement that he called the Retrospective Prime Directive.

Pro Tip

The Prime Directive should be taken very seriously. Don't think of it like *Star Trek*'s Prime Directive. This team shouldn't discard this directive when it's inconvenient, like Captain Kirk did all too often. It should be a concrete, shared commitment.

The Prime Directive is a pledge. It's a shared understanding about how to interact. Some facilitators even suggest reading the directive out loud. It is a little cringe-worthy to see a team reading the directive. It looks like a pledge to the state of agile. If you get the team to do it, then there is some evidence that this reinforces positive behavior.

The directive states:

> Regardless of what we discover, we understand and truly believe that everyone did the best job they could, given what they knew at the time, their skills and abilities, the resources available, and the situation at hand.

This statement does a couple things. One thing that you might notice is that it's very empowering. It puts the responsibility of the retrospective squarely in the hands of the team.

You can see this from the language, regardless of what "we discover" and what "we" believe or understand. There's no manager to light the candle. It's not about something brought up in last week's status meeting. It's about the team recognizing their strengths and weaknesses. They're transparent, exploring, learning, and adapting.

The second thing this directive does is that it takes the first step in separating people from the process. Two of the most dangerous statements you'll hear in an organization are "It's not personal" or "It's just business."

Most people take their work very personally. That's why organizational culture is very important. Employees usually want to be part of something that's personal and rewarding.

That's one of the reasons why it takes some effort to get the team to think creatively and not defensively. This isn't about looking for someone who did something wrong. Instead, this is about the team looking at their process. Then they discuss it and see how they can improve. What you'll commonly hear in a retrospective is that there is "no naming and no blaming."

Pro Tip

Often when people are afraid, they'll work hard to defend the status quo. Everyone on a team might acknowledge that there are challenges, but they don't want to change. A change will reshuffle things. They will have a new set of problems. They'll work to protect the process even though they know it doesn't work. They'll do this mostly out of fear—fear that things could always be worse.

It takes courage to make changes. That courage comes from the team being comfortable. Only after the team expects innovation will they start to come up with creative new ideas. If everyone turns on one another then it won't take long for everything to shut down.

Teams that don't have this level of confidence are the ones that benefit the most from good retrospectives. They're also the ones who have the most to learn from the prime directive. The vast majority of people on teams are genuinely interested in doing the right thing. When everyone accepts the directive, then it's much easier to start building that shared trust.

It's worth pointing out that Norm Kerth's retrospectives were originally after several months. Agile retrospectives are at the end of every sprint. That means you should use the prime directive, but definitely understand the limitations when applying it to agile.

Many agile teams will start out by heavily relying on the prime directive. Then they stop using it after they build up a sense of greater safety and trust. When the team is at this level, they're able to ignore some key aspects of the prime directive. One key element that they might want to ignore is the assumption that everyone is doing their best.

When things first start out, it's best to create this fiction that everyone is doing their best with what they knew at the time. As the team gets more advanced, it certainly makes sense to explore some of these avenues which the prime directive sees as off-limits.

One place you may see this is with developers who work from home. It takes a lot of self-discipline to work from home and maintain the same level of productivity. An advanced team might mention that the work-from-home developers are not as productive. The retrospective isn't a performance review. Still, it would be difficult to explore this process challenge while at the same time following the prime directive.

If you are the ScrumMaster for the team, try to keep in mind the strengths and limitations of the prime directive. It can be a great tool for teams that are just starting to build trust. Once the team feels safe, then you may want to revisit the prime directive and decide if the team still needs it for their retrospectives. You might find that the prime directive starts out by freeing the team, but as they become more open and trusting, it might start to limit the team's discussion.

Using A Facilitator

Sometimes a retrospective is misunderstood or misused. That's why some organizations have independent retrospective facilitators. Their job is to come in only for the retrospective. They help the team get the most out of the dedicated time. Sometimes they're outside consultants. Some organizations are large enough to have an independent facilitator who moves from team to team. Either way, it's an advantage to have an impartial voice.

Still, many organizations don't want to spend the time or money finding an independent facilitator. What inevitably happens is that someone from the team has to step up and facilitate the retrospective. This creates a unique set of challenges.

Many teams will ask the ScrumMaster to facilitate the retrospective. At first, this seems to make sense. They're the servant leader. They "master" the agile framework. It seems like a natural fit. In reality, the ScrumMaster's role is quite a bit different from the retrospective facilitator.

A retrospective is primarily designed for team reflection. The team looks back on the last sprint and tries to decide what could be improved or changed.

The ScrumMaster removes the obstacles for the team. Their role is about action. It's about fixing problems. In general, you don't want the same person fixing the problem to be the one who also helps identify the problems. It's a built-in conflict of interest. You'll know that whatever problem you find, it will be your job to fix. Whether you realize it or not, you'll have a bias toward minimizing or dismissing the problem.

Field Notes

I once worked for a team with a ScrumMaster who was the facilitator for the retrospective. The ScrumMaster knew a lot about agile and was very good at setting up the necessary space for the team.

When the team started the retrospective, they identified several challenges from the last sprint. One of the challenges they mentioned was that they couldn't get the hardware they needed to test out their software application. The ScrumMaster was the person working on that obstacle. The ScrumMasater responded to the team that the equipment was "on order." The team asked when the hardware would arrive and the ScrumMaster responded sometime next week.

This conversation would be fine if it was held immediately after the daily standup. The retrospective is different. It's about identifying challenges and opportunities to improve. The ScrumMaster was unintentionally keeping that from happening.

The team was talking about the problem of not having or knowing when the hardware would arrive. The ScrumMaster was just worried about removing the obstacle. There wasn't any effort to try and improve the process. If the team needed new hardware in the next sprint, they would most likely run into the same problem.

An independent facilitator would push the team to figure out how to improve the process. They would ask questions like "How did you communicate that you needed the hardware?" Or they might ask, "What was the process you used to order the hardware?" Once you had those questions answered then they would go on to ask, "What would you do to improve the process?"

This information is different from what a ScrumMaster would ask. The retrospective is about fixing the process, not removing the obstacle. By the time it reaches a retrospective, it is usually too late to fix the obstacle. The facilitator wants to find out how to keep that same problem from happening over and over again.

Because of the challenges the team will face with having a ScrumMaster as the facilitator, some teams will use one of the developers. This also presents a new, but different, set of issues.

Often, the developer will unintentionally favor some discussions. They'll bring their own set of biases and not even realize how that impacts the retrospective.

Field Notes

I once watched a retrospective where a longtime developer was the facilitator. When the team brought up issues, the developer would give verbal cues about which ones the developer wanted to discuss. If the team had ideas about new tools and technology, the developer would light up and say, "That's a great suggestion," and "Let's put that up so everyone can discuss it." When the team brought up ideas about how to improve testing or the process, the developer would change the verbal cues. The developer would say something like "I don't know much about that," or "Does anybody have any interesting ideas?"

These subtle differences changed the agenda for the retrospective. Instead of being about improving the process, it became a brainstorming session about new tools and technology.

Without realizing it, the developer had guided the entire team in a new direction.

If you're the facilitator for the retrospective, try to keep in mind your own biases. If you don't, then you will almost certainly guide the team in your own direction. The key is to understand your bias and try to do your best to fight your own instincts. Make sure the team doesn't easily pick up on your ideas.

If you're the facilitator then you have to give up your role as a contributor. If you don't, you will almost certainly start intentionally or unintentionally steering the team in a different direction.

Setting The Stage

A retrospective facilitator should work hard to make sure that everyone feels safe and engaged. Sometimes retrospectives bring out a lot of passion. Some team members have strong ideas about what went well and what could be improved. It's important to have a good space set up and geared toward making people comfortable and open to new ideas.

The space is a big part of that comfort. A good space can go a long way to making sure that everyone's in the right mindset. A bad space can quickly turn your retrospective into a passive-aggressive time waster.

Free Analogy

Think about the last time you went on an airplane flight. You walk through a tight corridor hoping that there is some space left in the overhead bin. None of the air vents are open so the plane feels overcrowded and suffocating. There are people sitting everywhere. Many of them are anxious and uncomfortable. They're looking at you and then back down at their smartphones.

When you finally get to your seat, think about how well you would receive some well-intended criticism from your neighbors about the size of your bag. Chances are it would be pretty unwelcome. You'd probably bark back something like, "Yes, I can get this bag under the seat in front of me!"

Now place yourself in a different setting. Maybe you're back at home and wearing a comfortable outfit. You're sitting in a reclining chair and someone says to you, "That bag looks a little big. Maybe you should try traveling with something smaller."

This person will probably get an entirely different response.

It's because settings matter. Where you are? What are you doing? Who's in the room with you? They all matter.

That comfortable feeling is one of the most important steps toward having a good retrospective. If you have a retrospective in a stressful workspace, then it's less likely to get good results. This is a time to be reflective and solve problems. For that you need to be comfortable and ready to listen.

There are a few things that you should try to do when picking a space. First make sure that there is *plenty of room*. Crowded rooms create anxious people. You also want everybody to be able to move around. People should be able to move closer to the conversation.

Also make sure that there is plenty of collaborative and colorful material. Teams tend to collaborate better when there are flip boards, index cards, blue tape, Post-it notes, and colorful markers. If someone has a good idea they should be able to have it up on the wall and sketched out without too much effort.

Teams also tend to perform better when there are lots of windows and *natural daylight*. Some teams find it difficult to be reflective in a windowless room under flickering fluorescent lights.

Field Notes

I once worked for an organization that didn't have the type of spaces that are needed for a retrospective. There were a few small rooms that were reserved months at a time by long-serving directors. These rooms were windowless and seated a maximum of five people. Even the team's shared workspace was just a break in rows of cubicles.

The team tried having the retrospective in their shared workspace. That didn't seem to have any positive impact. Other agile charts and reports took up all the wall space. It was also hard to communicate that this was a special activity.

I asked the ScrumMaster to consider some alternative spaces. The team tried meeting outside, but the wind and highway noise made it too distracting. The local Mexican restaurant was happy to host the retrospective, but it ended up taking too much of the team's time in the commute. Finally the team arranged to have the activity in the corner of the building cafeteria. It wasn't the perfect space, but it gave the team time to think creatively.

After a few retrospectives it started to feel more comfortable. The people who worked in the cafeteria even offered some snacks and left the soda machine on.

It was far from ideal but it was more comfortable than the shared workspace. Many people on the team associated the retrospective with the low-stress conversations they had over lunch.

After a while the retrospective started to take on the feeling of a friendly lunch meeting. The team began to collaborate and offer one another creative solutions. The ScrumMaster even noticed that some of the developers stayed behind and worked on their laptops in the same spot.

A comfortable space is key to getting out of the routine of thinking about daily tasks. A good space will communicate safety, creativity, and something new. Like the shared workspace, it's often a struggle to get this set up in a traditional organization. The retrospective facilitator should put a lot of emphasis on this requirement. It's one of the few but important details that keeps this activity productive.

Retrospectives With Distributed Teams

Even in agile, there's an allure to having distributed teams. The less expensive labor markets tempt some organizations. Others like the ability to reach around the globe for experts.

Either way, there's a good chance that your agile team will have at least one offsite developer. Offsite team members are not usually beneficial to the team's communication. It's a real challenge that agile teams try to overcome.

The retrospective is a good gathering for these types of discussions. The team will need to adapt the process to make sure that everyone is still doing a good job communicating. It can be a real problem for agile teams when they're depending on work from a developer in a different time zone.

Pro Tip

One of the biggest challenges is the lack of face-to-face communication. Even with modern tools such as inexpensive videoconferencing there's still something lost when you're not sitting next to the person. Human beings are just wired to receive useful information from nonverbal cues.

Another challenge is coordination. The retrospective needs to happen at the same place at the same time. That's a necessary part of getting a good discussion. A person is not really participating in the discussion when the facilitator is reading their email out loud or going through a bullet list.

Many teams are dealing with this challenge, and there are a bunch of tricks that can help the team adapt. If you're the facilitator for the team, then the first thing you should do is call out the remote person or teams as a challenge. It's not a value judgment about your organization's policy. It's a necessary question primer to let people know that it's okay to try and solve the issue.

Also try to address the issue of trust. Most teams have trouble building relationships with remote employees. They might just be a talking head in a video square. Worse, they might just be a disembodied voice coming through a speaker. It's hard to have a frank and honest conversation with someone that you don't really know.

Field Notes

I once worked for an organization where the facilitator was helping run a retrospective for a team that was split across three locations. It was not easy and the facilitator visibly struggled trying to get people to communicate. After each retrospective, they worked with the team to improve the process.

Field Notes (continued)

Some of the action items work better than others. If you're the facilitator for a distributed retrospective, here are four tricks that seemed to really help the team.

The first is to try to get the team to meet together at least once. Of course, this may not be possible if parts of your team are on a different continent, but you should really push for this if your developers are just a short plane or car ride away. When you do this, everyone on the team will have a picture in their head when that person is talking. It will help the rest of the team establish the video and voice is a real person and not just an image.

If that's not possible, then the second thing you could try is to make sure that the team is always using video. An audio-only participant is always outside the conversation. It's also very difficult for the team to connect with a voice coming out of a speaker. In most retrospectives, this is a distraction. Every so often you'll hear a voice come from a box like Charlie from *Charlie's Angels*. It takes everyone a few seconds to figure out where the voice is coming from and remember that someone is on the line.

It's also likely that the facilitator will ask the person to mute their phone. That way you don't hear traffic or dogs barking. Since the remote person is mostly eavesdropping on the conversation, they're very likely to start answering email or developing. The retrospective turns into background music for them, just like the music you hear when you get into an elevator. When this happens, there's really no reason for them to attend the retrospective at all.

If you're the facilitator and some of the participants are connected with audio only, you may want to stop the retrospective a few times and ask them if they have any opinions. You'll have to be patient as they take their phone off mute and gather their thoughts.

Some teams also put pictures of the people over the conference speaker. It serves as both a reminder that someone's online and humanizes the participant. It helps the team think of them as an equal participant. If you don't have a good picture, it is still helpful to put some object over the conference speaker. Some teams use a stuffed animal or even a koosh to remind the team that there's someone else participating.

If none of these tricks are working, then you may want to try just splitting the team up into two separate retrospectives. They should be as close to the same time as possible. You may want to have an offshore and an onshore retrospective.

Whichever team goes last should watch a short presentation video of the action items from the other retrospective. Then they should record their own video responding to their action items. There's no reason to record the entire retrospective—just a short video presentation about what the team decided would suffice. Try to avoid sending an email or memo that summarizes the retrospective with text. It would be difficult to understand without the context and will often go unread.

Pro Tip

Try to keep in mind that these are just tricks to try and improve a difficult situation. There is a big difference between distributed retrospectives and a typical collocate retrospective. Don't get too frustrated if you run into many challenges. It will take some time and tweaking before you can extract real value from these distributed discussions.

Keeping Track In The Retrospective

There are a number of different charts and methods that you can use to help ensure that your retrospective is successful and that all the points which are brought up are addressed.

Creating A Starfish Diagram

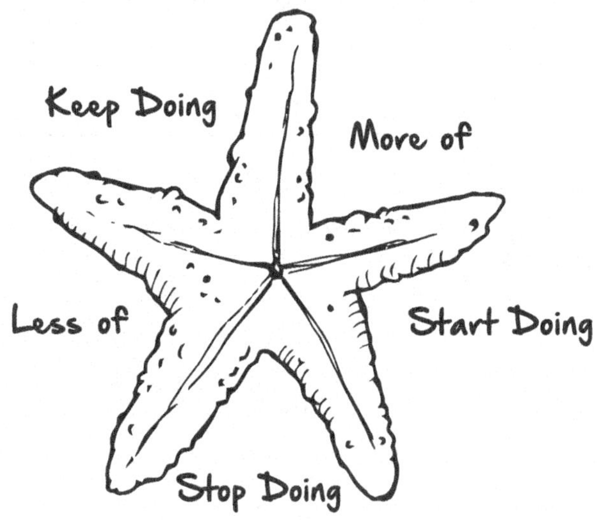

A starfish diagram is a scatter plot that is typically displayed on a whiteboard. The diagram shows the team how they can improve. The starfish has five equal quadrants. Each of these quadrants is a category. The categories are: "keep doing," "less of," "more of," "stop doing," and "start doing." The category dividing lines look a little like a starfish.

To use the starfish, each person identifies an activity that they would like to discuss. One team member might like the way the team holds their standups. In the retrospective, they would create an activity Post-it note called "having efficient daily standups." They'd put that activity in the "keep doing" quadrant of the starfish diagram.

The benefit of the starfish is that it allows the team to identify many day-to-day events. Then the team categorizes these events into what's working well or what might not be working at all. It can be very helpful to have a diagram that shows this in one place. That way the team can decide as a group what they need to improve or change.

Some teams keep the starfish prominently displayed in the shared workspace. Others use the diagram only during the retrospective. They take the items from the board and create action items for the next sprint. How often you display the starfish may influence the way it's used.

If you keep the diagram up all the time, then you might have some team members who will use the board a bit more than others. Team members are interested in improving the process at different times. If one or two developers are upset about something during the sprint, then this will be overrepresented on the board. There'll be a few similar issues that are clustered around a few people or activities.

Some teams display the diagram all the time as a way to continually improve. They feel there's no reason to wait until the end of the iteration for the team to start making improvements.

Other teams feel that the starfish is only for the retrospective. The team should only contribute to the starfish when they're in that timebox. The team can work together as a group to try and come up with solutions and not just identify challenges.

Everyone Contributes

If you want to make sure everyone contributes, then you should display the starfish only during retrospectives. When you use the diagram solely for the retrospective you have more control over how many people are adding events.

Pro Tip

One way to make sure that everyone has a voice is to create a one person, one Post-it policy. Each person gets a Post-it note for the retrospective. Since everyone will have a Post-it note in their hands, it's very easy to see who's not posting on the board. The facilitator can encourage each one of the attendees to put at least one of them on the board.

It's actually not very difficult to contribute something to the board. The five categories give you a wide range of events you might want to call attention to. Even the most satisfied team member could always post *something* in the "keep doing" category.

The categories are designed to be softer than the "more of" and "less of" T-charts that are used in traditional project management. This makes the starfish diagram much more open-ended in regard to the types of events the team will post.

The "keep doing" category is a good way to help keep the meeting positive and should be how the team starts the activity. The facilitator should try to help the team identify all the good things that they liked about the project and that sprint. One way they could do this is to ask what the team would miss the most if it was taken away. Sometimes this is a person, practice, or technology.

The next two categories are closely linked. They are the "less of" and "more of" categories.

The "less of" category usually displays events that were quite refined or helpful in the last sprint. A good question the facilitator can ask is, "What could be improved from this last sprint?" Remember that this category is not necessarily about stopping something. It is more about fixing something. It might be a new software tool that wasn't worth the trouble. It might also be a meeting that took a lot of time but didn't produce a lot of insight.

The "more of" category is usually about things that are underutilized or undiscovered. The facilitator can ask the group, "What would you like to see more of in the next sprint?" Try to be careful to clearly separate these events from the "less of" category. You wouldn't want to put an event on the starfish that said something like "more time developing." That's really the flip side of a "less of" event. Maybe the team wants less meetings or less planning. These events are really about bringing out more value in things that the team already does, such as an event that says, "more coordination with DevOps."

One of the clearest categories is the "stop doing" category. These are events that are not very helpful or not adding very much value. Some groups have trouble with this category because it's too definitive. They prefer to live in the more flexible "less of" category. The facilitator should get the team to commit to items they want to stop doing. If the team has a very negative discussion about an event, the facilitator should ask, "Should we stop doing this?"

The final category in the starfish is "start doing." These discussions sometimes seem like a mini-brainstorming session. They are new things to try or new ideas on how to solve a problem. Sometimes the team will want to spend the entire retrospective talking about this category. Developers and engineers almost always have a lot of ideas about how to solve problems. The facilitator might want to rein in these ideas to make sure that they can be translated into action items.

All of these events in one way or another should be actionable. At the end of the retrospective the facilitator should be able to create a list of action items to solve each item or event. If they don't take this crucial step, each time the team has a retrospective activity the same items will appear on the board.

Running PANCAKE Retrospectives

The starfish diagram is great for running open-ended retrospectives. It's a good simple chart and it works well for many agile teams. It has the benefit of being broad, but not too directed. It doesn't limit the team's conversation.

Still, there are times when a team needs a little more guidance. This is especially true for newer agile teams. For these teams, it's often better to have a **PANCAKE retrospective**. Unfortunately, this retrospective doesn't include a short stack of fluffy goodness. Instead, these PANCAKES are an easy way to remember the agenda.

The PANCAKE is a high-level list of a retrospective's agenda items. It stands for **puzzles**, **appreciations**, **news**, **challenges**, **aspirations**, **knowledge,** and **endorsements**. Sometimes the facilitator will put this list in the front of the room. They'll create a chart with a line through the middle. On one side, they'll list out the PANCAKE. On the other side, they'll place Post-it notes for items, topics, and discussions.

The PANCAKE should be used as a way to start the conversation. It gives the team a little bit more direction in their topics. You should still create action items. This is the same method that you'd use with the starfish diagram. Every item that the team calls out should have at least one action item.

Use the PANCAKE as a way to inspire the team and not as a way to control the agenda.

Puzzles: The first thing to do is to look at what puzzles the team. Have the team call out any items that are the source of confusion. You'd be surprised how far a team can get without some basic answers. As always, try to make the team feel safe. Some common puzzle items are "Why are we doing things this way?" or "I've never seen this before."

Appreciations: Always make sure that the team spends at least some time calling out things they appreciate. This does two things. First it makes the activity more enjoyable. It's tough to spend two hours just talking about things that went wrong.

Second, the appreciation is almost always the flipside of some challenge. You might hear in the retrospective something like "I really appreciate the organization's commitment to Scrum. Is there a way we can send more people through training?" You see there's an appreciation and at the end a new action item.

News: This is usually information about the organization. It can be news of a scheduled reorganization. It may even be unsubstantiated rumor and gossip. Try to keep the news relevant to the team. A common news item might be something like: "My understanding is that we're combining the offshore teams. Has anybody else heard that?" The type of shared understanding is very useful in planning out the team's process. If they do combine the offshore teams, then it might have an impact on the planning and other agile processes.

Challenges: The challenges are almost always a reflection of the other agenda items. You might hear something like, "Why are we reorganizing all the time?"

The facilitator needs to make sure that these challenges don't just sit on the board. Each complaint should be tied into an action item. Otherwise, the challenge will just reappear at the end of every sprint.

Aspirations: These are the hopes and wishes of the team. They may be mundane, like a new way to purchase servers. They can also be higher minded, like an opportunity to meet the offshore team. These shouldn't be pipe dreams or empty wishes. They should tie into action items that help the aspiration come true. This team might want to create an action item called "create budget for team get-together."

Knowledge. This agenda item is really a by-product of the group's discussion. The team should start to create shared knowledge. This will come out after they start talking about the other items. It will be knowledge from the news, challenges, or what puzzles them. Remember that one of the main goals of a retrospective is to get everybody to give their piece of the story. Once everybody shares their piece of the story, you'll start to create new knowledge.

If you're the facilitator for the team, you may want to call this agenda item out directly. You may want to poll the group by asking them, "What did we just learn?"

Endorsements: In many ways, this is the most challenging agenda item. This is about getting the team to agree on and to prioritize all the new action items. You want the team to have a shared understanding of how to address any new challenges. You don't want the team to have contradicting action items.

Let's say that the team has an aspirational action item about creating a group get-together. You'll want the entire group to agree that this is a worthwhile improvement. Some members of the team might think it's not a great use of time. This might be especially true if the team is about to be reorganized. The team needs to have a shared sense of direction. You wouldn't want people working toward meeting the offshore team while others are working toward reorganization. By the time you meet the team, they might be no longer be part of your project.

The PANCAKE is a great way to direct the team without controlling the conversation. It's not important for the team to spend equal time on each agenda item. Let the team think about the most important item for that retrospective. Once the team has more experience with the retrospectives, they may want to go back to the starfish diagram. They may even decide to have a completely self-directed retrospective.

Running The Retrospective

Now that we've gone through the pieces that make up a successful retrospective, it's time to look at how a retrospective is actually run.

We've seen the importance of having a good workspace for the retrospective—a place where the team knows they're doing something different. We've also seen the benefit of using the starfish and the PANCAKE retrospective to focus the discussion of what went well and what could be improved.

Now the team is in the room and has created the chart. It's time to actually go through the business of starting your retrospective.

When you start, it's important to keep in mind that people communicate differently. In fact, many of the people who sound the most convincing are the ones who are most unclear. It takes a lot of skill to identify your own blind spots.

Bonus Fact

The disconnect between confidence and clarity is often referred to as the Dunning–Kruger effect. It was based on a study at Cornell University that showed that students who identified themselves as having the best logic skills were often the ones who scored the lowest when tested. It suggests that people who are riddled with self-doubt are often those with the greatest understanding. It's a little like the Shakespeare quote that the "wise man knows himself to be a fool."

If you're the facilitator for the team, make sure that the quietest people are given the chance to speak. They will often be a great source for some of your best insights. It pays to listen to the quieter voices.

A good way to make sure that everyone participates is to give everyone a Post-it note asking them to identify a process or event that they would like to improve. Then ask everybody to just sit and quietly write them down. Have the group write down as many as they can identify.

Keep people from talking to one another as a way to discourage groupthink. If you let people talk during this time, they're more likely to converge around a few issues. The loudest and most aggressive people will drown out quieter team members.

The facilitator should gather up everybody's Post-it notes and start putting them up on the starfish diagram. They should read each Post-it note out loud. The facilitator might start by saying, "I have a Post-it here that says coordinate more closely with the DevOps team." Then the facilitator should ask the group, "Is this something you'd like to do more of, less of, start, or stop?"

The facilitator should give everyone a chance to understand what the author is saying. They may want to ask the person directly. They may want to just present the questions to the group. Let the team clarify any open questions. There might be more than one DevOps team. In that case, the facilitator can edit and change the Post-it note.

Once everyone agrees on the meaning of the note, they should figure out the best category. In this case, it seems that the team wants to have *more* coordination with the DevOps team, so the facilitator should put this in the "more of" category on the starfish.

The team has identified something that they want to improve or change. Now comes the hard part. The facilitator has to encourage a group discussion around some action item that will help resolve or improve this process or event. For this Post-it note, they have to figure out *how* they're going to coordinate more with DevOps.

This is where the discussion can get a little challenging. Should the team have more meetings? Most agile teams run a pretty tight timebox. Developers are usually not very happy about giving up development time for more meeting time. If they do decide to have an extra meeting, then they need go through the details of that meeting.

The solution needs to be actionable. They have to put improvements in place for the next sprint. Who's going to be in the meeting? How often will it happen? How long will it be? These are the answers they need to improve for the next sprint.

There are a number of ways that you can turn the identified issues into actionable items.

Developing Action Items

A retrospective needs action items. It is the best mechanism for addressing the team's ongoing challenges. Without action items the team would just be on a treadmill without making any improvements. The action items are how the team adapts. Each one is a little step in the right direction.

Action items also give every team member a piece of the solution. It's usually easier for the team to talk about challenges in the abstract. It's more challenging for the team to break down the solution into individual actions and have each person deliver their piece.

For most organizations, this isn't much of a challenge. The starfish diagram almost always has items the team wants to do "less of," "start doing," or "stop doing." Yet identifying the challenge is only the first step. The team still needs to find action items so that they can figure out *how* to make the process better.

Developing SMART Goals

One mistake that some teams make is to think of a retrospective as a casual get-together. It's a good time for the team to kick around new ideas. It's almost like a scheduled version of an office birthday party. You stand around with cake on a paper plate and chitchat about the project.

The real agenda of the retrospective is much different. It's true that the team should be in a comfortable space. As always, the team should be self-organized. You don't want this setup to encourage an easy and loose agenda. The open setting shouldn't lead to an open agenda. An agile retrospective is about identifying challenges or opportunities. Then the team works together to create action items to change the outcome.

Once the team has these items on the starfish or the PANCAKE, they should start getting into the serious business of making real improvements. To make these improvements, the team can't think in the abstract. Instead, they need to focus on small changes that would lead to some measurable improvement.

If you come from a project management background, you may have heard of the SMART criteria. This is a checklist that is often attributed to management guru Peter Drucker. This list helps the team create clearly defined goals. For your retrospective, it will help the team form their action items. At the end of the retrospective each of the items on the starfish should have at least one action item.

These action items should all pass through the SMART checklist. The checklist has five questions: Is the item **specific?** Is it **measurable?** Are you sure the action item is **achievable?** Is it **relevant** to the project? And finally is it **timeboxed** to something that could be done in a sprint?

If the answer is yes to all these questions, then you probably have an action item that will lead to some result. It's a small tangible step in the right direction. It's not just an open discussion. It's a small commitment from the team.

Often teams will have trouble with the **specifics** of an action item. Maybe the team has some communication challenges. When this happens, they might be tempted to create an action item that says, "better team communication." That might be fine as a discussion topic, but for an action item, it isn't very clear.

The team needs to create actions detailing *how* they will be better at communicating. That can often be a much more difficult question.

That's why you have to quickly get into **specifics**. Maybe the team wants to meet more often. Maybe they'll create a listserv. Each one of these has to be clearly defined. How many times do you want to meet? Who's going to be in charge of the listserv? These are all the action items the team has to figure out.

Another challenge is to make sure that the action items are **measurable**. How will you know when the action item is finished?

Say the team does decide to have one extra meeting a week just to try and avoid miscommunication. It's pretty unlikely that one extra meeting will solve all the team's communication challenges. How would you measure progress? How much are you expecting your communication to benefit from this one meeting? You may want to tie the meeting into some measurable outcome.

This meeting could be specifically around making sure the team has the correct hardware. That way you can measure the number of communication challenges around hardware and software issues.

Another question the team needs to ask is whether the item is **achievable**. This is one of the biggest challenges for action items in the retrospective. It's much easier to describe problems than it is to solve problems. Bigger problems almost always need to be solved with smaller incremental fixes. Solving a big problem with a big solution will almost always make the action item difficult to achieve.

If you're trying to improve communication, one of the most attainable things you can do is make sure a smaller number of people are talking about a smaller number of things. You can create a specific meeting with a small number of people and measure how well they're talking to one another. Then you can see if they've achieved anything by looking at the decrease in miscommunication.

One challenge that doesn't come up as often in agile teams is whether the action item is **relevant**. Where this does come up is around tools and software. Sometimes, the team will create action items to install new software that may not be relevant to the project. It is interesting for the team, but might not add value to the product. For example, a team member may want to create something like a wiki server to help with communication issues.

The team needs to take a critical look at this type of action item. Developers have the tendency to try and solve problems with software solutions. The team needs to be very careful that these solutions are not taking too much time away from delivering the project.

Finally the team needs to make sure that all of the action items are **timeboxed**. The retrospective happens at the end of every two-week sprint. That means you need to break down the action item to something that can be achieved in that timebox. When you can't finish it in that time frame, it will just roll over into the next retrospective. Then your action items will double because the one you didn't finish from last time will be added to the new ones the team is creating this time.

The timebox and whether you can achieve your action item are closely related. If you keep your action item small and achievable, then you're more likely to fit it in your two-week timebox.

Flushing Out The Issues

Most projects run like an ancient Greek warship called a trireme. These ships skimmed the waterline and had dozens of oars along each side. The team of oarsmen would row in a rhythm. Each side would coordinate in real time with the other. They didn't have time to reflect on the direction or on each other's actions. Each member of the team sits down, grabs an oar, and starts rowing. There's no debate and no consensus. There's no time for improvement.

Agile breaks this pattern by running a team retrospective at the end of every 2-week sprint. They look for the project's impact on one another and the organization. You can use this time to ask questions. Are there ways the ship can move faster? Do we need to change course?

Like the warship, there are only a few people who know the big picture for the entire venture. Most of the information is held in the collective experience of the team. Each person holds a small piece of the larger effort. They may know their side and who sits next to them. They know their row or the people sitting across from them. This is just how most people work. You don't need to know everything about the project to be able to positively contribute to the outcome.

The downside to this reality is that everybody gets stuck focusing on their own tasks. That might work fine if the team is managed like a traditional project, but an agile team is self-organized. They need to do the work and help set the direction. They're also responsible for their own process improvement. For this you need to set aside some time for reflection.

Norm Kerth first described project retrospectives in his 2001 book. He called retrospectives a "ritual gathering" to learn from one another's "experience" and collectively tell a story. Then the team would mine that "experience for wisdom." Kerth places a great deal of emphasis on positive action. It's about making things better and not about pointing fingers.

Pro Tip

Many projects will have a small postmortem at the end. The challenge with this approach is that you're only learning lessons after the project is complete. There's no room to improve the current project. You'll only know more for the next one.

An agile retrospective happens midstream. It's while everyone is still rowing. This is what Esther Derby and Diana Larsen call the "heartbeat retrospectives."[33]

[33] *Agile Retrospectives: Making Good Teams Great*

> It may take time away from delivery, but it increases the team's overall efficiency.
>
> These heartbeat retrospectives are like miniature versions of what Kerth described. Instead of helping at the end of the project, there's a smaller retrospective that happens at the end of every sprint. You follow the same form and format of retrospectives but you do it more often.

Kerth writes that the agenda should be the same. The team should ask three questions: "What went well?", "What did we do less well?", and "What still puzzles us?"

Asking "What went well?" is a very important start to the activity. It gets everything off to a positive start. It celebrates the team's successes. It also recognizes any improvement. Be sure to take enough time at the beginning to celebrate accomplishments. You might need that positive energy to keep everything moving if things become drearier later on.

Usually the second question, "What did we do less well?" takes up the bulk of a retrospective. It's here where most of the experience "mining" happens. Everyone tries to identify the team's challenges and inefficiencies. Once these are all out in the open, the team can go through and try to look for common themes. Then try to get some shared understanding for what is causing the issues. Only after that can the team begin to identify an improvement.

The third question, "What still puzzles us?" is usually a catchall for issues that aren't answered by the previous two questions. Many organizations start moving forward before everyone has a chance to figure out what's going on. Decisions are made and some people miss the meeting or the memo. They might just grab the oar and start rowing because that's what everyone else is doing. But they won't really have an idea of what they're doing and why they're doing it.

That's why it's very important for retrospectives to flush out any issues that still puzzle the team.

Field Notes

I once worked for an organization where the team was going through an enormous effort to upgrade their data cluster. They were rewiring the entire project so they could fit this upgrade in with their current workload. It was decided that it was very important for the project to integrate with the existing active directory servers.

At a project retrospective, one team member finally pointed out that the servers were never going to use active directory. The developer was puzzled that the team's effort was being put into the upgrade. If it weren't for the retrospective, everyone would've kept on rowing. It would have taken a substantial amount of the project's resources.

It's very important to ask these three questions in your retrospective. Get everyone to stop what they're doing and look around. See what everyone thinks went well, what issues the team has, and if anyone is confused about where the team is going. These heartbeat reflections will more than make up for the time the team sets aside each sprint.

Playing Games

Some organizations don't like the idea of playing games. It seems to conflict with professionalism. It is different from a traditional corporate meeting. Traditional notions of professionalism may be fine for status meetings, but retrospectives are about creative reflection. A retrospective is about coming up with ideas to improve the process. When you're trying to be creative, it helps for the team to feel energized and comfortable. That's where games can really help.

The Question Circle

One popular retrospective game is the question circle. Diana Larsen and Esther Derby created this game to help the team level out the conversation. It forces everyone on the team to come up with a few questions.

Pro Tip

One challenge with some retrospectives is when a few strong personalities do most of the talking. Sometimes this happens when one team member bulldozes everyone else. Other times this happens when some people on the team are just more passionate about improving. Either way, it ends up with the same result. You have a few people contributing while the rest of the team holds back.

A question circle is a good way to get everyone to participate while at the same time quieting louder voices.

It starts by having the facilitator sit everyone in a circle. After they are seated, a team member starts by asking a question to the person on their left. It could be any question. That person then answers the question and asks another question to the team member on *their* left. It could be the same question or a new question.

Sometimes they ask the same question if they feel that someone else can give a better answer.

This game works best if you do two rounds of questions. You should start out clockwise. When you reach the end you can start again going counterclockwise.

Many teams find questioning much easier than making suggestions. Take a simple question like: "How do you think we could improve our team estimates?" This question is much more likely to start a good discussion. It is less judgmental. Compare that to: "We really need to improve how we do our estimates." That doesn't really stimulate conversation. It might even make everyone defensive.

As a facilitator, you should listen for common questions. If any question is asked more than once, you should write it down for later discussion.

This exercise should yield a lot of new information from the team. It will mostly come from the team's quieter voices. Don't spend too much time managing the questions. It's okay if a few people ask funny questions or add something that's irrelevant. It might even help everyone feel more comfortable.

The question circle is for when the team has different levels of participation. Everyone has ideas on how to improve the process, but sometimes people have trouble getting them out. If you're the facilitator, then you don't want to use this game when the team is having trouble coming up with new ideas. For that, you may want to try a different game.

The Futurespective

Sometimes when the team is having trouble coming up with new ideas they can try thinking about the future. One common way to do this is to have a "futurespective."

For this game, you want to have the team imagine that they're having a retrospective at least one year in the future. What are the problems they've solved? What are the questions that continue to bog the team down?

The futurespective flips the retrospective from reflection to prediction. This might help the team come up with new ideas. They have to see through their day-to day constraints. They're not reflecting on what they've done. Instead, they're imagining new things that could be done.

To run a futurespective, the facilitator sets the team up for a virtual time journey. They start by having the team imagine that they're one year in the future. The project was successful and the team is having their final retrospective.

The future facilitator asks the team to reflect on the final product. What were its best characteristics? What were the key events that happened in the past year that contributed to its success? They also ask about crazy ideas that ended up working. What were the key turning points in the project? What were the biggest surprises?

The facilitator in the present records all this future information. After the team has finished their futurespective, the facilitator takes them back to the present. Then they talk about the main points. The facilitator asks the team what they need to accomplish to reach these goals and avoid any future pitfalls.

The team should then turn these challenges and goals around and create action items for the present. How can the team take the next step toward creating that successful future?

The question circle and futurespectives are creative ways to get the team to contribute to the retrospect. Both of these games are about stimulating thinking and discussion. The question circle gets people contributing and gives everyone a voice. The futurespective helps the team think openly and creatively.

If you're the facilitator for the retrospective, try to keep these games fun. At the same time, make sure that you're helping the team record the action items to apply real changes.

Asking Good Questions

Even during a retrospective, teams don't usually spend their time asking the right questions. It makes sense. Most agile teams are filled with developers and managers. These professionals have spent most of their careers providing answers. They're not usually hired to be inquisitive. If they ask questions, then they may even look unqualified.

Pro Tip

If you search one of the job-listing sites, you'll see how most of these organizations hire teams. Search for words such as *expert*, *solution*, and *experience*. Then search for words such as *curious*, *inquisitive*, or *learn*. The second search will give you much fewer results. The first search would probably include most of the listings.

What this suggests is that teams are not rewarded for being good at questioning. The problem with this is that without good questions, it's very difficult to find real process improvements. You have to step back from the structure of answers. Then you have to examine all the solutions that were put in place. It takes a strong personality to look at something that everyone accepts and ask, "Why?"

Yet this is a key part of a successful retrospective. The team will call out items that can be improved. They'll also celebrate things that went well. Yet most of these are symptoms. Most teams still need an extra step to get at the process.

Without good questions, teams will get hung up only trying to improve the status quo. They'll often feel that what's in place is there for a reason. They don't want to poke at it too much with a stick. It falls to the facilitator to make sure that they're answering the right questions.

Asking good questions is a skill. Like any skill, it takes practice. It's not realistic to assume that everyone on the team is going to be an expert. A good facilitator will take the burden away from the team.

If you don't have a facilitator, then you may want to start out asking broad questions. You should have someone on the team who asks some basic questions when an item goes on the starfish. Think about these questions as what, how, who, and where.

A Question Primer

Start out with a primer. A question primer is a way to get more information about what the team identifies. A good way to ask it is to start by saying, "Let me make sure I understand you. . . ." Then have the team explain the item in plain language.

Let's say the team identified an area for improvement. They put "full-time ScrumMaster" in the more of quadrant of the starfish diagram. Whoever's facilitating the retrospective might say, "Let me make sure I understand you. Is the ScrumMaster not available to the team?"

That will probably spur the team to add more information. After that, the facilitator should ask what have you done, tried, or considered?

The team might mention that they talked to the ScrumMaster and sent an email to the senior manager. Either way will help the team figure out an action item for the process.

Now the facilitator should ask them how they would prepare or proceed to improve the issue. A good facilitator will want to ask questions of the team. They don't want to present solutions. The question should give the team some structure to find their own process improvement.

The team can now start to think about how to improve the process. Should they push to have the ScrumMaster sit with the team full time?

What will that mean for the other team? Why are they sharing a ScrumMaster? Is it financial, or is it because so few people have the required skills? These questions will help the team create action items. They'll know what to ask for.

Now the team needs to figure out who the key people are. For this issue, you would certainly have the ScrumMaster as one key person. Other key people might be the agile team that shares the ScrumMaster. The team might also want to talk about the ScrumMaster's manager. There also might be an executive sponsor.

Finally, the team should decide where you would like to be at the end of the fix. Here, they're asking for a full-time ScrumMaster. Do they want their current ScrumMaster for more time?

When the team asks what, how, who, and where, it helps them break through the status quo. Many teams will unintentionally settle on just improving the broken process. A good retrospective will shed light on what needs to be fixed.

Field Notes

I once worked for an organization that had the developers separated from the testers. The developers all worked for one senior manager and the testers all worked for quality assurance. This proved to be a significant challenge for the agile team. Some testers only worked on the team part time, which could cause a bottleneck in development. The developers would have to wait for the testers.

They brought this up as a challenge in the team's retrospective. What they came up with was that they needed more part-time testers. Then the facilitator asked them what, how, who, and where. After a little more questioning, the team realized that the real challenge was that the work was improperly divided up because of the way the team was set up. An agile team should be cross-functional and self-organized.

It was a real challenge to be either of these things with part-time testers floating in and out of the team. Now that the team understood the core problem, they were able to come up with better fixes.

Asking The "Five Whys"

Agile uses some of the same tools as lean manufacturing. Remember that lean software development is still considered under the agile umbrella. That means that many of the items in the lean tool belt also work for agile. One of the oldest is the "five-whys" technique.

The five-whys technique is used to get to the root cause of a process failure. The root cause is the original issue. It is the initial problem that caused all the later fixes. Often this original problem gets buried under a pile of solutions. That's why many manufacturers use the five-whys technique. It gets to the root cause of a product defect.

One of the best things about this technique is that it's very intuitive. You just need to ask "why" five times. It's easy to start and then gets more difficult as you get further along.

The biggest challenge with this technique is to try and find the right place to ask your "why." The answers are almost always more difficult than the question. A good retrospective facilitator will know how to strip away the extra information and find the right place to question.

Field Notes

I once worked for an organization that used the five-whys technique in almost all of their retrospectives.

In one retrospective, the team brought up an issue about closing their hardware user stories. They were creating stories to install server and other computer hardware.

The facilitator asked the first why, "Why are there hardware stories on the task board?"

The team answered that they were assigned a DevOps person to join the team. This person was the only one who could install the hardware. The team needed the hardware for the project. So they wanted to keep track of their work.

The facilitator asked the second why, "Why does the team want to keep track of their work?"

The team answered that the project was dependent on a few of the items that this person was responsible for delivering. If that person was overwhelmed, they needed to know so they could reorganize the other stories.

The facilitator asked the third why, "Why is the team depending on something that this person is delivering?"

The team answered that the organization doesn't want anyone on the agile team installing or configuring hardware.

The facilitator asked the fourth why, "Why does the organization keep the agile team from installing or configuring hardware?"

The team answered that the hardware group was an entirely different functional area. The senior managers felt that the agile team didn't have the expertise to install production hardware. They didn't want to be held responsible for equipment that people outside of their team configured and installed.

Field Notes (continued)

The facilitator asked the fifth why, "Why does the team need to install production hardware?"

That fifth "why" was the root cause of the issue. It turned out to be a miscommunication between a few of the senior managers. They felt that since the team was having agile product demonstrations they needed to make sure that all the hardware was "production ready."

In reality, the team didn't really need that level of security or configuration to just have a product demo. The action item for the retrospective was to investigate a process where the team could configure a temporary server to demonstrate the software. It would coordinate with the infrastructure team, but they didn't need their expertise every sprint.

The five-whys technique helped to root out the cause of the problem and not just the symptoms. It wasn't about getting better at finishing hardware user stories. It was about the miscommunication and misunderstanding about the purpose of a product demonstration.

As a retrospective facilitator, you may want to use this technique when you see something that doesn't seem to make sense. These are the strange fixes that are not much of a concern for the team. This can be particularly useful for solutions that everyone accepts just because that's the way it's always been.

This is another reason why you might want the retrospective facilitator to be someone outside the team. When you use the five-whys technique, it's often best to have a fresh perspective. Otherwise, you might have a tough time finding the right "whys."

Finding Actions

The result of every retrospective should be a clear list of action items. These action items are applied in the next sprint. They shouldn't be big-picture items. They should be small, measurable, and attainable. If you're the facilitator, make sure you're using your SMART goals.

For some teams, SMART goals aren't enough. They're not getting to the next step. The team isn't thinking about well-formed goals. Instead they're having trouble converting their conversations into real improvements. There are three challenges that you should watch for when you're trying to create action.

The first challenge is too much talk and not enough action. Sometimes this is called a "kvetchrospective." The second challenge is the opposite. The team is creating too many actions without enough discussion. They get bogged down with too many small fixes. The final challenge is when a project manager takes all of the action items. The team doesn't take responsibility for their own improvement and throws it to an overwhelmed project manager.

Kvetchrospective

The first challenge is perhaps the most common. It is the dreaded "kvetchrospective." For those of you who don't speak Yiddish, this term is derived from the word *kvetch*. When someone is kvetching, they're complaining without any thought toward making things better. It's when someone complains that their soup is too cold or it's raining outside. The teams can't think that way. They need to put on a jacket or warm up their soup. The team needs to figure out how to solve the problem.

If you're the facilitator for the retrospective, try to limit any negative input that doesn't lend itself to improvement. Try to keep everyone focused on improvement and not kvetching.

Field Notes

I once worked on a project where the team ended every sprint with a kvetchrospective. They would bring up issues that couldn't be solved. They would complain that the facilities and people changed too often. They also complained about one person who used permanent marker on the window. These are not issues that can be solved in a retrospective.

Being an agile team is hard. People will make mistakes and there will be unanticipated challenges. The retrospective is not the place to air grievances. It is designed to improve the team. It's not about group support. If you're the facilitator for a kvetchrospective, be sure to clarify the agenda. Make sure that everyone on the team is forced to create action items and not just find problems.

Limited Discussion

The second challenge is the opposite of the first. This is when the team focuses too much on action items. This usually happens when the team recognizes challenges but can't agree on the scope of the problem. There's much more danger of this happening if your team is filled with engineers who immediately get into debating fixes.

Field Notes

At one retrospective, a team member mentioned that the task board was not up to date. The developers sprang into action talking about the different software packages. They pointed out that they could view the task board from

Field Notes (continued)

their computer, smartphone, or tablet. The software would even show you the history of the task board. You could roll back changes and make mistakes.

The team came up with a list of action items. They were all about getting trial subscriptions for two or three different software packages.

The facilitator had to back the team up. They needed to have some shared understanding of the challenge. Why was the task board not updated? Were team members not working in the shared workspace? If not, was this a problem for the team?

These are the process challenges that the team needed to debate. The real action items were about making sure that the team was collocated. If members of the team were not located, what does that mean for the rest of the project? One of the action items that came out of that retrospective was to make sure everyone was in the shared workspace for the next sprint.

Project Manager Dependence

The final challenge happens when the development team depends too much on project managers. Some organizations have a powerful project management office, or PMO. Long time developers in that organization might be used to depending on project managers.

In these retrospectives, the team finds several action items, but they're tasks that need to be completed by the project manager. When this happens, the facilitator needs to make sure that the team is creating action items that improve the process. If the project manager is taking responsibility for the action items, then this is not about improving the team. It's usually about improving circumstances. Maybe it's about buying a new software package, or trying to increase the budget.

Another challenge is that it sends the opposite message that you want the team to take away from the retrospective. It communicates that the team needs a project manager to make meaningful changes. It doesn't allow the team to self-organize and create a shared responsibility for their process. Instead, it creates a bottleneck, where the team waits for the project manager to complete their list of tasks. There's no creativity and no ownership.

If you're the facilitator for the team, be sure to keep the project manager from taking responsibility for all the action items. You may want to ask the project manager if they want to skip a few retrospectives to send the right message. The retrospective is not a time to update the project manager. Be sure to keep the team reflecting on their own process and not looking to others for action.

Following Up On Actions

Once the team has come up with actions, it's important that these actions are addressed. It's important that in every retrospective, each person contributes something to the fix before the end of the sprint. There are a few things that the facilitator can do to encourage this level of ownership.

The first is that at the end of the retrospective, each action item should have one person listed as the action "owner." The best way to do this is by asking for volunteers. Remember that the team needs to self-organize. The facilitator should never assign owners. They should also keep the project managers, ScrumMasters, or managers from assigning action owners.

Each person on the team should volunteer to work on at least one action item. Keep in mind that you can have the same volunteer for more than one action item.

The facilitator should also keep an eye on any abandoned action items. The team should discuss any item that doesn't have an owner. This is usually a red flag. Don't assume that the team doesn't want to do the extra work. Most of the time an abandoned item means that no one really understands what it takes to fix the issue.

Pro Tip

Once everyone has an item, they should display it in their shared workspace. Some teams create a "tweak wall." This is an information radiator similar to the task board.

The tweak wall is usually a much simpler chart. It's just a whiteboard with the title across the top. Then each person on the team has a Post-it note with the action item and their name.

Some teams put action items on the task board. This usually makes the task board seem too cluttered. It also makes it difficult to see if the team is delivering the highest-value stories.

Action items are important but they're not as important as delivering the highest-priority stories from the product backlog.

Ideally, the action owners should self-organize and deliver their fixes for the next retrospective. In many organizations, it's still a challenge to get the team to self-organize on action items. It's much easier for developers to accept that they're responsible for delivering valuable software.

Action items are usually different. They're much more administrative. Unfortunately, this means that even self-organized teams can usually benefit from a little nudging.

The best way to nudge the team is to set aside time at the end of the daily standups. The ScrumMaster should work with the team to figure out which days they should address the tweak wall. For most teams, talking about their action items every day would be too much time. Agile teams usually have a pretty strict timebox. It's often enough just to dedicate a few days a week to updating the tweak wall.

Some teams will have the ScrumMaster ask the team for a status update on the action items every Monday and Wednesday. The ScrumMaster will usually facilitate the meeting at the end of the 15-minute daily standup. The ScrumMaster should use the tweak wall in this meeting. They should point to individual Post-it notes and ask each owner to update the team on their action item.

Action Items Versus Obstacles

Sometimes there's confusion between action items and the ScrumMaster's obstacles. The individual team members are responsible for completing the action items, while the ScrumMaster removes the team's development obstacles. The key difference between the two is that obstacles are an impediment to delivering software. The action items are the output of the retrospective activity. They improve the team's process.

Let's say in the team's last retrospective they put "better user stories" in the "more of" area of the starfish diagram. The goal is pretty vague. It takes real skill to create good user stories. So the facilitator encouraged them to create good action items to improve the process. The team created two action items to improve the stories. The first was to recommend a good book. The second was to have a long time product owner from a different team sit in on the estimation session.

These two action items are not simply about improving the team's process. These items are about *the team*. The team knows that they're not doing a good job with user stories. The action items are some of the steps they're taking to improve.

The ScrumMaster is more focused on keeping development moving. The ScrumMaster can provide training and help the team maintain their timebox, but the ScrumMaster can't force the team to be better at working together. It's a little like being the coach of a sports team. A coach could tell the team the rules of the game and give them strategies to succeed, but it is still each team player's choice whether to be excellent.

The action items are part of a team's agreement to be excellent. It's an individual commitment from each team member on how they can help the team improve.

Chapter 10

Wrapping Up

We're at the end of our "Leading Agile Teams" journey. You started out seeing how important it is to have **strong agile teams**. This is especially true if you're just starting agile in your organization. The first team will be your crucial change agents. Hopefully they'll spread the word about the benefits of agile. They will talk about their work in the lunchroom and spread agile by "contagion."

You've seen how an agile organization splits their groups into cross-functional **self-organized** teams. These teams are critical for creating an agile mindset. Some of the most valuable changes will come by having a cross-functional team in a shared workspace.

Each agile team should have a **customer representative**. In Scrum, this is typically called the product owner. This role is responsible for creating and maintaining the product backlog. They'll gather up the work and split it into user stories.

When the product owner has enough user stories, the team will start developing the product. The product owner will work with the team to get a relative estimate of effort for each story. Then they'll rank the list so that the team knows the **highest-value** items.

At the beginning of each sprint the development team will split the stories into Post-it notes. Each one of these notes will represent one day of work. Then they'll place the notes on a **task board**. The task board is a key information radiator. It will communicate how much of the work is planned, in progress, or done.

Each team will deliver in a two-week, timeboxed iteration. In Scrum these are called "sprints." At the end of each sprint the team will have a shippable product. This is much different from a milestone or phase. It should be a functioning product.

This product should be demonstrated at the end of each sprint. The product owner is usually the best person on the team to give the demonstration. They have the closest connection to the customer. It also helps keep the product owner plugged into the team from the sprint. The public demonstration will help the team gain insights into the mind of the customer. The customer can apply these changes in close collaboration with the rest of the team.

At the end of the demonstration the team should hold a sprint retrospective. This activity is about optimizing the process. It's the team getting better at being agile.

By now all of these topics should only serve as a reminder. If you are hearing any of this information for the first time please go back through the table of contents and check out each of the related chapters.

Putting The Bell On The Cat

By now you should have a better understanding of agile processes and practices. That brings us back to where we started. How to put the bell on the cat? This book gave you a broad overview of the *ideal* way to transform your organization. There were quite a few "pro tips" that gave you an idea of how to put these concepts into practice.

Leading your team to greater agility means that you need to know when to push and when to compromise. There are quite a few places where you should stay as close as possible to the ideal. Try to ensure that the team has a shared workspace. Always push the team to self-organize. Make sure that the team has a dedicated product owner. Without this foundation it seems unlikely that your transformation will succeed.

Other areas are more flexible. It's not ideal to share a ScrumMaster across several teams, but it can be done. You can still be an agile team if some of your developers are offsite. It just presents a lot more challenges. Finally you can create some traditional project artifacts. Upper-level managers can get a Gantt chart and milestones. It just might take a little creative thinking.

Each of these as a single challenge shouldn't be too difficult to overcome. If you have to deal with them all at once it might be too much for your new agile effort.

When you're an agile team, try to be a "happy warrior." In general, organizations don't like to change. Change usually means job losses and frustration. They're much more likely to get onboard when the change comes from an upbeat person. If you get frustrated or overwhelmed, it will come through in your efforts. You'll be an obstacle to your own change efforts. Try to smile and have a good sense of humor. This is a significant change. If you are happy, people will be more likely to see this as a friendly change.

Trying to stay upbeat is not easy. Change efforts are time consuming. Don't be surprised if you find yourself in the same meeting with the same people saying the same thing over and over. Leading an agile team takes a lot of patience. There are a few common challenges that you're likely to run into as part of your overall change effort.

One of the first challenges you'll run into is that people do not usually understand the role of the ScrumMaster. This role is very different from what you find in many organizations. Most managers have authority over the development team. The ScrumMaster is a new role. They are a combination of a trainer, coach, and administrator. Make sure that you repeat this consistently and often. You might be several months into your transformation effort and still have people going to the ScrumMaster to help "push" the team.

It is very common for organizations to misread the levels of authority on the team. The true roles of authority on the team are the developers and the product owner.

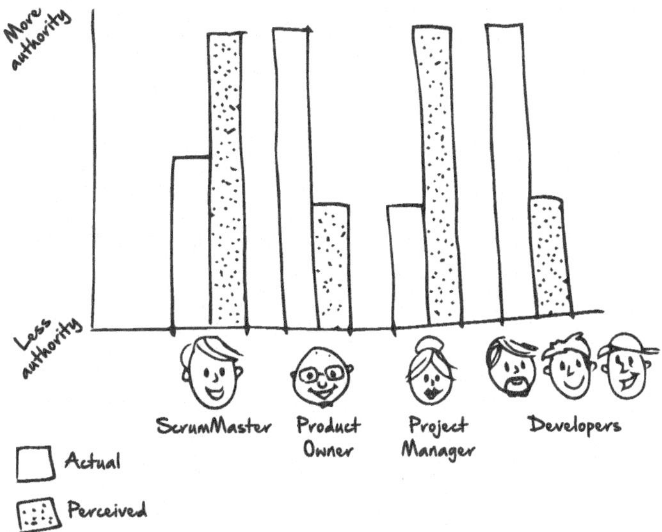

Another challenge is that people will generally not understand project iterations. Project milestones are pretty deeply ingrained in product delivery. Most people still think of work as divisible by time. When you have a month-long project you should be one-quarter finished by the first week and halfway finished by the second week and so on. The idea that you can start building the whole thing and then improve it over time is still pretty foreign to most organizations.

Use your team's demonstrations to clarify what it means to deliver in project iterations. Most teams have an easier time understanding iterations once they see a few of them displayed.

This leads to the final common challenge. Often the team will not get the point of the product demonstrations. Remember that the demonstrations are designed to make sure that the product owner and the customer share the *same understanding* about the product. When they're starting out, most teams use the demonstration to celebrate the work. They want to show the customer how much they've accomplished.

When you're leading the team, try to make sure that the product demonstrations are performed correctly. If you use them to celebrate the work it won't take long for the customers to stop attending. It's very important to have the product owner drive this event.

The key difference between a leader and a manager is the ability to get people to come around to your way of thinking. I hope this book has helped you understand what it means to be "agile." Hopefully you now have a vision for your agile team. We have covered the key places that will likely cause you trouble when convincing others to change. Now all it takes is your knowledge, patience, and upbeat persistence. I wish you the best success in leading your agile team.